Black Comics

ALSO AVAILABLE FROM BLOOMSBURY

Comic Books and American Cultural History, edited by Matthew Pustz
Comics and the City, edited by Jörn Ahrens and Arno Meteling
Do the Gods Wear Capes?, Ben Saunders
The Power of Comics, Randy Duncan and Matthew J. Smith

Black Comics

Politics of Race and Representation

**EDITED BY
SHEENA C. HOWARD AND
RONALD L. JACKSON II**

Bloomsbury Academic
An imprint of Bloomsbury Publishing Plc

B L O O M S B U R Y

LONDON • NEW DELHI • NEW YORK • SYDNEY

Bloomsbury Academic

An imprint of Bloomsbury Publishing Plc

50 Bedford Square
London
WC1B 3DP
UK

1385 Broadway
New York
NY 10018
USA

www.bloomsbury.com

BLOOMSBURY and the Diana logo are trademarks of Bloomsbury Publishing Plc

First published in 2013
Reprinted 2014

British Library Cataloguing-in-Publication Data
A catalogue record for this book is available from the British Library.

ISBN: HB: 978-1-4411-7276-1
PB: 978-1-4411-3528-5
ePDF: 978-1-4411-6847-4
ePUB: 978-1-4411-3849-1

Library of Congress Cataloging-in-Publication Data
Black comics: politics of race and representation/edited by Sheena C. Howard
and Ronald L. Jackson II.
p. cm.
Includes bibliographical references and index.
ISBN 978-1-4411-3528-5 (pbk.)–ISBN 978-1-4411-7276-1 (hardback)–ISBN 978-1-4411-
6847-4 (ebook (pdf))–ISBN 978-1-4411-3849-1 (ebook (epub)) 1. Comic books, strips,
etc.–Social aspects–United States. 2. African American cartoonists. 3. African Americans in popular
culture. 4. Race in literature. I. Howard, Sheena C. II. Jackson, Ronald L., 1970-
PN6725.B56 2013
741.5'973 dc23
2012039414

Typeset by Fakenham Prepress Solutions, Fakenham, Norfolk NR21 8NN

For my mom, the first one is for you.
– Sheena

To my children, Niyah and Niles, that their imaginations take them to
levels of life success that outmatch their dreams.
– Ron

Contents

PART TWO Representing race and gender 95

PART THREE Comics as political commentary 189

Foreword

William Foster III

"It was the best of times, it was the worst of times"

CHARLES DICKENS, *A TALE OF TWO CITIES*

It has been said that the more things change, the more they remain the same. But today at least in one particular venue, things are appreciably better. In the landscape of comics, we now can choose from a much more diverse selection of reading. Because of a number of changes in the industry, comic book fans have been gifted on a number of fronts with a point of view that is finally in full color. The number of players of color has grown and the proud history of Black people is finally being told in all its glory.

As a comic book fan and historian, this is the fascinating journey that I have been chronicling for years. Long fascinated with the changing image of people of color in comics, I have found this work a worthy pursuit and one that has lea me to the discovery of many long forgotten efforts, as well as a growing list of new and exciting contemporary creators.

That is why I am so excited about the book you hold in your hands right now. This is a long-awaited and important collection of essays.

I have long believed that it is impossible to truly appreciate literature if you do not have a sense of history. It is not just that certain references will be lost on you as a reader. Everything has a historical context that the reader must be familiar with in order to truly appreciate and process the story being told. Here is your opportunity to obtain that historical reference point.

As the title suggests, this collection presents the reader with two different levels of enlightenment. The famous science fiction writer, Robert A. Heinlein, once said, "Politics is the only game for adults." I tend to agree. We may not like what happens in this arena, but we cannot stay out of it if we want to get things done. This then is an examination of the *representation* of the history of how Black people have been portrayed in the media in general, and in the powerful medium of comics specifically. *Race*, a topic that has always fought for a proper hearing on the agenda of major issues in America, finally gets a fair hearing here.

Telling a story that must be told, including our unique point of reference, is what this book is all about. We must stand up and tell the story of how a people have been represented, or misrepresented or have been totally left out in the official history of a birth of a country. Here is a collection by scholars who take the mission of bearing this necessary accounting very seriously.

These researchers are paying tribute to a group of artists and writers who toiled, almost anonymously, to reveal the truth about their lives. It is important to note they did so with little or no fanfare when the population at large did not offer them much support. They have looked back to examine trends that have changed the way people of color are viewed in comics.

The power of the written word combined with drawn images is still to be discovered by folks from every generation. It is still hard for me to grasp that there are those who have not yet been exposed to the brilliant political cartooning of Ollie Harrington (*Bootsie*) or the esoteric art of George Herriman (*Krazy Kat*).

We can now more appreciate the brilliance of innovators like Morrie Turner, whose *Wee Pals* cartoons became the first integrated strip in American history, or Barbara Brandon, a second-generation Black syndicated cartoonist. We can celebrate the story of Jackie Ormes, the first female African American syndicated cartoonist, and her signature character, *Torchy Brown*. We can share with our children the pioneering comic books of Bertram Fitzgerald, who single-handedly created a series of comic books that documented the history of Black people in America (*Golden Legacy*).

The landscape on the comics canvas has truly broadened to include the works of past comic strip and comic book pioneers like E. Simms Campbell (*Esquire Magazine*), Alvin Hollingsworth (*Negro Romance*), Charles Johnson, Buck Brown, Matt Baker, Tom Floyd (*Blackman*), and George Winners. These are individuals who literally and visually altered the worldview with their creative wit and unique points of view.

We can revel in the outstanding work of contemporary artists and writers such as Alex Simmons (*Blackjack*), Ho Che Anderson (*King*), Kyle Baker (*Nat Turner*), Kevin Taylor (*Girl*), Aaron McGruder (*The Boondocks*), Jerry Craft (*Mama's Boyz*), and so many others whose combined body of work has forever changed the way people of color are perceived by the world at large.

But it is not just a time to pay tribute to our noble past and to the men and women artists and writers who were determined to leave footprints on the pages of time. We can also promote the ever-expanding presence of women of color both as characters and creators, and talented artists and writers of every ethnicity who appreciate our stories and tell them with style and panache. All this speaks to it being the best of times.

This book is a ready testament to that idea that there has never been a more exciting time than right now in the field of comics research. It is my hope that it will inspire other chroniclers of this unique history as well.

Respectfully submitted,
William H. Foster III
Comic Book Historian

Acknowledgments

Sheena C. Howard

This project has truly been a collective effort. It all began with my dissertation topic, *The Continuity and Extension of African-American Communication Dynamics through Black Comic Strips*. From that, a book project was birthed.

First, I wish to thank Ron Jackson, my co-editor, for his hard work, support and mentorship throughout this process. I would also like to express deep appreciation and gratitude to the contributors of this volume. Thank you for sharing your research, insights, thoughts, as well as your time.

I am thankful for the support, guidance and dedication of my dissertation committee at Howard University—Dr Melbourne Cummings, Dr William Starosta, Dr Chuka Onwumechili, and Dr Carolyn Byerly—as well as my outside examiner Dr Pierre Rodgers.

Finally, one special person participated in virtually every phase of this project—my mother, Jacqueline A. Howard. I dedicate this work to you.

Ronald L. Jackson II

A special debt of gratitude goes to my co-editor and friend Sheena Howard for bringing this project to my attention and allowing me to be a part. Also, I appreciate that her sense of humor and diligence made this an easy collaboration. I am also thankful for the contributors of this volume, many of whom have already made their mark in the study and/or production of comics. My mentors and influences are countless, but I must say I am grateful for the constant guidance of my mother Sharon Prather, my father Ronald L. Jackson, Sr., my wife Ricci Jackson, my brother Bruce Jackson, and good friends Brad Hogue, Carlos Morrison, Keith Wilson, Theo Coleman, Torrence Sparkman, Shaun Gabbidon, and Lawrence Griffith. Thank you for your endless support and love.

Introduction

Sheena C. Howard and Ronald L. Jackson II

Black comics: An introduction

Every political campaign is based on it. Every adolescent's life begins with it. Every motivational speaker tries to convince us of its power and potential. Your reflex might be to guess that the answer is hope; and you would be half-right. The answer is imagination, or imagining what is possible. From an early age we are socialized to consider life through the lenses of others. As we come to learn more about social ways of being, we begin to develop our own lenses for seeing the world. This is when we start to explore the possibilities of our imaginations. We are reminded of the old biblical adage "as a man thinketh, so he is." How we conceive of the world defines the parameters and limits of what we can do within it. If you think you are defeated, you are. If you think you are incapable of doing something and therefore never try, then you have only actualized your own incapacity. In a country where Blacks are seldom recognized and celebrated for their exceptional historical contributions and achievements beyond sports and entertainment, Black children often turn elsewhere to fuel their imaginations. The fantastical worlds of comic strips, cartoons, and comic books have the powerful potential to weave imaginary narratives that offer possibilities for seeing Black heroism. Nonetheless, it is possible to engage with these worlds and walk away with little understanding about either how Blacks have contributed to these genres or how Blacks have used these genres to transmit positive, political messages to consumers. This is the impetus for the book you hold in your hands. We want to offer a resource that chronicles and celebrates the form, function, and contributions of Black comic strips, cartoons, and comic books (hereafter referred to simply as comics, a term we embrace to also refer to graphic novels and animated cartoons) and their producers.

Comics have functioned to sustain our imaginations. They have aided readers, artists, and general consumers in stepping outside of themselves to become something beyond what is real. They have also been quite adept at taking what is real and turning it topsy-turvy to demonstrate the idiosyncrasies or wrong-headedness of our thinking. At a young age, when most people are first introduced to comics, they use them as an escape. They are visually fascinated by storyboards depicting people flying through the air like Superman, turning green as a sign of anger like The Incredible Hulk, or swiftly transforming into a superhero costume to save the day like Wonder Woman or Spiderman. Kids gradually come to identify with, attach themselves to, or simply admire these superheroes. And who would not? These protagonists are endowed with superhuman strength and special skills that show their magnanimous larger-than-life personalities. This is not to mention that they fortify at an early age what we have been taught about right and wrong, justice and evil, as well as friends and enemies. Comics, perhaps, are many people's first glimpse at a social justice pedagogy in action.

Even still there is something that lies beneath the seemingly innocent veneer of comics pedagogy—White patriarchal universalism. In other words, oftentimes comics tell a story about White heroes and minority villains, White victors and minority losers, White protagonists and perhaps a minority sidekick. This sets up a dialectic that, although is quite public, leaves a concealed residue of minority inferiority. These kinds of comics signify hidden meanings within broad comic messages purporting that minorities could not be winners or expect to win. This is indeed a tragedy, because although these are "just comics" as some would say, they imprint on young impressionable readers' imaginations a sense of minority incapacity, incompetency, and impossibility. Until the work of George Herriman, there was never a minority hero in comics.

The closest Blacks came to exploring Black heroes was through oral narratives shared by a community storyteller or Griot, who was very often the eldest in the community. The eldest in a family was well respected in African communities, and this became a carryover in African American families from the "middle passage" of slavery. Although Griots were the eldest community members in Africa, they became the eldest family members within the African American family who held the critical responsibility of keeping the oral tradition alive. This oral tradition was not anti-literary. It was a way of transmitting community values while growing the bond between community members. As generations passed, the responsibility of the eldest to function in the role of Griot began to fade. Stories were preserved spottily and community histories died as the elders passed away. This is one of the reasons the work of comics is important, because it is a way of preserving community and cultural values. George Herriman understood this and developed a comic strip to give life to those communal values he learned as a Creole growing up in New Orleans.

Of course, Herriman became famous when his comic strip entitled *Gooseberry Sprig* emerged in 1909. Within a year, he started publishing a sub-strip called *The Family Upstairs*, which was followed a few years later in 1913 with *Krazy Kat*. As you read the chapters in this book, you will learn about Herriman's mulatto and Creole identity, which scholars have explained is probably why not only the color of the characters in this strip would vacillate between Black and White, but also why Krazy and Ignatz had this rivalry around their color in which Ignatz would exhibit hatred toward Krazy only when he was Black. This was a powerful message that was filtered through the narrative and signified something deeply problematic about society. These filtered commentaries were indicative of a legacy of racism during this time period that is now well documented.

The popular emergence of Black comics via Herriman's illustrations coincided with the beginnings of what would become known as the Harlem Renaissance. In the early 1920s, the United States was shaped by a post-World War I economy and society. During this time many African Americans pursued educational and cultural opportunities, as well as industrial or domestic employment. Furthermore, many African Americans migrated to metropolitan areas such as Detroit, Chicago, Washington and New York. Even still, it was difficult for African American writers and artists of the 1920s to find well-established White publishers who would accept their work (Porter, 1992). Nonetheless, Elmer Simms Campbell and Ollie Harrington, who you will read about in more depth throughout this volume, were two of the first African American artists to connect illustrations with satirical or political humor with great success.

Soon after the birth of Black comic strips, in 1935 Oliver "Ollie" Harrington conceived of the first Black cartoons. Perhaps his most popular cartoon was *Dark Laughter*, which was a single panel cartoon created for the *Amsterdam News*. In this comics, his main character Bootsie would explore issues related to racism and social injustice while maintaining a markedly well-adjusted, positive personality. It was important to him for his audiences to see a character who was astute, sensible, proud, and plainly honest about the struggles he was confronting. Though there is documented evidence of Black cartoonists' contributions within the medium of comics since the 1930s, in American society Black cartoonists have struggled to impact the funny pages, as well as the broader spectrum of "comics" (i.e. graphic novels, animated cartoons, etc.).

Not long after that, Orrin C. Evans became the progenitor of Black comic books. For the first 28 years of his adulthood, Evans worked as a Philadelphia journalist who wrote about social injustice among other things. In 1947, after having worked for two Black periodicals, the *Chicago Defender* and NAACP's *Crisis Magazine*, he decided it was time to develop a vehicle for getting his messages in the hands of many more people. So, he worked with fellow friends and artists to create *All Negro Comics*, the first comic book intended, written and developed by, for, and about a Black audience. He did this in spite of threats on his life. For many more years, he boldly continued publishing a series of other Black hero comics. He understood the significance of his work to the psychological and social well-being of Blacks. He wanted to make a difference.

Since then, many artists and writers have ventured to create Black comic strips, cartoons, and comic books. This book seeks to not only chronicle some of the early development of comics, but also to explore the variance, political messages, and social implications of these many contributions as a way to highlight the evolution of these genres and a way to remember the works that have now become part of the landscape and legacy of American comics.

Comics today

Despite the early works of George Herriman and Ollie Harrington, many newspapers still struggled to bring color, in the use of strips by and about minorities, to their comic pages (Kent 2006); instead they buckled under political pressures to keep the pages non-political (i.e. all White). Strangely, more than half a century after Harrington's first work emerged, in the late 1990s *The Chicago Tribune* finally made a concerted effort to incorporate more diversity in the newspaper. A result of this effort was the publication of Aaron McGruder's strip *The Boondocks*. Prior to *The Boondocks* there were a limited number of nationally syndicated comic strips with diverse characters; *Curtis* by Ray Billingsley, which began in 1988, was one. Today, each African American cartoonist who is afforded the opportunity of syndication paves the way for future African American artists.

The media of comics are still only peppered with representations of the multifaceted Black experience by Black artists. *The Boondocks*, *Candorville* and *Doonesbury* are the most recent syndicated comic strips that have displayed representations of minorities. In addition, Milestone Media, Inc, a Black-owned and-controlled comic book publishing company offers a variety of African American superheroes and multicultural approaches to comic book characters.

This book offers a historical to contemporary analysis of the contributions Black artists have made within the media of comics, as well as the ways in which Black artists have depicted the Black experience through comics. Documenting the history and contributions of Black cartoonists is vital as it relates to American history. This text attempts, whenever possible, to focus on Black comics that emphasize and represent the composite Black experience. This helps to drive the critical exploration of the evolution of Black comics. There is a scarcity of research that seeks to illumine the contributions of Blacks in regard to the evolution of American comics. Frankly, when seeking to do research on the history of Black comic strips, comic books or cartoons researchers are hard pressed to find any material, let alone anything comprehensive, that does this work. This volume is unique in that it highlights the innovative perspectives and contributions of Black artists from the early twentieth century to present. These perspectives include a historical look at Black comics' commentary on capitalism, sexism and racism among other variables. These perspectives also include the uniqueness in which Black artists use humor.

Historical knowledge of the use of humor within the African American community is imperative to understand the complexity of humor, satire, signification, metonymy, double entendres, and various other figures of speech within Black comics that represent the Black community. The point of any comics, whether it is a comic strip, graphic novel or single panel strip, is to entertain audiences and also to provoke thinking about the latent meanings. American slavery provides the backdrop of tragedy against which African Americans developed their distinct form of humor, in which the material of tragedy was converted into comedy (Gordon 1998). These elements of humor within the Black community cannot be and should not be ignored.

The soul of African Americans is revealed in humor, which oftentimes is racial because it is impregnated with historical context, convictions, customs, and associations (Gordon 1998). This very statement can be found within and across Black comedy today, including comics. These unique approaches to comics have never been purposefully illuminated or appreciated—until now.

Over the last three decades there have been very little overt representations of the Black experience, though there have been several Black superheroes, including *Spawn* and *Black Panther*, among numerous others. Comics dealing with issues specific to the African American experience, such as racial profiling, discrimination, integration, etc. have been scarce, perhaps because these realities are swept under a rug in order to avoid state responsibility for them. This is an unfortunate reality for American youth, consumers of comics and popular culture at large; especially, given the political and social commentary found within comics. It is not only odd in contrast to our general sense of what is true in our society, but it flies in the face of our public pronouncements embracing diversity and global awareness. Furthermore, not including these diverse perspectives severely limits the medium and the progression of popular culture as we strive to move into the twenty-first century. The aforementioned realities of the history of American comics has enthused the need for this volume. Another element that has spurred interest in completing this volume is that, though scarce, the contributions that Black artists have made within this medium have largely gone unrecognized. Said another way, nearly every documented discussion or major text on the history of American comics is devoid of the contributions of Black artists. Black artists should be considered in any discussion of the history of American comics and it is our objective to create a volume that will illuminate these contributions. Thus, *Black Comics: Politics of Race and Representation* aims to engage with a broad range of issues around a central theme by taking a closer look at the prevalent themes around the history and evolution of Black comics.

The contributions of Black cartoonists from past to present across three genres—comics strips, cartoons and comic books—allow the reader to compare and contrast the prevalent and salient themes within and across each genre. Consequently, the volume that you hold in your hands is invaluable in that it allows the reader to gain insight into critical-theoretic explorations of the content and commentaries inherent in Black comics and it illuminates the ways in which these genres resonate with one another over time.

Summary of book by chapters

Black Comics: Politics of Race and Representation is organized into 14 chapters that are organized into three themes. These themes address: (1) critical-theoretic explorations of the content and commentaries inherent in Black comics through the comparison of past and present representations, (2) representations of race and gender, and (3) Black comics as political commentary. Chapter 1, "Brief history of the black comic strip: Past and present" by Sheena C. Howard, introduces the book with a historical documentation of Black comic strips by tracing the history of the Black comic strip in the United States, with a specific focus on African American comic strips by African American artists. In a broader sense this chapter traces back to the inception of the comic strip in the United States while situating the Black comic strip in an art historical perspective. Thus, Chapter 2, "The trouble with romance in Jackie Ormes's comics" by Nancy Goldstein, focuses on the role of the visual in the development of and social impact of Jackie Orme's artistic production of characters. Chapter 3, "Contemporary representations of black females in newspaper comic strips" by Tia C. M. Tyree, examines how comic strips hold insights into how Black women are perceived by themselves and others, as well as providing the reader with a social critique of how mass media may continue, as it has in the past, to marginalize Black females within the understudied medium of comics. Chapter 4, "Black comics and social media" by Derek Lackaff and Michael Sales, continues to explore the artistic progression of comics by addressing the relationship between Black comic art culture and online social media through interviews with creators and case analyses of several online sites and communities. This chapter further explores the crossover appeal of comics and the significance of digital technologies in the twenty-first century. Chapter 5, "Beyond b&w? The global manga of Felipe Smith" by Casey Brienza, examines the depictions and representations of elements of globalization, multiculturalism and cultural hybridity as we move through the twenty-first century.

Chapters 6, 7, 8, 9 and 10 turn to gender and racial representations in Black comics. Chapter 6, "Studying black comic strips: Popular art and discourses of race" by Angela M. Nelson, constructs a theoretical framework for studying Black comic strips based on American race relations and African American culture. In Chapter 7, "Blowing flames into the souls of black folk: Ollie Harrington and his bombs from Berlin to Harlem," Christian Davenport takes a deeper look at Ollie Harrington's work from a period of overt racism and, paradoxically, a period of hope and public policy directed toward some change in racial politics (from the 1930s through the late 1960s). The chapter reveals the complexity, as well as the power, of the artistic medium and the intersection between the political, personal and artistic. Chapter 8, "Panthers and vixens: Black superheroines, sexuality, and stereotypes in contemporary comic books" by Jeffrey A. Brown, explores the ways in which Black female superheroes are sexualized and portrayed as sexual spectacles. Specifically, this chapter will review and analyze how Black superheroines in mainstream comics have been depicted according to racial and sexual stereotypes. Chapter 9, "Gender, race and *The Boondocks*" by Sheena C. Howard, raises complex questions around the gendered tension in Black comic strips while offering an exploration of Black masculinity within modern comic strips. In Chapter 10, "From sexual siren to race traitor: Condoleezza Rice in political cartoons" by Clariza Ruiz De Castilla and Zazil Reyes Garcia, discuss the ways in which Black female politicians are depicted and the ways in which readers are encouraged to make sense of the intersections of race and gender. This chapter provides a nice transition into exploring comics as political commentary.

Chapters 11, 12, 13 and 14 focus on comics as political commentary and explore the complex dynamics of ideology in more depth, appropriation and cultural production of comics. Chapter 11, "'There's a Revolutionary Messiah in our Mist': A pentadic analysis of *Birth of a Nation*: A comic novel" by Carlos D. Morrison and Ronald L. Jackson II, takes a rhetorical approach to examining the way in which Black cartoonists communicate ideology through the comic strip as text. Chapter 12, "Inappropriate political content: Serialized comic strips at the Intersection of visual rhetoric and the rhetoric of Humor" by Elizabeth Sills, builds on previous literature about the rhetorical power of the comic strip, by examining comic strips as a synthesis of visual rhetoric and the rhetoric of humor that combines the appeal of both schools to become a powerful catalyst of ideological tensions. Chapter 13, "Will the "Real" Black Superheroes Please Stand Up!" by Kenneth Ghee, explores cultural identity and the sociocultural value system by addressing the fundamental theoretical question: does the sparse but "mainstreamed" Black superheroes in both Black and American popular culture (e.g. Black Panther, Storm, Spawn, Green Lantern, Static Shock, Hancock, etc.) have any real, or redeeming, value for socializing young Black men (and women) into a healthy cultural identity or value system for improving the social, political, educational and achievement parameters of young Black males in American society?

In the final chapter, Chapter 14, "Culturally gatekeeping the black comic strip," David Deluliis looks at the ways in which the comic strip and the newspaper are reflections of the social and racial world. This chapter is the first to investigate cultural gatekeeping at three levels—the cartoonist, the comic strip and the newspaper.

The goal in *Black Comics: Politics of Race and Representation* is to call attention to the salient themes around race, gender and representation prevalent in historical and contemporary comics. Though not always explicitly addressed, the centerpiece of this volume is the exploration of inherent stereotypes, the influence of racialized, as well as gendered, scripts and the tracking of cultural changes across comic books, comic strips and animated cartoons. In other words, in many ways, this book is a reconnaissance of various visual messages, ideas, and identity referents within comics that reflect the zeitgeists throughout time. The question is often asked whether popular culture imitates reality or whether reality imitates popular culture. Of course it is a little bit of both; therefore, inasmuch as popular culture and reality imitate one another, the contents, flow and momentum of this volume facilitate a remembrance of how Black comics have visually interpreted what has moved generations of citizens over time. Enjoy!

References

Gordon, D. (1998), "Humor in African American discourse: Speaking of oppression". *Journal of Black Studies*, 29, (2), 254–76.

Kent, A. (2006, March 1), "Lack of Black comic strips, no laughing matter." *Austin Weekly News* Retrieved from: http://austinweeklynews.1upsoftware. com/main.asp?SectionID=1&SubSectionID=1&ArticleID=544&TM=2578.561.

Porter, J. (1992), *Modern Negro Art*. Washington, DC: Howard University Press.

PART ONE

Comics then and now

1

Brief history of the black comic strip: Past and present

Sheena C. Howard

Introduction

There is a scarcity of literature on the history and development of newspaper comic strips created by Black (of African descent) artists; thus, this chapter will provide an overview of the salient comic strips created by Black artists, from the inception of the comic strip in the United States through the twenty-first century. I find it necessary to trace the history of newspaper comic strips created by Black artists in order to establish, maintain, and preserve African American history, as well as to situate the Black comic strip within an historical and societal context. The primary goal of this chapter is twofold: (1) provide descriptive historical information about newspaper comic strips created by Black artists, some of whom may not be well known and (2) bring attention and structure to this area of study within the field of comic art scholarship.

The American comic strip

A comic strip is a sequence of drawings that tells a story. More specifically, comic strips are "open-ended dramatic narratives about a recurring set of characters, told with a balance between narrative text and visual action, often including dialogue in balloons, and published serially in newspapers" (Inge 1978: 77). The art form of combining words and pictures gradually evolved and began to exist in print form in the late nine-tenth century. *The Yellow Kid* is usually credited as the first newspaper comic strip. The first appearance of *The Yellow Kid* was on July 7, 1895 (Berger 1973).

In the United States newspaper comic strips are divided into daily strips and Sunday strips. Strips were initially published in black and white; however, beginning in the later part of the twentieth century, strips published in color became more frequent. Most newspaper comic strips are syndicated. Syndication makes it possible for a successful comic strip to be distributed to multiple newspapers. Cartoonists are typically paid half of the strip's revenue, while the syndicate keeps the other half. The amount cartoonists are paid depends on the size of the newspaper's circulation (Spurgeon 2004).

In America, the popularity of comics can be accredited to the war between Joseph Pulitzer and William Randolph Hearst. In 1895 the *New York World* newspaper introduced *The Yellow Kid* comic by Richard F. Outcault, the first newspaper comic printed in color. Under Joseph Pulitzer's direction circulation grew substantially, making it the largest newspaper in the country. The then rival newspaper was the *New York Journal*, which was purchased by William Randolph Hearst from Pulitzer's own brother; this led to a circulation war. The competition between Hearst and Pulitzer, coupled with the coverage of the Spanish-American War, catapulted the popularity of the comic strip. Hundreds of comic strips followed, with many running for decades, such as, but not limited to, *The Phantom, Prince Valiant, Dick Tracy, Mary Worth, Modesty Blaise*, *Tarzan*, and *Peanuts*.

From the beginning, comics have been used for political and social commentary, evidenced through the right-wing views of *Little Orphan Annie* to the liberalism of *Doonesbury*. For example, *Little Orphan Annie,* created in 1924 by Harold Gray was originally aimed at children but later morphed into a political and social commentary. Conan Tobias (2010: 27) states:

> As the Second World War approached, Gray became one of the first newspaper cartoonists to inject politics into his **strip**. The cartoonist often used Warbucks—who believed in an honest day's wage for an honest day's work—as a mouthpiece for his own conservative/libertarian views, with stories targeting communism, labour unions and even U.S. President Franklin Roosevelt's New Deal.

Undoubtedly, comic strips have traditionally mirrored contemporary society and presented alternative views of society through the lens of the artists, thus making strips meaningful and poignant to a large number of people. *Doonesbury* (created by G. B. Trudeau), for example, has been touted for its "left-wing political stance" and the creators "gift for blending sociopolitical commentary" according to *Publishers Weekly* ("Comics review: 40: A Doonesbury Retrospective", 1990: 30). Comic strips, such as *Doonesbury*, are often printed on the editorial or op-ed page[1] rather than the comics page because of their regular political and controversial commentary.

Most discussions around comic strips in America exclude the contributions of Black artists; thus, the remainder of this chapter specifically focuses on newspaper comic strips created by Black artists. Specifically, this chapter will: (1) trace the history (though not an exhaustive account) of newspaper comic strips published by Black artists in the United States, and (2) illume the unique contributions of Black comic strip artists—including social and political commentary within these cultural works.

Black comic strips: 1920–60

Black comic strips (newspaper comic strips created by Black artists and featuring Black characters) are a form of popular art that has embodied the hopes and dreams of their cartoonists, the editorial heads of the newspapers that feature them, and middle-class African Americans (Nelson 2005). Comic strips published in Black newspapers for more than half a century provide interesting insights into Black aspirations and frustrations, drawn as they are by Blacks for Blacks (Stevens 1976). Comic strips by Black artists depicting Black characters are often unmentioned in any conversation of American comic strip history.

The four largest Black newspapers in the United States from the 1920s to the 1940s were the *Pittsburgh Courier*; the *Chicago Defender*; the *Afro-American*, headquartered in Baltimore and serving five eastern cities; and the *New York Amsterdam News* (Goldstein 2008). During this time a few notable Black cartoonists appeared off and on including but not limited to: Wilbert Holloway (*Sunnyboy Sam*) and Jay Jackson (*Bungleton Green*).

According to John Stevens (1976), "most of the [early comic strips featuring Black characters] were drawn by editorial cartoonists for the largest Black papers in their 'spare' time" and often had more than one artist. For example, *Bungleton Green* at the *Chicago Defender* had four creators (1920–63) and *Sunny Boy Sam* had two (Wilbert Holloway and Clarence Washington) since his introduction in the *Pittsburgh Courier* in 1928 (Stevens 1976). According to Stevens (1976):

Both strips featured fall guys or schlemiels. "Sunny Boy Sam" has always been a gag strip, but "Bungleton Green" switched from gags to an adventure continuity during the early 1930's and again during the mid 1940's.

Though these strips dealt with adventure and the daily dealings of a common man, these strips did not shy away from social and political satire. Stevens (1976: 240) states:

> As the traditional last-hired and first-fired of industry, the Depression hit [Blacks] faster than it did most Americans. In that gloomy atmosphere, they found Bungleton, their fantasy self, an eccentric millionaire. Nothing will do for his honeymoon but a lavish trip to Africa where Bung slays six lions and is made chief of the Congo. The reader learns on April 12, 1930: "All Africa is his-its diamond fields, coal lands and copper mines. With this he will conflict with the leading powers of the world." Bung heads home, only to find his palatial estate on the auction block and his stocks worthless. Luckily, he remembers to send his valet to fetch the gold and diamonds from Africa. His oil wells come in and by June he is on top of the world again.

Thus, though many Blacks fell on hard economic times during the stock market crash of 1929, Blacks could turn to the *Bungleton Green* strip for comic relief and a sense of escapism from the trials and tribulations of unemployment and financial uncertainty.

In 1934 Jay Jackson took over the comic strip *Bungleton Green*, which up until this time had been authored by Henry Brown. Before *Bungleton Green*, Jay Jackson had drawn panels for the *Pittsburgh Courier*. Under Jay Jackson, Bungleton continued to grapple with the everyday problems that troubled Black Americans.

> Bung couldn't enlist in World War I because of his family responsibilities. A few weeks after Pearl Harbor, he mused while looking at a bond poster: "This country is like life--It's not perfect but I do all I can to preserve it because what might follow could be worse." On that note, he moved to the country to raise chickens to aid the war effort. The strip was full of references to shortages and high prices. When he struck oil while digging a post hole, he decided to cover it up again because there wasn't anything to buy with money, anyway. He rebelled at the idea of paying 25 cents a dozen for eggs and spending $5 for groceries that fit into a small bag (Stevens 1976: 240).

Here, you can see the strip laden with ideological content that, one can reason, resonated with the Black community as the predominate readership of these strips were African Americans. In the early 1960s the *Chicago Defender* changed to a daily newspaper and the artists could not keep up with creating the strip on a consistent basis. *Bungleton Green* faded in 1963.

During *Bungleton Green*'s run in the *Chicago Defender,* the *Pittsburgh Courier* tried to rival the strip with several unsuccessful attempts. Finally, the *Pittsburgh Courier*'s editorial cartoonist introduced "Sunny Boy Sam." Stevens (1976: 241) states:

In that first strip on October 5, Sunny Boy announced, "Well, well, well. Heah I is folks right back on Wylie Avenoo. Doggon if dis place sho' don't look natchul. Sho do." Shorty, his buddy in the strip, then rushed up to tell him the exciting news about the local election. "Nemmineth' 'lection. What's da numbah t'day?" Sunny Boy asks. And that set the pace. This strip began with a heavy African American dialect, as well as exaggerated African American features—big lips and heavy features—which are reminiscent of a minstrel show. Later the dialect and minstrel features disappeared. By 1947, Sunny Boy was speaking like a college graduate: "its evident people are influenced by environment" (Stevens 1976). In the strip, the heavy dialect was reserved for encounters with evil Whites. In 1950, the *Pittsburgh Courier* added the color press; as a result, *Sunny Boy Sam* was printed in color.

During *Bungleton Green* and *Sunny Boy Sam*'s run in the *Pittsburgh Courier* and *Chicago Defender*, one of the most notable African American artists to connect illustration with satirical or political humor for the *Amsterdam News* was Ollie Harrington. In 1935, Harrington was employed as a cartoonist with the *Amsterdam News.* The *Amsterdam News* was a New York newspaper aimed at an African American audience. Harrington first had his work published in May 1935 (Goldstein 2008). His cartoon ran under the title *Dark Laughter.* Harrington used satire to comment on social issues, specifically capitalism and racism. Satire is a socially conscious art form used to expose abuses, inequality, and human vices through irony. Within the comic strip the end goal of satire is making the readers laugh, while simultaneously providing a level of awareness of some social issue. In a 1993 essay, Harrington described the motivation for his comics' messages: "I personally feel that my art must be involved, and the most profound involvement must be with the Black liberation struggle" (Goldstein 2008). Harrington's comment signifies the importance of comics as one among the many outlets African Americans used to speak out against the dominant society, other than the well-documented folk tales and slave songs.

Harrington's work ran as a single-panel cartoon, oftentimes alongside Jackie Ormes's upscale single-panel cartoon *Patty-Jo 'n' Ginger.* Jackie Ormes is the first African American female cartoonist (Brunner 2007). Ormes' began publishing her work as a cartoonist during the late 1930s in the *Pittsburgh Courier.* Ormes's first comic strip was *Dixie to Harlem,* starring Torchy Brown. At this time the daily newspapers rarely carried stories about the African American community or showed a Black face in photographs, except perhaps in the sports section (Goldstein 2008). Brunner (2007: 24) states:

Not only was *Torchy Brown* almost certainly the first strip to be written and drawn by an African American woman, but its appearance in all editions of the *Pittsburgh Courier* (as many as fourteen) was as close to syndication as an African American strip could expect.

Although *Dixie to Harlem* was a big hit, it only received a 12-month run before it was terminated. According to Nancy Goldstein (2008: 17), "It's possible her contract simply ran out or that the strip was not renewed because it's subject matter—the escapades of a madcap young woman—was not particularly of the editor's liking."

Before the mid 1960s Jackie Ormes's *Torchy Brown* challenged racial stereotypes and provided social commentary on a variety of issues. Torchy was an attractive, sexy, intelligent, and self-motivated young Black woman who, within the course of her romantic adventures (the binding theme of the strip), managed to fight racism, sexism, warmongering, and environmental pollution (Jones 1986).

Black comic strips: 1960–90

In 1965, Morrie Turner created the *Wee Pals* comic strip as a way of bringing more Black characters to the funny pages. His goal was no easy task; Black comic strips were still few and far between on the funny pages. The strip originally appeared in only five newspapers because many newspapers refused to run a strip featuring Black characters. The strip did not receive full syndication until three years later after the assassination of Dr Martin Luther King, Jr. The number of newspapers carrying the strip grew to over 60. *Wee Pals* became the first comic strip syndicated in the United States featuring a diverse ethnic cast.

Wee Pals centered on the activities of a variety of children from various ethnic backgrounds including but not limited to: Randy, an African American character, Diz; an African American character with impaired vision; and George, an Asian American character. At 85 years old Morrie Turner continued to draw the syndicated *Wee Pals* comic strip. The strip, at its height, appeared in over 100 newspapers; today it appears in 40 (Newhouse 2009).

The Black activism of the late 1960s led to new individualized portrayals of Black characters in the mainstream press. Among these were action-adventure strips like *Dateline: Danger* (1968), *The Badge Guys* (1971), and *Friday Foster* (1970–4) (Jones 1986).

In 1988, the Detroit City Council Youth Advisory Commission urged Detroit newspaper editors to bring diversity to the funny pages. At this time *The*

Detroit Free Press counted the number of characters in its comic pages in a given month, and came up with 5,250 Whites and 31 Blacks (0.6 per cent). Detroit at the time was 63 percent Black (as cited in Gardner 2008: para. 3). In September 1988, Ray Billingsley was offered a syndication contract by King Features for *Curtis*, which sold to nearly 100 newspapers by the year's end (as cited in Gardner 2008: para. 3). Curtis features a cast of decidedly African American characters. The strip involves the daily activities of Curtis at home and school. One of the main story lines is Curtis trying to get his father, Greg, to quit smoking. This story line won Billingsley the American Lung Association President Award in 2000.

In 1989, Barbara Brandon's comic strip *Where I'm Coming From* was featured in *The Detroit Free Press* Sunday edition. *Where I'm Coming From*, a nationally distributed strip by Universal Press Syndicate, is made up of "the girls," fictional characters based on Brandon and her friends. There are about a dozen women, ranging from the issues-conscious Lekesia to the self-absorbed, man-obsessed Nicole. Universal Press Syndicate syndicated the strip nationally in 1991. To date, Brandon is only the eighth Black cartoonist to reach syndication (as of October 2009) and the only female African American cartoonist to reach syndication ("Crusaders with pen and ink" 1993).

Black comic strips: 1990–twenty-first century

Historically, the comic strip in the United States has been politically and socially driven; however, "only recently have African Americans become authors and protagonists in a handful of comic strips" (Rockler 2002: 2). Comic strips for and by African Americans from the 1990s through the twenty-first century include but are not limited to: *Quincy* (Ted Shearer), *Jumpstart* (Robb Armstrong), *Herb and Jamaal* (Stephen Bentley) and *Curtis* (Ray Billingsley).

In the late 1990s, there was still a lack of lead minority characters on the funny pages. In 1999 Geoff Brown, an African American, became the associate managing editor of features for the *Chicago Tribune*. Brown felt it was an embarrassment not to have a diverse set of characters on the funny pages. Annette Kent (2006: para. 7), in an article titled "Lack of black comic strips, no laughing matter" states:

[W]hen Brown, an African-American, stepped into his role overseeing the comics section in 1999, he made it a point to include more diversity. He decided to do away with segments that had "lost their mojo," and go with "fresher" cartoonists. One of those was Aaron McGruder, creator of "The Boondocks," a nationally acclaimed strip that zeros in on Black consciousness and political aspects of American culture.

As of 2012, the funny pages are still only peppered with representations of African American comic strips. *Candorville* and *Doonesbury* are at the forefront of syndicated comic strips displaying representations with minority appeal. *The Boondocks*, initially a cultural icon on the funny pages featuring predominantly Black characters, ceased in 2006 to become an animated cartoon on *Comedy Central.*

The Boondocks is one of the most popular, yet controversial, Black comic strips to be syndicated by an African American about the African American experience within the twenty-first century. Aaron McGruder's *The Boondocks* has enjoyed tremendous media, as well as scholarly attention.

Since its strikingly successful debut in over 160 newspapers in 1999, *The Boondocks* provoked controversy in newspapers and on the internet, especially on *www.boondocks.net*—as Cornwell and Orbe (2002) argue in their analysis of African American readers' comments on this website (Rockler 2002). *The Boondocks* comic strip depicts Huey Freeman and his younger brother Riley, two young African American children who have been moved out of Chicago by their grandfather to live with him in a predominantly White suburb. The title word "boondocks" alludes to the isolation from primarily African American urban life that the characters feel, and permits McGruder some philosophical distance. Huey is a politically perceptive devotee of Black radical ideas of the past and is harshly critical of many aspects of modern Black culture. The comic strip focuses on an issue that is often silenced in mass media: race.

Though Aaron McGruder's *The Boondocks* received much acclaim, it is still evident that Black cartoonists face some of the same racist ideological hegemony faced by early Black cartoonists in the early 1900s when it comes to tokenism and outlets for their work. The funny pages are still only peppered with comic strips that feature lead minority characters.

As previously mentioned, racially aware comic strips by Black artists that attack social ills in the twenty-first century include but are not limited to: *Jumpstart* (Robb Armstrong), *Quincy* (Ted Shearer), *Herb and Jamaal* (Stephen Bentley) and *Curtis* (Ray Billingsley). These will be discussed briefly in turn.

Jumpstart created by Robb Armstrong brings a well-illustrated Black family to the funny pages. *Jumpstart* portrays a hard working middle-class African American family.

The daily lives of Joe, a policeman, Marcy, a nurse, and Sunny—along with a supporting cast of family and friends—have helped make Armstrong, 34, one of the country's hottest young newspaper cartoonists. His **strip**, which runs seven days a week, is syndicated in 200 papers, and HarperPerennial has just published **JumpStart**: A Love Story, a novel in cartoons (Neill and Calandra 1996: 69).

Quincy created by Ted Shearer features "a little Black boy coping with inner-city problems" ("Crusaders with pen and ink" 1993: 42). According to *Ebony* ("Crusaders with pen and ink" 1993: 42) magazine:

> After 15 years as art director of a Madison Avenue advertising agency, [Ted Shearer] quit his job to create the daily comic strip, "Quincy," which for 16 years was syndicated by King Features in the United States and abroad.

It has been said that Ted Shearer has been vastly overlooked in the history of comic strips.

Herb and Jamaal (Stephen Bentley) has appeared in more than 60 newspapers including the *Chicago Tribune* and the *Seattle Times*. Bentley studied Art and English at Rio Hondo College. His comic strip, *Herb and Jamaal*, was inspired by a high school reunion he attended, where he was reunited with an old friend. *Herb and Jamaal* depicts a long-lasting friendship in which the main characters go through everything together; topics span from problems with their wives to household chores.

Curtis, created by Ray Billingsley, traces the trials and tribulations of a Black youth growing up in the inner city. Ray Billingsley's early strip *Lookin' Fine* ran in over 30 newspapers from 1979 to 1982 but received minimal success. Billingsley tried again with *Curtis* in the late 1980s. Through the 1990s, Curtis appeared in over 150 newspapers across the United States. "[Billingsley] gets many of his ideas for his strip by listening to people in Black barbershops" ("Crusaders with pen and ink" 1993: 38). As of 2012, *Curtis* is still syndicated by King Features.

Black humor and language

This chapter will conclude with the unique location of humor found within past and present day Black comedy. This final section speaks to the unique contribution of Black cartoonists and the distinctive communicative patterns employed by Black cartoonists—which is germane to understanding the unique contributions and work of Black cartoonists.

Historical knowledge of the use of humor within the African American community is imperative to the study of Black comedy, which includes Black comic strips. No inquiry into the consciousness and inner resources of African

Americans can ignore the content and structure of African American humor (Levine 2007).

A large component of the success of comic strips is the artist's ability to make people laugh. Humor must characterize any comic strip and is not unique to African American cartoonists; however, the location of the humor and the way in which humor is utilized within African American discourse is distinctive.

Humor is an eminently social phenomenon and must have a social significance. Humor is primarily an interactive process among those who share a sense of commonality of experience and situation (Levine 2007: 358).

American slavery provides the backdrop of tragedy against which African Americans developed their distinct form of humor, in which the material of tragedy was converted into comedy (Gordon 1998). The use of humor provided a small, yet significant, form of relief from the brutality and hardships of slavery. Black slaves faced with the demand of White masters for rigid discipline, unconditional surrender, acceptance of Black inferiority, and White superiority, survived these emotionally crippling conditions through dignity, integrity and a rich sense of humor (Gordon 1998). Verbal play, specifically playing the dozens, loud talking, testifying, and calling out are unique modes within the history of African American rhetorical practices that served as methods of channeling aggression and controlling anger and that still exist today (See Chapter 9, "Gender, race and *The Boondocks*," for an analysis of the African American rhetorical practices within Black comic strips). In this sense, humor functioned as a safety valve, as it facilitated a venting of anger and aggression while providing the community with a sense of solidarity. Humor within the African American tradition still serves this purpose today. Though slavery has long been abolished, racism still exists in various, yet more subtle, forms. Contemporary comic strips (such as *Curtis, The Boondocks, Jumpstart*) and others mentioned throughout this chapter have dealt with and illumined race relations through parodies and satire, alchemizing inequality, economic disparity and various other social/political issues into a humorous narrative.

The soul of African Americans is revealed in humor, which oftentimes is racial because it is impregnated with historical context, convictions, customs, and associations (Gordon 1998); these associations cannot be isolated from the history of the Black community. It is this continuity from past to present that distinguishes Black comic strips and their creators from those of other ethnic and racial histories; thus, the chronicle, documentation and glorification of Black comic strips is worthy of being highlighted within the American comic strip history. This chapter is by no means an exhaustive history of Black comic strips created by Black artists; however, it seeks to begin to fill the void within the field of comics scholarship.

References

Berger, A. (1973), *The Comic-Stripped American: What Dick Tracy, Blondie, Daddy Warbucks and Charlie Brown Tell Us About Ourselves*. New York: Walker Publishing.

Brunner, E. (2007), "'Shuh! Ain't nothin' to it': The dynamics of success in Jackie Ormes's *Torchy Brown*". *MELUS*, 32, (3), 23–49.

"Comics review: 40: A Doonesbury Retrospective". (2010). *Publishers Weekly*, 257, (36), 30.

Cornwell, N. C. and Orbe, M. P. (2002), "'Keepin it real' and/or 'sellin' out to the man': African-American responses to Aaron McGruder's *The Boondocks*", in R. M. Coleman (ed.), *Say It Loud!: African American Audiences, Media and Identity*. New York: Routledge, pp. 28–43.

"Crusaders with pen and ink". (1993). *Ebony*, 48, (3), 36–42.

Goldstein, N. (2008), *Jackie Ormes: The First African American Woman Cartoonist*. Ann Arbor, MI: University of Michigan Press.

Gordon, D. (1998), "Humor in African American discourse: Speaking of oppression". *Journal of Black Studies*, 29, (2), 254–76.

Inge, M. T. (1978), "Comic Art", in M. T. Inge (ed.), *Handbook of American Popular Culture*. Westport, CT: Greenwood Press.

Jones, S. L. (1986), "From 'under cork' to overcoming: Black images in the comics", in C. Hardy and G. F. Stern (eds), *Ethnic Images in the Comics: An Exhibition in the Museum of the Balch Institute for Ethnic Studies*. Philadelphia, PA: The Balch Institute for Ethnic Studies, pp. 21–30.

Kent, A. (2006, March 1), "Lack of Black comic strips, no laughing matter." *Austin Weekly News* Retrieved from: http://austinweeklynews.1upsoftware.com/main.asp?SectionID=1&SubSectionID=1&ArticleID=544&TM=2578.561.

Levine, L. (1977), *Black Culture and Black Consciousness: Afro-American Folk Thought from Slavery to Freedom*. New York: Oxford University Press.

Neill, M. and Calandra, B. (1996). "Life's a sketch". *People*, 45, (17), 69.

Nelson, A. M. (2005), "*Swing Papa* and *Barry Jordan*: Comic strips and black newspapers in postwar Toledo", in *Proceedings of the Ohio Academy of History, Muskingum College, New Concord, 7–8 April 2005*, pp. 61–74.

Newhouse, D. (2009, July 9), "Dave Newhouse: 'Wee Pals' harmony extends to its executors'. *Oakland Tribune*. Retrieve from: http://findarticles.com/p/articles/mi_qn4176/is_20090419/ai_n31577222/.

Rockler, N. (2002), "Race, Whiteness, lightness, and relevance: African American and European American interpretations of *Jump Start* and *The Boondocks*". *Critical Studies in Mass Communication*, 19, 398–418.

Spurgeon, T. (2004), "Getting published—Comic strips". *The Comics Reporter*. Retrieved from: http://www.comicsreporter.com/index.php/all_about_comics/all_about/76/.

Stevens, J. D. (1976), "Reflections in a dark mirror: Comic strips in Black newspapers". *The Journal of Popular Culture*, X, (1), 239–44.

Tobias, C. (2010, August 16), "The Ode: Little Orphan Annie (1924–2010)". *Canadian Business*, 83, (11/12), 27.

Note

1 Opposite the editorial page; a newspaper article that expresses the opinions of a named writer who is usually unaffiliated with the newspaper's editorial board.

2

The trouble with romance in Jackie Ormes's comics

Nancy Goldstein

Several cartoon historians have confessed to me that although they are fond of Jackie Ormes's other comics, her 1950–4 *Torchy in Heartbeats* that chronicles Torchy's search for romantic love holds little interest for them. Possibly the 1950s *Pittsburgh Courier* newspaper editors had a similar distaste for the ongoing love story when they dropped *Torchy in Heartbeats* from the *Comic Section* while continuing all the other strips. Just as curious, on the few occasions when writers today have taken up *Torchy in Heartbeats* at all, they tend to focus on singular episodes in the strip that deal with racism and environmental justice, glossing over or remaining indifferent to the central character's four-year pursuit of love (Jackson, D. 1985; Jackson, T. 1998; Jones 1986; Reib and Feil 1996; Robbins 2001). Of course the politically charged episodes in *Torchy in Heartbeats* are extraordinary for their originality and courage and they well deserve writers' admiration, including my own. In those episodes, Ormes was probably the first cartoonist to depict industrial pollution's disproportionately ill effects on people of color; in addition, she was one of the few who challenged racial prejudice in a comic strip. My 2008 biography of Ormes explores these remarkable *Torchy in Heartbeats* episodes at length, as well as Ormes's other social and political commentary in her comics and cartoons (Goldstein 2008). I will extend that discussion here to show ways she was just as bold in depicting romantic love in a comic strip, unusual for its time since Black characters were rarely seen in love scenes in print or film. Indeed, in the mainstream media passionate, fulfilling, or even enduring love relationships between African American men and women were virtually invisible.

Jackie Ormes (1911–85) is considered to be the first African American woman newspaper cartoonist. Most of her work appeared in the *Pittsburgh*

Courier, one of the largest Black press weekly newspapers, which by the late 1940s claimed a coast-to-coast readership of over a million through its 14 big city editions. She produced four different comic strips and cartoons from 1937 to 1956, a time period that includes an unexplained seven-year break from cartooning. Although she also produced single panel cartoons, this essay will focus only on Ormes's two comic strips. Specifically, I will discuss the romantic love elements in *Torchy in Heartbeats* (titled *Torchy Brown Heartbeats* for its first few months), and will offer a brief overview of her earlier comic strip, *Torchy Brown in "Dixie to Harlem"* (1937–8), as it relates to different kinds of romantic situations. In addition to the two comic strips, Ormes also produced two single panel cartoons. *Candy*, set at the home front of World War II and featuring a wisecracking housemaid, ran for four months in the *Chicago Defender* (March to July 1945). Ormes's single panel *Patty-Jo 'n' Ginger* in the *Pittsburgh Courier* (1945–56) was her longest-running work. With plenty of eye candy in the person of shapely Ginger, *Patty-Jo 'n' Ginger* was a big sister–little sister setup that made jokes about domestic life while satirizing society and politics, and protesting racial injustice. In 1946 Ormes contracted with the Terri Lee company to produce a Patty-Jo doll, one of the first upscale Black dolls on the market. Although this essay focuses on romance as a unique aspect of her comic strips, I would be remiss to not mention Ormes's political activism and her FBI file of nearly 300 pages that the Justice Department compiled during 12 years of the communist-hunting Cold War era of the 1940s and 1950s. Certainly not a communist, her left-leaning activities and some of her associations nevertheless made her a target for investigation. Despite what must have been a worrisome situation, she continued to criticize in her *Patty-Jo 'n'Ginger* cartoons such powerful entities as segregated school systems, the HUAC (House Un-American Activities Committee), and the US military machine, defying some of the most entrenched American institutions.

As we consider Ormes's artistic production in the context of mid-twentieth-century cartooning, it is useful to review some of the formal elements of comic strips and cartoons. She drew and wrote in both formats, at times simultaneously, a practice somewhat unusual for a cartoonist and one that required dexterity of skill and imagination. Generally speaking, comic strips work differently from single panel cartoons, each using distinct strategies of elapsed time and, sometimes, of language (Eisner 1985; McCloud 1993). While single panels deliver the goods in one moment, comic strips build tension over time for an eventual climactic payoff. In her single panels the reader's gaze surveys one scene, taking in settings, postures, clothing, and faces, before dropping to the one-liner at the bottom that may be funny, insightful, or even somber. By contrast, her comic strips are read as a series of panels that sustain action and tell stories that continue from week to week. Successful mainstream cartoonists were paid well enough to be able to afford assistants, but, like most Black press cartoonists, Ormes did all the work herself, dreaming up the stories, penciling, erasing, inking, coloring, and lettering the balloons. She followed the pictorial convention of horizontal strips of uniform panels read from left to right, building to a last panel that ends with a bang or a cliffhanger promising to be "Continued next week!" thus enticing the reader to buy another paper.

Recovering newspaper comic strips and cartoons

One of the problems in discussing cartoons and comics in the historic Black press is that few people have actually seen them. Until recently, most writers have restricted their recovery of historic newspaper comics to the mainstream press, for various reasons overlooking the rich legacy of African American newspapers. This is not to suggest that there was any particular animus toward African American cartoonists on the part of comics historians; more likely, Black newspapers were not considered part of the accepted canon of comics history, a lapse of inclusion that some critics might identify as racial prejudice. One simple way to find evidence of this neglect in the past is to peruse the indexes of pre-2000 comics encyclopedias and retrospectives where such names as Ollie Harrington, Samuel Milai, Jackie Ormes, and Leslie Rogers will not be found. Black press cartoonists were, to use the term made famous by novelist Ralph Ellison, invisible.

But surely the main reason today for any perceived neglect is the difficulty of locating microfilm or original issues of such papers as the *Chicago Defender, New York Amsterdam News, Afro-American,* and *Pittsburgh Courier,* the largest Black-owned newspapers of mid-twentieth century America. Since these were weeklies, fewer were produced than the daily mainstream newspapers, leaving behind a relatively small number of Black press papers in libraries, museums, and private collections. Unfortunately, they mostly met the fate of mainstream papers when in the 1970s libraries turned their newspapers over to be microfilmed and then sold or trashed the newspapers (Baker 2001; Goldstein 2008). Today a persistent collector or researcher might get lucky and find an ephemera dealer selling original format *Pittsburgh Courier* newspapers, or sometimes a cache of papers— even original drawings—are found in a deceased cartoonist's belongings and donated by a family member to a library. This happened recently with the family of Samuel Milai (*Pittsburgh Courier* and others) donating to the Billy Ireland Cartoon Library at Ohio State University, or the family of Chester Commodore (*Chicago Defender*) donating to the Vivian G. Harsh Research

Collection of Afro-American History and Literature at a South Side Chicago public library. Viewing the newspaper in original format is something of a revelation. Enormous in size compared to today's papers, the 1947 *Pittsburgh Courier*, for instance, is 23 inches high by a fully open 43 inches. No wonder back in the day kids read the funnies lying on the floor propped on their elbows; the paper was just too big for a youngster to hold. Although print quality was often lacking in Black press papers, many of the best *Pittsburgh Courier* funnies pages compare favorably to any on the newsstand. With two single panels on the left side (Ollie Harrington's *Dark Laughter* starring the character Bootsie, and Ormes's *Patty-Jo 'n' Ginger*), and five or six cartoonists' strips on the right (Ollie Harrington, Wilbert Holloway, Samuel Milai, Clovis Parker, Jerry Stewart), the *Pittsburgh Courier* funnies pages made for exciting and pleasurable reading.

Microfilm archives and digital databases now make available Ormes's black-and-white 1937–8 *Torchy Brown in "Dixie to Harlem"* comic strip (as well as her *Candy* and *Patty-Jo 'n' Ginger* single panels) that were in the regular news pages. Like other Black press papers, the *Pittsburgh Courier* embedded cartoons and sometimes a strip or two or a full page in its regular news pages and these were duly microfilmed, presently making them available through libraries that subscribe to Black history digital databases such as ProQuest Historical Newspapers and Black Studies Center. Unfortunately the digital image of cartoons, comics, and illustrations can be of poor quality since its original source is celluloid microfilm that often bears the vicissitudes of time and use. While text is usually legible, graphics often appear blotchy, distorted, or scratched, corrupting the crisp lines and clear space created by cartoonists like Ormes. Researchers such as Allan Holtz, Tim Jackson, and others have toiled in microfilm archives and online to find obscure comics that were filmed, to clean them up and post them on their websites.

But the difficulties of recovering comics in black-and-white newspaper pages pale beside the problem of locating what was probably the only Black press color newspaper comics supplement, the *Pittsburgh Courier's* 1950–4 eight-page *Comic Section* in which Ormes's *Torchy in Heartbeats* appeared. This tabloid-size color insert was overlooked—or discarded—in the microfilming process and the few issues that were filmed of course appear in microfilm black and white. Produced by the White-owned Smith-Mann Syndicate based in New York, it appears that the *Pittsburgh Courier* was this syndicate's only customer in its short existence. Of the eight comics with all-Black casts of characters, only three cartoonists can be identified as African American: Wilbert Holloway, Samuel Milai, and Ormes; Edd Ashe and Carl Pfeufer are White men and the other two comics are unsigned. Diligent tracking on eBay and other auction sites can occasionally turn up an original format *Comic Section*. Recently the University of Michigan Special Collections

Library acquired from a collector 23 heretofore lost issues starting with its inception in August 1950 through early 1951; about 160 intact *Comic Section*s can be found in the Chicago edition of the *Pittsburgh Courier* from 1951 to 1954 at the Center for Research Libraries, Chicago, though access is limited due to the fragile condition of the newspapers; the Library of Congress Prints Division has one copy; and a good guess of a count among private collectors is perhaps two dozen *Comic Section*s.

One hopes that in the future funding will become available to gather, scan, and publish the entire color comic strip lineup of African American cowboys, space rangers, detectives, crime-fighters, fighter pilots, and secret agents. But presently there are only a few ways to see the *Pittsburgh Courier* color comics in reproduction. I was fortunate to find and photograph many of Ormes's *Torchy in Heartbeats* strips that appeared in the *Comic Section* and have reproduced 18 of them in my book along with more than a hundred of her other cartoons and comics. In the "Obscurity of the Day" section of his blog, Holtz presents an entire eight-page color *Comic Section* from August 1953, "Over the next week or so I'm going to present all the comics from a rare copy of the section that I recently acquired (only the third I've found, though I've been searching them out for years)" (Holtz 2006). Because few people have actually seen full runs of Ormes's comic strips, it will be necessary—and quite fun, at least for this writer—to describe the narratives and how they relate to the evolving art of comic strips in Black newspapers and to romance fiction.

Romance in *Torchy Brown in "Dixie to Harlem"* (1937–8)

Before television, videos, and electronic games took over as the national pastime, comic strips provided a large part of Americans' in-home entertainment and were a major player in newspaper marketing. So popular were the comics in the mainstream press, and such a draw for the purchase of a paper, that often comics titles were on the front page, with "Dick Tracy ... p. 13" and "Orphan Annie ... p. 15," for instance, listed with the page numbers for "Editorials" and "Obituaries." The Hearst and Pulitzer newspapers and their mighty cartoon syndicates conducted reader polls of favorite comics and the trade journal *Editor & Publisher* reported on cartoonists' contracts and work arrangements. For the smaller Black press, we are left mostly to deduce a cartoonist's popularity from evidence in the comics pages themselves. Either a comic strip continued over time or it disappeared, leaving us to guess that its absence indicated low reader interest though other factors may have been at work as when, for instance, the cartoonist may have moved on to other projects. No statistics were published, few interviews were recorded, and only an occasional letter to the editor about comics can be found. It is impossible to know exactly why *Torchy Brown in "Dixie to Harlem"* lasted only a year but the answer likely lies with Jackie Ormes's working relationship with the *Pittsburgh Courier*. Many Black press cartoonists worked on staff for the newspapers producing anything that was needed from editorial cartoons to story and features illustrations and even display ads as well as their comic strips. In contrast Ormes had an independent contract to produce *Torchy Brown in "Dixie to Harlem"* and she spun the story out over precisely the one-year term of her agreement. By the time the story wound to an end, Ormes and her husband had moved from Pittsburgh to a small town in Ohio where perhaps her mind had turned to other matters and she chose to not continue. It is possible that this woman cartoonist was brought on board to spark the interest of female readers, and perhaps that did not happen to the publisher's satisfaction. Or, maybe, in the dark days of the Great Depression, the *Pittsburgh Courier* was financially unable to renew an independent cartoonist.

Another consideration is that an ongoing narrative by and about a woman did not appeal to the tastes of all-male editorial staff or even to the readers. Indeed Ormes peppered the *Torchy Brown in "Dixie to Harlem"* story with themes that were considered feminine like tender feelings, girl talk about men, and of course shopping, high fashion, and glamour while the other *Pittsburgh Courier* strips were mostly one-shot humorous vignettes starring men and boys who pulled pranks, took pratfalls, played the numbers, and uttered sardonic punch lines. When Ormes was asked much later in life how it happened that she left the *Pittsburgh Courier* in 1956, she hinted at gender bias: "It was strictly a man's world" (Jackson, D. 1985: 25). Even today the number of women cartoonists in print lags far behind that of men.

Though hardly a love story, *Torchy Brown in "Dixie to Harlem"* is nevertheless romantic in a classical sense with its protagonist as an excitable, quixotic—and very funny—young woman seeking adventure. Farm girl Torchy who "[d]oesn't know much about life but suspects an awful lot" runs away from her loving Mississippi family, defying the perils of the "Big Apple" to win a spot as a performer in what is suggested to be the Cotton Club. Torchy claims her spot as a nightclub headliner through sheer talent, but not without using feminine wiles of flirting, wheedling, cajoling, and begging, pausing once or twice to pine over the loving family she left behind. Both male and female readers surely appreciated the poignancy of *Torchy Brown in "Dixie to Harlem"* as an amusing allegory to real-life experiences of the Great Migration. One scene, for instance, shows young Torchy boarding a northbound train, pondering ways to confound the conductor in order to sit in the more comfortable "White" section of the segregated train, and in another scene in New York City a frightened Torchy dodges a procuress' entrapment. Several panels are unusually tender for a comic strip when Torchy pours out her heart in a letter home to her Aunt Clemmie and Uncle Jeff, telling them of her loneliness and how she misses them. Soon enough Torchy gathers her courage, defies the obstacles and begins to conquer the city. "Golly gee—I guess all New Yawk gals are pretty nifty … I'm gonna get me a hat like that" Torchy exclaims in one panel. She finds herself inside a stylish boutique trying on dresses and gowns. "Clothes do make the woman," the shop girl tells Torchy who, more than a little out of her element replies, "Sho' nuff?" The cartoonist's detailed, delicate line work wonderfully animates Torchy's humorous facial expressions and dance movements, and her character's entertaining words ring with soft southern idioms that sometimes evolve into comic northern hipster patter (Brunner 2007). In cameo scenes that were unique on the page, real-life people add immediacy to the story. After auditioning for choreographer Leonard Reed, getting an admiring approval from columnist Billy Rowe, singing with bandleader Cab Calloway, and dancing with Bill "Bojangles" Robinson, Torchy finally becomes a nightclub star. Ormes ends the tale with a funny but tender moment when Torchy's long-lost mother emerges from the audience in the unmistakable profile of Josephine Baker. One can imagine that Ormes's own emotions inspired this mother-daughter reunion since she and her husband had lost their only child, three-year-old Jacqueline, to a brain tumor a few years before. (Earl and Jackie Ormes would have no more children but they did enjoy a happy 45-year marriage.) Though now wrapped in humor and gaiety, episodes such as these nevertheless speak to deeply felt emotions, fears, and longings in scenes that many readers could identify with and ones that were rarely seen in other comic strips on the page.

Romantic love in *Torchy in Heartbeats* (1950–4)

It was clear that 1950 was a banner year for romance fiction, and Jackie Ormes jumped at the chance to bring this best-selling genre to the pages of a newspaper. It had been thirteen years since she created comic strips, filling about half that time with her weekly humorous single panel *Patty-Jo 'n' Ginger* that would, in fact, go on another six years. By the time the *Pittsburgh Courier* tapped Ormes to bring Torchy back in its new color *Comic Section*, much had happened in the world of comic strips. For one thing, cartoonists like Milton Caniff had emerged. The art in his phenomenally popular adventure strip *Terry and the Pirates* that began in 1934 had evolved into a realistic, painterly style that also used such cinematic techniques as overhead shots and close-ups, long shot landscapes and factual settings. Ollie Harrington, probably the most famous Black press cartoonist whose single panel cartoon *Dark Laughter* appeared next to *Patty-Jo 'n' Ginger*, was already adopting Caniffian methods in his *Jive Gray* adventure strip in the *Pittsburgh Courier* (Brunner 2005; Inge 1993: xx-xxii). Another revelation for Ormes must have been *Brenda Starr, Reporter*, a comic strip by Dale Messick, a Chicagoan like Ormes, that began in 1940. Beautiful, independent, and smart Brenda must have inspired Jackie Ormes as the only female character starring in a comic strip that was also written and drawn by a woman.

She knew she would have to modernize her style, her Torchy character, and her story. For fresh ideas Ormes needed to look no further than the corner drug store's comic book racks, brimming with romance comics. By 1950 when she began to reimagine the Torchy character, "comic book creators, editors and publishers, the vast majority of them male, and the romance readers of America, the vast majority of them female, went love crazy. Stark, raving crazy ... Love was on the racks everywhere ... more love begat more love," Michelle Nolan explains in *Love on the Racks*. She further notes, "One of the enduring American pop cultural myths is that Superman and Batman created the greatest explosion of comic book success in the industry's history. That's not quite true. In 1949, comic book publishers learned there was nothing more super than a kiss," and 22 companies parlayed the frenzy by churning out 256 romance issues under 118 titles like *Young Romance* and *First Love* (Nolan 2008: 43–4). As the titles suggest, romance comics were aimed at a youthful market, generally for young women aged 12 to 20 for whom the ten-cent cover price was affordable. Along with thrilling stories of young love, romance comic books were thoroughly steeped in cautionary tales. An inexperienced girl paid the consequences in remorse and humili-ation for going out, for instance, with the devious and vain rich boy whose flashy car mysteriously would run out of gas on the way home. Though such narratives aimed to satisfy readers' expectations of practical life lessons, the artwork and dialogue were meant to titillate. Handsome men and beautiful women brilliantly tinted under a moonlit sky gaze soulfully into each others' eyes; or a lovesick girl, going down in the swirling blue surf for the third time, would cry "I don't care—I'd rather sink than call Brad for help!"—a line and image that years later Roy Lichtenstein would parody in one of his famous pop art paintings. It did not take long for critics and others to point out the emotional excess in romance comics' art and dialogue and indeed some of the terms used to describe the genre became outright negative, like "kitsch," "junk," and "trash," or perhaps more kindly "camp."

Ormes probably knew about another Black cartoonist who was famous for working in the romance comics field, and also about a short-lived Black romance comic book that joined the love glut of 1950. Matt Baker (1921–59) was the only African American who drew for major comic book publishers such as St John Publications, Atlas/Marvel, and Fox. He specialized in GGA or Good Girl Art ("good" referring not to the girl but to the art) and for these comics his characters were of course White. He was such a prized cartoonist that his employers reserved him for cover art, and had him only penciling the inside pages, with other artists doing the inking "so that he could do as much work as possible" (Benson 2003: 12). Matt Baker, whose last known work was on "I Gave Up The Man I Love!" for Atlas/Marvel, was posthumously inducted into the Will Eisner Comic Book Hall of Fame in 2009. The only

Black-oriented romance comic book of the time was something of an exper-
iment by Fawcett Publications, a power in the mainstream industry. In 1950,
they tried tapping into the African American market with *Negro Romance*
that featured stories such as "Possessed," "Love's Decoy," and "My Heart's
Dilemma." However, after three issues Fawcett discontinued the comic book,
making extant copies highly desirable for comic book collectors.

There was even more love in pulp novels and magazines. African American
women's magazines had been around since the 1910s providing important
information for the woman learning to navigate urban spaces; importantly as
well, the magazines also had love stories. In the same year that Ormes began
her love story in the funny papers, *Ebony* publisher John H. Johnson brought
out the first issue of *Tan Confessions*, a women's magazine with articles that
furnished "home-making coverage in the Negro field" sprinkled among "the
more sensational stories of sexual intrigue that formed the bulk of the publication" (Rooks 2004: 121). Living in Chicago, the home of John H. Johnson's
publishing empire, Ormes undoubtedly read some of these magazines, and,
being active in the city's social and arts scene, she was probably acquainted
with some of their writers, photographers, and editors. But as a cartoonist
her excitement lay beyond the black-and-white magazine pages, and for the
new *Pittsburgh Courier* color section she planned to model her next work
after the romance comic books that splashed "four color love" across its
pages.

Considering Ormes's past work, her inclinations, and her temperament,
one could predict that she would inevitably draw and write a love story in the
funny papers, essentially creating a sub-genre of her own design. Tales of love
were not unheard of in Black newspapers, and in the late 1930s Ormes drew
an illustration for a *Pittsburgh Courier* "Short Story Complete in One Issue"
about a misbegotten romance. In the illustration that bears her signature,
a beautiful woman glances flirtatiously and the caption reads, "He pictured
in his mind her creamy brown complexion and sloe-eyes." By the early
1940s, when Ormes did some stringer reporting for the *Chicago Defender*,
her penchant for overwriting apparently vexed news editor Ben Burns who
lamented, "Another staff short-timer was pert Ormes, who was always
upbeat but who, for all my attempts to shape her clumsy writing, never
could measure up as a competent reporter" (Burns, 1996, p. 20). To be sure,
Ormes strayed from objective reporting, leaning rather toward flowery prose
and interviews that uncover—as she put it herself—the subject's "affairs
d'amour." When she spoke to singer and actress Lena Horne, for instance,
Ormes got right to the point with a question about her love life: "'Tell them
marriage is nowhere on my program,' she [Horne] replied almost wearily. But,
the gesture of shrugging her pretty shoulders and clasping slender hands,
revealed an agate-sized star sapphire on her third finger. The queen pin-up

of a million men in uniform explained, 'All I know about my love life is what I read in the papers!'" (Ormes 1944: 7). A better fit for Ormes was writing the *Defender*'s "Social Whirl" column where for a few weeks in the early 1940s she was hired to enthuse about dating, engagements, weddings, and couples a-courting, as well as reporting other social news. But her journalistic writing came to an end when "I said, well that's fun but I want to draw" and the *Defender* gave her a four-month trial run with single panel *Candy* (Jackson, D 1985: 18). Soon she returned to the *Pittsburgh Courier* where she embarked on the long run of producing *Patty-Jo 'n' Ginger* and where her romance comic strip *Torchy in Heartbeats* made its debut in 1950.

When asked to explain their disregard for *Torchy in Heartbeats*, my comics historian colleagues usually say something like, "Well, it's mostly a predictable love story, you know, hearts and flowers and a happy ending." Of course these critics are right. But as Thomas J. Roberts suggests in *An Aesthetics of Junk Fiction*, they are missing the point. Romance love stories belong to a vernacular fiction genre that invites readers "to predict what they will get but then surprises them ... This is a fiction that is read for its twists and turns and sparks of interest" and when we do not know how to read a certain genre "we are unconsciously looking for the wrong things" (Roberts 1990: 171–2). The *Pittsburgh Courier* color comics pages with their detectives, spacemen, cowboys, and others, was all about genre reading. Most women young and older understood the logic of the romance genre in *Torchy in Heartbeats* from the multitude of radio soap operas, magazines, and romance comic books flooding the market, but for others—men especially—romantic love must have been inconceivable in the funnies. Even in mainstream newspaper comic strips heroines and heroes were not known to pursue serious love relationships. Some male lead characters occasionally had strong feelings for girlfriends or were pursued by girls, like Superman/Clark Kent and Lois Lane, but none of them suffered in the name of love, as did Torchy in *Torchy in Heartbeats*.

Closest to the true lovelorn convention perhaps were the main characters in *Mary Worth* (so titled in 1940; previously titled *Apple Mary* from 1934, and *Mary Worth's Family* from 1939) and *Rex Morgan, M.D.* (from 1948) who dispensed advice about intimate affairs, as well as about taboo subjects like teen pregnancy and drug abuse, though they themselves were not entangled in relationships. But these strips were written and drawn by men, and as Janice Radway put it in *Reading the Romance*, "a man's story always gives the hero's point of view more extensively than that of the heroine ... the crucial passages about emotional satisfaction were not centered on the heroine's experience at all but expressed the male fantasy..." (Radway 1991: 179). *Torchy in Heartbeats* is often compared to *Brenda Starr, Reporter* and indeed both were drawn by women, starred women, and had romances, as well as other similar elements like exotic settings and fashionable clothing. But Brenda was above all else a newspaper career woman and most of the excitement in *Brenda Starr* involved pursuing the story, helping to solve crimes, and getting the goods on racketeers and corrupt politicians. Torchy, on the other hand, never did settle on a career, and in fact most of the time it is hard to figure out just what kind of work she does. Her overriding journey seems to be the pursuit of love, but she finds surprising, exciting twists and turns along the way. They differ in other important ways as well. The *Brenda Starr* strip could be humorous and ironic and it was drawn in a flamboyant, fanciful style; sometimes Brenda even had stars in her eyes. *Torchy* was portrayed realistically, with the settings and interiors taken from real life and the storyline was earnest and thoughtful. And throughout the strip, almost all the characters were drawn and colored as Black persons, from mobsters to ship's captains, villains to heroes, sly romantic rivals to trusted true loves.

Torchy in Heartbeats tells the story of an independent-minded young woman who searches for love and finds adventures in a variety of colorful settings; she is a romantic character with whom readers would vicariously identify. The word *heartbeats* in the title prepares readers for tales about a tender heroine whose caring nature leads her to intimate relations that sometimes end up hurting her. From August to December 1950, Torchy appeared as a lovelorn ingénue whose boyfriend was killed while pursuing a life of crime; between January and October 1951, Torchy's role was love-struck rescuer of a young man in distress who was a musical genius; during November 1951 to January 1953, she is trapped in and then escapes from a jungle with a new love; finally, from January 1953 to its ending in September 1954, she appears in her most celebrated role as a campaigner for environmental justice and racial equality in the US South. The very last strip brings the Torchy story to a—yes, predictable—happy ending when handsome Dr Paul Hammond proposes marriage.

From the very beginning, Ormes places the Torchy character in a scene of domestic stability and middle class plenty that defines her status and careful upbringing, and, perhaps not incidentally, echoes Ormes's own family history. Mother places a vase of roses on a table, "You're tired Torchy, you're wearing yourself out looking for just the kind of job you want," and father puts down his newspaper for a moment, saying to the young woman "I still wish you'd come work for me in the store, Torchy" who replies, "I know, Dad, but I've got to try making my own way." Independence was standard fare in romance stories but this convention had added meaning for young, urban African American female readers who could identify with Torchy looking for employment beyond the want-ad listings for "domestic help" and yearning to step beyond the bounds of patriarchal control. Torchy personified the very desire for economic freedom, self-improvement, and emotional happiness that would resonate with Ormes's readers. Along the way, and in contrast to the often sexually scandalous stories in women's magazines, Torchy provided a model for virtuous behavior. *Torchy in Heartbeats* appeared in a family newspaper, one that was known for its editorials and features promoting good behavior, thrift, manners, and family values, all elements of racial uplift that the *Pittsburgh Courier* promoted. While some readers of the more daring *Tan Confessions*, for instance, "were enthusiastic   others complained   " No respectable colored woman would allow herself to be in these situations and she certainly wouldn't write about them if she did'" (Rooks 2004: 125). As a realistic girl-next-door type, Torchy sometimes made bad choices but her own common sense and strength of character helped her to learn from her mistakes, an essential ingredient of romance fiction. Her first mistake was involvement with Dan. They landed a job dancing as a pair in a nightclub and when she learned he was part of an illegal gambling racket and that he was taking up with other women, she still stuck to him, " No, Dan, I'm not walking out!—(sob)—you need me—more than you know!" In shadowy side scenes of Dan deal-making, readers could see that Torchy's efforts to reform him would fail and inevitably he was killed in a police raid, leaving her "an aching heart."

Throughout her cartooning career Ormes often drew sensuous images of women that bordered on erotic while keeping the women's behavior virtuous and proper. The nightclub setting had given her a chance to show shapely Torchy dancing in slinky evening gowns and appearing scantily clad in her dressing room, and Ormes lost no time undressing Torchy in the next episode. Leaving behind her broken heart, she fled on a bus that crashed ("KA-RAASH!") on a rainy night. Torchy was unhurt and rushed to the aid of a young man, bandaging his wounds with her blouse that left her only in a lacy bra and trousers for several subsequent comic strips. The man was Earl, her next love-to-be, who needed weeks of her tender care for his crushed fingers to heal so he could return to his virtuoso piano playing. That Earl had been composing for jazz piano must have struck a chord with readers who would have recognized the jazz tradition as originating in African American communities. (And the clever in-joke here was naming the hero Earl after Jackie Ormes's own husband, Earl Ormes!)

Readers understood that a romance required the woman searching for love to project sex appeal and desirability in order to attract the man of her dreams. The image of a comely and partially clad Black female in heroic performance fit perfectly with the *Pittsburgh Courier*'s effort to be at once eye-catching and racially uplifting. Pin-up poses sold papers and the newspaper often placed photos of statuesque bathing beauty contest winners, as well as modest headshots of pretty college graduates, on the front page. In a fascinating unpublished dissertation, Kim T. Gallon describes how photojournalism enhanced the ability of Black newspaper readers to view and debate issues of sexuality. "Photographs of attractive women were another aspect of life which African Americans could also be proud ... A fit body, healthy sexuality oriented toward men, and physical attractiveness reconfigured the face of respectability and demonstrated a larger shift in the integration of it with sexuality. Black women's bodies, however, also signified Black progress and accomplishment ... the bodies of Black women stood for the entire race" (Gallon 2009: 128, 148). As if taking her cues from these photos, and probably also from other Black press cartoonists, Ormes transformed the bathing beauty idea to create Torchy as a wholesome charmer with a real-life story. Others also drew attractive women. Jay Jackson and Wilbert Holloway were staff artists whose humorous cartoons with leggy women were sometimes seen on the editorial page, and during World War II Jackson even advertised in the *Chicago Defender* a packet of what were called military morale kits, "Pin Up Girls—These solid senders sketched from beautiful brown models are strictly whistle bait! 6 for $1." (Jackson, J. 1942–5) In the *Pittsburgh Courier*'s color *Comic Section* Samuel Milai, a Black cartoonist who drew *Don Powers*, as well as other comic strips and cartoons, included women though in minor roles where, most often, they required rescuing by the male hero. Interestingly, people who knew her often commented that Ormes looked a lot like her striking cartoon characters, and indeed in the archive of her papers at the DuSable Museum of African American History, Chicago, there are photographs of her in sweater-girl pin-up poses.

By early 1951, Ormes was producing fashion shows and training models on the South Side of Chicago and she was intimately, as well as commercially, involved with dressing the female body in the latest styles. In late January she added *Torchy Togs*, a paper doll cut-out panel, next to *Torchy in Heartbeats*. *Torchy Togs* was a perfect way to report fashion news and from the time it started in late January the topper[1] often covered half the *Torchy* page. Dressed in strapless bra and panties, and surrounded by dresses, gowns, sportswear, hats, gloves, and lingerie, Torchy in *Torchy Togs* says, "Girls! Get those scissors ready! Here are some items from my new wardrobe. Cut carefully along the heavy black outlines so they'll fit me! And *please* ... do right by my figure, too. Go slow around the curves." Paper doll collectors who own much of the *Torchy in Heartbeats/Torchy Togs* pages in private collections say that Torchy is the only paper doll in history that speaks directly to readers, instructing them on how to dress. Her many female comic strip predecessors like Jane Arden, Mopsy, Tillie the Toiler, and, of course, Brenda Starr also had paper doll cut-out panels but they stood mute on the page.

Torchy's friendly, informal chatter aimed to create a fan base of women for whom reading *Torchy in Heartbeats/Torchy Togs* would become almost like a social event. In *Torchy Togs* Ormes welcomes readers with "Here we go again, gals," "Come on, girls!," "Hello, Everybody!," "Hi, Courier pals!," "Hello, you wonderful people," "Hi there, friends!," "What's happening, kids?," "Hi, girl friends!" and as a nod to men who may have occasionally enjoyed glancing at the topper, Torchy offers her pin-up possibilities, "Get out the scissors gals, but for a guy a pin is all you need!" Usually the words spoken by paper doll Torchy have nothing to do with the narrative; they are breezy and chatty in upbeat messages, and, one intuits, they are really spoken by Ormes herself. Romance reading assumes physical attractiveness and sex appeal and while Ormes could not always work those elements into her story, they took center stage in *Torchy Togs*. Just below dramatic scenes of Torchy suffering in the name of love, a quite different Torchy would appear in the topper, dressed, for instance, in strapless bra and a girdle with garters attached to nylon stockings. Here Torchy cheerily enthuses with advice, "This week I'm showing my favorite curve-controls. Such are a must for perfect grooming." This was valuable information for the young African American woman following her mother's and grandmother's admonitions to wear respectable clothing that would, incidentally, defy White stereotypes of the loose Black female in revealing clothing.

At the same time Torchy's smart image countered the demeaning images in mainstream comic strips where Black women were stuck in what were meant to be humorous mammy-type roles, or as domestic servants and laundresses with oversized, lumpy clothing covering portly bodies. It was a pleasure to see in Torchy an attractive, confident, modern Black woman who knew how to read the social and sartorial rules, and who, in her friendly chatter, shared her tips. Moreover, the visible consumption of goods that Torchy models in *Torchy Togs* signified racial progress to her readers, promoting what Susannah Walker calls "consumer citizenship," a term that defines full participation in the marketplace and signifies entry into the American middle class (Walker 2007: 11–28). Indeed Torchy's sumptuous wardrobe leaves little doubt of her high expectations and that her search for love will end, predictably, in a happy marriage that provides material well-being. In *Torchy Togs* Ormes also begins to flirt with romantic notions of a fantasy world, this one transporting readers into a realm of high fashion. Sometimes she named actual designers as when she drew gowns whose hourglass designs she attributed to Christian Dior, or when she included real hats by African American milliner Artie Wiggins, well-known in Chicago fashion circles. And at the same time, the extra *Torchy Togs* panel freed the Torchy character from the confines of *Torchy in Heartbeats's* workaday wardrobe and allowed Ormes free rein to create imaginative clothing.

Over and above these diverse attractions, though, the main reason women would have read *Torchy in Heartbeats* was for pleasure and satisfaction, and for simple escapist fun. A work of "junk fiction" is form-intensive and readers returned again and again to such formal romance reading pleasures as narrative design, scene construction, tone of language, and a well-defined heroine (Roberts 1990: 9). *Torchy in Heartbeats* was pleasurably diverting, to be sure, but, as romance reading should, the strip also imparted useful information. Just as Torchy was instructing women on how to dress in *Torchy Togs*, she was also modeling ways to learn from failed love experiences in the *Torchy in Heartbeats* narrative. Finally comprehending what readers knew all along, that her boyfriend Earl was more in love with his music than with her, and with large, sad, wet eyes and knitted brows, Torchy figures it out, "He'd be mine, and his love would be wonderful—but still a part would be missing. Or am I being a fool? Am I looking for something that can't be had?" To heighten the emotional impact Ormes sometimes used color in surprising and innovative ways. Here, with Torchy in a blue mood, Ormes places her face in a close-up and tints it cornflower blue. Readers were looking for deeply felt emotion in such depictions, but there were other reasons a woman would pick up the newspaper to follow *Torchy in Heartbeats*.

On a practical level, newspapers were readily available and a serialized story was made for a quick read, perfect for busy women with a limited amount of leisure time. Comic strip installments were short, undemanding, and could be enjoyed even when the reader was tired—aspects of storytelling that could be taken as negative but actually are elements of strength for the romance genre. The language in this type of story—and certainly Jackie Ormes's florid prose—could also come in for criticism; her purple passages and expressions ("sob!," "choke!," "gasp!") might not wear so well if one were to sit down with, say, two hundred pages of the stuff. But for romance readers who were looking for drama, such emotional expressions would have been satisfying and, of course, expected. And after all, it was partly the language in the narrative that inspired artists like Matt Baker and Roy Lichtenstein to translate the romance-comics genre into a visual vocabulary of love, suffering, and triumph. About this time, Torchy was ready to leave her suffering behind. As the musician boyfriend episode ends, a story recap says, "Torchy has decided to leave, quickly, before Earl comes to try to stop her. Her heart, though an empty shattered thing, tells her this course is the best for them both and so now ..." she runs again, this time far away, hopping a "dirty old tramp freighter" to Brazil where an ill-defined job as bookkeeper on a banana plantation awaits her.

The next installment takes a gothic turn with sadistic villains, physical danger, and a fantasy romance in exotic settings, all familiar tropes in romance reading. Torchy had been sunbathing on deck in a brief swimsuit days before, and when a lecherous ship hand makes her his prey during a battering storm she smacks his face, "CRACK," and he falls back and is swept overboard. Sexual violence against women was unusual for the funny papers but certainly not for romance reading. Ormes brings real-life issues of male dominance, control, and even aggression to the page in ways that force her heroine to redefine herself as courageous and physically strong. Romance fiction was known to occasionally include brutal violence, validating "the very pressing need to know how to deal with the realities of male power and force in day-to-day existence" (Radway, 1991, p. 76). Torchy also learns another lesson familiar to her era, that to survive as a single woman who would be so bold as to travel alone, she must avoid giving the wrong signals. We would not again see Torchy sunbathing in public display (but of course on the page there was plenty of flesh in the *Torchy Togs* topper). She is met at the port by Manu, her employer's minion, whose flat affect and evasive replies portend danger. On the page, the edges of her face and his are shown in a large crimson circle as she fixes a wary eye on the creepy, heavy browed servant who says, "You wait! You see yourself! Manu no talk!" By now Torchy has grown in experience and knows to keep a safe distance from LeGran, the overseer who runs the plantation hidden deep in the jungle. A shriek—in large red letters—pierces through her bedroom window, "'AI-I-I-I-E-E-E-E!' Suddenly, Torchy's thoughts were cut short by a scream ... a blood-chilling cry of terror!" Black press readers in their collective understanding would certainly have held special scorn for plantations and cruel overseers and probably would have caught the allusion of the name of LeGran to Simon LeGree (*Uncle Tom's Cabin*) and the cry of terror as coming from slave quarters. "There's something inhuman about him—something frighteningly inhuman! He warned me no one leaves here! I must be careful—very careful!" LeGran stalks Torchy in several episodes, "I want you to regard me more—shall we say—warmly, my dear, you will I'm sure!" Later, Torchy spies a light in the jungle and follows it to a dilapidated cabin where she meets another captive, Dr Paul Hammond, his handsome face edged in stubble and his clothes shabby, underscoring the adversity of their situation.

Throughout the series, Ormes would portray such scenes with detailed, documentary-like exactitude using the illustrated reference books she kept near her drawing table, and drawing in the realistic style of such popular cartoonists as Hal Foster (*Prince Valiant*), Alex Raymond (*Jungle Jim*, among others), Ollie Harrington in the Black press (*Jive Gray*), and, of course, Milton Caniff (*Terry and the Pirates* and *Steve Canyon*). Ormes plumbs some of a woman's worst fears in a shocking scene of attempted rape, unheard of in newspaper comic strips. LeGran pins Torchy down, his body on top of hers, "You've put me off long enough! It's time you learned who's master here!" She is saved when a fire calls him away, and the story continues for a few weeks with cat-and-mouse scenes of Torchy evading LeGran while she and Paul plan an escape, and, predictably, they begin to fall in love. Another image that probably would not have gotten past mainstream syndicate editors but apparently was acceptable in the Black press was Torchy bathing nearly nude in a jungle pool. Fleeing through the jungle, Paul and Torchy are beset by a swarm of angry stinging insects, as well as by Manu with his fearsome machete, huge snakes, and a watchful, hungry-looking leopard. "These insects … they're eating us alive!" Torchy cries. In her near-delirium, Paul must take charge, "Beside the clear waters of a jungle pool fed from an underground spring … 'In you go, Torchy … get those insect bites washed before they become infected!'" One of Ormes's most sensuously drawn strips shows Torchy nude from her cleavage up, bathing in the blue pool among pink water lilies, a tropical yellow bird flying overhead. Feeling better, Torchy muses, "I'm sure the Garden of Eden must have been like this," and from a respectful distance Paul reflects, "Eve was no more beautiful." Apparently, Ormes was pleased by the allegory of Adam and Eve in the Garden of Eden, and she extended it to her *Torchy Togs* panel with Torchy wearing panties, and cups over her breasts, made of green leaves. After twists and turns and exciting adventure running from LeGran, they escape and work their passage on a ship headed for the States, ending up in the US South.

Readers would begin to hope that our heroine has finally found the ideal romance, one with the emotional support that promises a happy ending. Paul embodies the inevitability and reality of male power that Torchy needs to ensure her survival in a cruel world, yet he is tender and gentle, loving her, protecting her, and putting concern for her above all else. And she would prove invaluable to him with her intelligence, moral courage, and with what would become her partnership in his work. Now begins the last episode of *Torchy in Heartbeats*, from January 1, 1953 to September 18, 1954, which would catch the attention of comics historians for its elements of social protest and environmental racism. Here Ormes turned from exotic adventures to real-world problems that faced her daily. She was all too familiar with racism of course, but also with the impact of air and water pollution. In 1953, citizens in South Side Chicago where she lived united to protest a defective landfill that released untreated runoff into swamps and lakes. Many parts of the South Side were low-income neighborhoods whose residents were mostly people of color, and these neighborhoods were well known as dumping grounds for the waste from more affluent communities and industry. About this time, probably not incidentally, Ormes has Torchy arriving in the little town of "Southville," where she first encounters racial prejudice when she asks a White farmer for help finding Paul's clinic. Urging his horse on to avoid giving her a ride in his cart, he replies, "There be some folks ye ask about thet sawbones and some ye don't! … Giddap, thar!" leaving Torchy to wonder, "My gracious! Now what was that all about?" Colonel Fuller, a White man and factory owner, is aptly named to suggest a denizen of the Old South who personifies the racist attitudes that blind him to Dr Paul Hammond's entreaties about the Fuller Chemical Company's pollution, which is affecting the health of the people of the town who are mostly Black and poor. Now aiding Paul in the clinic, Torchy confronts the Colonel with the doctor's evidence but he laughs off the idea ("Haw – haw! that's rich!") that a Black doctor could make such a discovery. Twists and turns ensue and eventually Fuller comes around to accept the blame, strike an enlightened friendship with Paul and Torchy, clean up the pollution, and build the town a sparkling new clinic.

With the larger drama over, Ormes had eight weeks left on her yearly contract. This was plenty of time to build suspense for the ending when Ormes introduces a rival for Paul's affections. Workaholic Paul barely notices that beautiful and rich Sandra is making a play for him, but Torchy begins to worry and imagine the worst. Radway explains that in romance reading the rival performs as a character foil, as a "*suspected* rather than actual" rival when the hero or heroine misunderstands what is really going on. But "Because the reader always knows that the principal in question is not attracted to the rival, that rival functions for her as a true foil, a point of comparison and contrast for hero or heroine" (Radway 1991: 122–3). Readers would be able to see the evidence of Sandra's sly machinations in her glances framed in close-up, as well as Torchy's suffering in her sad face and words, "I ... I've got to take care not to let Paul know I'm concerned about this girl! I mustn't magnify anything. Besides maybe I'm wrong ..." Finally Paul proposes marriage to Torchy, bringing *Torchy in Heartbeats* to an end. Even resolute romance readers might have felt a little disappointed at the ending. Ormes strung it out with several digressive strips that seemed to signal that the cartoonist was abandoning the story. The drawing became flatter and less detailed, and *Torchy Togs* lost some of its exuberance and audacity. Perhaps this was related to Ormes's health and the rheumatoid arthritis that had begun to affect her hands. Also, about this time, the color *Comic Section* itself was coming to a close and this must have been dispiriting for Ormes. For unexplained reasons probably related to financial considerations, on August, 28 1954 the Smith-Mann Syndicate that supplied both sections shuffled its color comics into the black-and-white *Magazine Section*. The once full-page and splendidly colorful *Torchy in Heartbeats* with *Torchy Togs* finished its career on a black-and-white half page with, incidentally, an inglorious cropping of the paper doll that cut off her feet and the bottoms of two dresses. Other comics continued in the magazine section for years.

Conclusion

With this revaluation of the romantic theme in Jackie Ormes's comic strips, perhaps some critics will be inspired to take another look. Perhaps not. Roberts describes some readers' chronic "allergies" to certain genre fiction, "We do not think of ourselves as having an allergic reaction, of course, but as truth seeing … this or that story *is* obscenely violent, or viciously snobbish, or stupid, or grossly ignorant, and those who read it are themselves violent, brutish, stupid" (Roberts 1990: 82). My contention that there existed among male editors, readers, and comics historians a distaste for the romantic love genre is not to suggest that men are allergic to narratives of the heart or other stories of romantic love. But in mid-century comic strips we just do not see the all-male editors or the mostly all-male cartoonists taking up an extended story of serious romantic love. And in fairness, it should be said that women who turned to *Torchy in Heartbeats* for touching tales of love probably also had some allergies of their own and were unlikely to follow the *Comic Section*'s shoot-'em-up western *The Chisholm Kid* or *Lohar,* the jungle leopard. Considering the bias that worked against the genre, it is actually surprising that her romance love story lasted four years, a longer run than many comic strips in other papers. Probably Ormes's *Torchy in Heartbeats* would have fit better in a romance comic book instead of a newspaper. And, one wonders if, had Fawcett Publications enlisted Ormes, *Negro Romance* may have succeeded beyond its scant three original issues. Or if John H. Johnson had signed her up to show "four color love" in *Tan Confessions*, Ormes might have had a longer life on the racks. The trouble with romance in Ormes's comic strips was that they were in the wrong place.

References

Baker, N. (2001), *Double Fold: Libraries and the Assault on Paper*. New York: Random House.

Benson, J. (ed.) (2003), *Romance Without Tears*. Seattle, WA: Fantagraphics Books.

Brunner, E. (2005), "'This job is a solid killer': Oliver Harrington's *Jive Gray* and the African American adventure strip". *Iowa Journal of Cultural Studies*, 6 (Spring), 36–57.

—(2007), "'Shuh! Ain't nothin' to it': The dynamics of success in Jackie Ormes's *Torchy Brown*". *MELUS*, 32, (3), 23–49.

Burns, B. (1996), *Nitty Gritty: A White Editor in Black Journalism*. Jackson: University Press of Mississippi.

Eisner, W. (1985), *Comics and Sequential Art*. Guerneville, CA: Eclipse Books.

Gallon, K. (2009), "Between respectability and modernity: Black newspapers and sexuality, 1925–1940". Unpublished dissertation. Philadelphia: University of Pennsylvania.

Goldstein, N. (2008), *Jackie Ormes: The First African American Woman Cartoonist*. Ann Arbor, MI: University of Michigan Press.

—(Forthcoming), *Fashion in the Funny Papers: Cartoonist Jackie Ormes's American Look*.

Holtz, A. (2006), *Stripper's Guide* [blog]. Retrieved from: http://strippersguide. blogspot.co.uk/.

Inge, M. T. (ed.) (1993), *Dark Laughter: The Satiric Art of Oliver W. Harrington*. Jackson, MS: University Press of Mississippi.

Jackson, D. (1985, August 16), "The amazing adventures of Jackie Ormes". *Chicago Reader*, 16–25.

Jackson, J. (1942–5), [Examples may be found as display ads between May 23, 1942 and March 25, 1945]. *Chicago Defender*.

Jackson, T. (1998), "Pioneering Cartoonists of Color". Retrieved from: http:// whgbetc.com/englewood/englewood-esimms-camp.html .

Jones, S. (1986), "From 'under cork' to overcoming: Black images in the comics", in C. Hardy and G. F. Stern (eds), *Ethnic Images in the Comics: An Exhibition in the Museum of the Balch Institute for Ethnic Studies*. . Philadelphia, PA: Balch Institute for Ethnic Studies, pp. 21–30.

McCloud, S. (1993), *Understanding Comics: The Invisible Art*. Northampton, MA: Kitchen Sink Press.

Nolan, M. (2008), *Love on the Racks: A History of American Romance Comics*. Jefferson, NC: McFarland.

Ormes, J. (1944, October 21), "Lena Horne sets a new box office record". *Chicago Defender*, p. 7.

Radway, J. (1991), *Reading the Romance: Women, Patriarchy, and Popular Literature* (2nd edn). Chapel Hill, NC: University of North Carolina Press.

Reib, S. and Feil, S. (1996), "Torchy Brown faces life". *American Legacy*, 2, (2), 25–32.

Robbins, T. (2001), *The Great Women Cartoonists*. New York: Watson-Guptill Publications.

Roberts, T. J. (1990), *An Aesthetic of Junk Fiction*. Athens, GA: University of Georgia Press.

Rooks, N. M. (2004), *Ladies' Pages: African American Women's Magazines and the Culture That Made Them*. New Brunswick, NJ: Rutgers University Press.

Walker, S. (2007), *Style & Status: Selling Beauty to African American Women 1920–1975*. Lexington: The University Press of Kentucky.

Note

1 A newspaper "topper" is a panel that accompanies a comic strip for added entertainment like a cut-out, puzzle of some sort, game, and such. "Topper" can be something of a misnomer since it often appeared not on top but rather under the main feature, as with *Torchy Togs* that was always underneath *Torchy in Heartbeats*.

3

Contemporary representations of black females in newspaper comic strips

Tia C. M. Tyree

Introduction

Newspaper comic strips hold great insights into American culture and they should be investigated, analyzed and critiqued through the proper lens. While research about minorities in comics is not dense, results from a few groundbreaking studies over the past three decades uncovered concerning statistics about the presence of both women and Blacks. Glascock and Preston-Schreck (2004) completed a study analyzing minority and gender roles in daily newspaper comics, and two key findings were drawn. First, 96 per cent of characters were White and only 2.5 per cent were Black. Further, many of the representations of women were stereotypical, including women always nagging and being more emotional than their male counterparts. This study occurred nearly 20 years after one completed by Deborah Chavez (1985), which addressed how gender inequality in comic strips can be detrimental and position women as inferior to men. She noted gender identity and inequality is continued, in part, by socialization and repetitious propaganda that reinforce women's inferiority (Chavez 1985). The reinforcement is done through stereotyping, which is the categorizing of a group of individuals based on their common outstanding attributes or a few select features (Chafetz 1978).

What is missing in scholarship is exactly how Black females are represented in comic strips. Black women have long since lacked power positions within media production companies and must work to maneuver within a society that consistently reproduces stereotypical images that have pigeonholed and falsely identified them as lazy, child-bearing, overprotective, sexualized beings and other things. From the long-standing mammy and Jezebel images to the newer stereotypes of the chickenhead and baby mama, numerous Black female stereotypical images are ingrained in our mass media culture. With many scholars agreeing that comic strips reflect American culture (White and Abel 1963; Saenger 1963; Alley 1991; Nelson 2005), it is also said that empirical investigations show they do not offer a "true" picture of society (Reitberger and Fuchs 1971). Instead, images within comics depict an idealized America reflective of the "good old days," which did not really exist (Reitberger and Fuchs 1971). The ideology and representations within US comic strips begs the question: How does the marginalized Black female fit within this perfect American society?

Currently, research on the roles of marginalized people, including Blacks, Hispanics, homosexuals and women, can be found, but there is little research with a primary focus on representations of Black females in daily comic strips. More specifically, as the role of Black females, and women in general, have changed over the last century, it is important to see how Black female representations are characterized today.

The purpose of this chapter is to analyze how Black females are portrayed within newspaper comics. The primary objectives are: (1) to determine if gender inequality is present in comic strips with Black female characters, (2) to analyze whether Black females are stereotyped, and (3) to uncover if the gender and race of cartoonists influence Black female representations in comic strips. Authorship is critical, because with less than 5 per cent of comic creators being Black (Astor 1998) and only 15 of the more than 200 syndicated comic strips being created or co-created by women (Astor 2000), the gender and race of authors (i.e. Black males, White males, Black females and White females) could play a role in how Black females are portrayed.

Literature review

Importance of newspaper comic strips as a mass medium

As powerful mediums within our mass-mediated culture, comics are an extremely influential part of popular culture. Nachbar and Lause (1992) assert "popular beliefs and values are those unseen convictions about the world which form a culture's mindset and thus mold and color the way that that culture sees and interprets reality" (p. 82). They further explain that the cultural mindset encompasses influences of history, present circumstances and the culture's future hopes and dreams (Nachhar and Lause 1992). Nelson posits that popular culture is concerned with amusement, pleasure and enjoyment, and comic art is a form of popular culture dating back to the 1890s (2005). It was at this time America was first introduced to *Yellow Kid* on Sunday, May 5, 1895 (McAllister, Sewell and Gordon 2001). This comic strip about a small child in a yellow nightshirt who lived in Hogan's Alley is often heralded because of how it was promoted, merchandized and influential in establishing the importance of comics in US newspapers (Gordon 1998; Witek 1999).

Since *Yellow Kid*, comic strip panels have been reflections of America life, but in their early representations, "comic strips often portrayed different races, ethnic groups and genders in a negatively stereotyped manner" and "solidified a striking occurrence within the nation's psyche – the dichotomy between blacks and the rest of society" (White and Fuentez 1997: 72). However, scholars observe finding representations of Black life or Black people in newspapers comics have historically proven difficult, and when Black representations are present, they are stereotypical ones (White and Fuentez 1997; Glascock and Preston-Schreck 2004). Therefore, it is important for scholars to continue to investigate what, if any, representations do exist and the meanings of those texts to society and those who read them. For with representations being so scarce, those existing ones bear "the burden of representation," which is "the impossible attempt to speak on behalf of 'the Black community' as if any singular object exists" (Hall 1996: 13).

From a theoretical standpoint, the absence of Black images in the media is problematic for other reasons. Gerbner et al.'s (1994) groundbreaking work involving cultivation theory concludes heavy exposure to media lead people to cultivate expectations about the real world that were consistent with the media images presented to them. Harrison and Frederickson (2003) further explain that cultivation theory predicts that messages in the media teach those who absorb them to adopt certain views of each other. Klein and Shiffman (2006) note this theoretical model assumes that individuals develop beliefs, attitudes, and expectations by what is seen and heard via television, video, film, magazines and other media, and they take what is developed to make decisions in the real world. According to Nabi and Kremar (2004), cultivation theory has been studied in relation to many social factors relevant to this study, including racism (Volgy and Schwarz 1980), marital discord (Shrum 1996), occupational roles (Shrum 1996) and sex-role stereotypes (Morgan 1982). Several studies acknowledge the media still create bias and prejudice in connection to representations of Blacks, which causes concern regarding the media's role in the "cultivation of race-based stereotypes that associate Blacks as being disproportionately indigent, uneducated, violent, and criminal" (Abraham and Appiah 2006: 184).

Stereotypical representations of blacks and black females in mass media

Black images in mainstream popular culture have traditionally been negative and degrading portrayals based on stereotypes (Berry 1998; Lichter et al. 1987). Mass media play a crucial role in the reproduction of racial ideology and stereotypes (Abraham and Appiah 2006). Stereotypes work to limit and label members of a specific group by assuming all members share similar traits (Gibson 1988). The creation and activation of stereotypes can occur for a variety of reasons, including group conflict, power differences and the urge to justify the status quo (Hilton and von Hippel 1996). Browne, Firestone and Mickiewicz (1994) address the power struggle issue in relation to the development of stereotypes. They note "majority cultural domination often carries with it the power to stereotype. It is in itself a way to maintain power, in fact, because it underlines the ability of those holding power to determine how to portray those who do not" (p. 8). These scholars also posit that media are ideal to carry stereotypes throughout society because of their pervasive nature, production of "raw material for daily conversation" and ability to serve as trendsetters, tastemakers, labelers (Browne, Firestone and Mickiewicz, 1994: 8).

Black female stereotypes date back centuries, and Americans have long been accustomed to digesting negative images of Black females. Yet, as society changes, stereotypes also evolve. Therefore, not only have some old stereotypes updated and morphed into new stereotypes influenced by old cultural beliefs, but additional stereotypes have developed, including the welfare queen, hoodrat and angry Black women. To name every Black female stereotype—both old and new—would be unwieldy for this chapter, but it is important to note some of the most key Black female stereotypes to help frame this work.

While identifying the most popular Black stereotypes in film, Bogle (2001) included several stereotypes relevant to this study, which are the coon, tragic mulatto, mammy and pickaninny. The tragic mulatto is often fair skinned, tortured and confused as a result of the societal and personal pressures of dealing with her biracialism (Bogle 2001). The pikaninny is a subcategory of the coon and portrays the young Black child as harmless, pleasant and used for diversion or comic relief (Bogle 2001: 7). The pickaninny was born from the slavery period and widely used in late nineteenth century as a marketing tool to sell products (Myers and Dean 2005). According to Bogle (2001), the pickaninny image associated with Black females is usually one of a young Black female with prominent lips, braids pointing in the air accented with bows and sometimes eating watermelon. He notes modern coon images make dialectical mistakes, are mentally incompetent, have ludicrous physical features and dress in unordinary ways. The mammy is one of the oldest and most notable Black mother stereotypes (Adams and Fuller 2006). The mammy is an obese, cantankerous, asexual female servant who is nurturing toward the White family who employs her (Stephens and Phillips 2003; Bogle 2001). Other Black mother stereotypes include the emasculating, scornful and controlling matriach who berates her male loved one (Bond and Perry 1970; Ransby and Matthews 1995; Wallace 1978); the welfare queen who lazily collects government handouts nearly ensuring that poverty passed down to her children (Sklar 1995); and the baby mama who often pushes her personal life goals aside to rear a child against the wishes of her lover and then proceeds to take his money (Stephens and Phillips 2003; Stephens and Few 2007; Wyatt 1997).

Sexuality, arrogance and aggression play a role in Black female stereotypes. According to Stephens and Few (2007), sexual scripts are present in the diva, gold digger, freak, dyke, gangsta bitch and other stereotypes. The Jezebel stereotype is characterized as a young, promiscuous woman who uses sex for love, attention and material gain (Collins 1990; Morton 1991). The Jezebel has evolved into the freak with no inhibitions who engages in dangerous and morally unacceptable behavior (Stephens and Phillips 2003; Cleage 1993). The freak has further evolved into the chickenhead and hoodrat (Stephens and Phillips 2003), who are usually outspoken, poor urban Black females. The gold digga, also known as a hoochie mama or pigeon, is portrayed as an uneducated woman with little social status who is willing to trade sex to increase her status in society (Stephens and Phillips 2003). Aggression is found in both the gangsta bitch and angry Black woman stereotypes. The gangsta bitch is an aggressive, self-sufficient female who lives in tough urban American environments (Mitchell 1999; Hampton 2000). The angry Black woman is the contemporary version of the "mouthy harpy" (Tasker and Negra 2007: 258), and she is aggressive, confrontational, overbearing and may even threaten or engage in violent physical behavior against others. The BAP, Black American Princess, has an "expectation of mainstream and acceptance that borders on arrogance" and her feelings of privilege can come from family heritage or personal will (George 1992: 2).

All Black stereotypes are not gender-specific. Instead, some are based on socioeconomics, behaviors and other factors present in the daily lives of Americans. One persistent stereotype is that Blacks are not smart and do not have the same level of success in school as their White and Asian-American peers (Bobo 2001; Steele 1997; Swim and Stangor 1998). Blacks are also portrayed as possessing natural music and sports talents (Grant, 1985; Lee and Browne 1995; Sailes 1991; Hardin et al. 2004). In terms of portrayals in animated cartoons, Blacks are more likely than other races to be involved in entertainment-related activities, such as singing, dancing and playing music as well as commit antisocial behaviors, including lying to or deceiving other characters, verbal aggression, physical aggression and violence (Klein and Shiffman 2006). Blacks are also frequently portrayed as incompetent, poor, jobless, passive and lazy (Graves 1996; Merritt and Stroman 1993; Stroman 1991; Bristor et al. 1995; Oliver 1994; Mastro and Greenberg 2000). Many Blacks were seen as living in "ghettos and slums," and Black families were portrayed as conflict ridden, dominated by females and having "little love toward their children" (Ward 2004).

Gender inequalities and race representations in comics

Within comic art, gender influences content, ideology and audience (Wong and Cuklanz 2002). Analyzing it within comics is worthy of study for numerous reasons. Traditionally, the humor in comics was used to stereotype and objectify female characters for the purpose of entertaining predominantly male audiences (Wong and Cuklanz 2002). Humor is a masculine form or mode of communication, because it is often seen as a manifestation of aggression (Walker 1991: 61). By understanding this aspect of humor, it is easier to comprehend why women have long been discouraged to participate in the humorous work, such as stand-up comedy and comic art (Wong and Cuklanz 2002). For a woman to use humor, it is seen as a "politically charged act" (Wong and Cuklanz 2002: 254), because the history of the production of humor is a male territory (Sheppard, 1991). Female cartoonists occupy an outsider position and use the power of the medium as a vehicle to critique patriarchal ideology from a female perspective (Wong and Cuklanz 2002).

Within society, there are many vehicles responsible for the perpetuation of gender inequality (Bowles and Gintis 1976). The mass media is one of those mediums. One vehicle reinforcing this "detrimental" practice of gender inequality is comic strips (Chavez 1985). Gender is not a reference to the biological characteristics of individuals. As a part of society and social relations, gender is a system of "social difference whose utility lies in the assumption that actors classified in one category may be expected to behave differently from those classified in another category" (Ridgeway 2006: 269). Gender inequality is the process by which the belief that women are inferior or subordinate to men is transmitted within society, and part of this socialization process is the daily repetition of "propaganda" reinforcing women's inferiority of men (Chavez 1985: 93–4). Gender plays a fundamental role in the organization of social relations and through the stereotypes, status assumptions, and cognitive biases existing within those relationships (Ridgeway 2006). Socially shared descriptive gender beliefs are stereotypes as well as cultural rules used to perceive and enact gender within a system of difference and inequality (Ridgeway 2006).

With comic strips presented every day to US audiences, they have the potential to be the daily "propaganda" needed to perpetuate gender equality. Scholars agree they often perpetuate and not challenge gender stereotypes (Chavez 1985; Brabant and Mooney 1986, 1997). In her study, Chavez concluded comics do perpetuate gender inequality: men were represented more than their true ratio in US population, while women were underrepresented versus their true proportion; and the strips provided a reflection of American society that gave a distorted view of reality (1985). Similar to the Chavez study, in an investigation of the role of gender and race in daily comic strips, Glascock and Preston-Schreck (2004) found women were underrepresented and character behaviors and activities were divided along gender lines. Women were less likely to have a job, and when employed, they had lower job statuses than men. Women were twice as likely to be seen in the home, more likely to be married and have children, and performed most of the domestic work. They noted women as "seemingly otherwise powerless" outside of their homes and perhaps their verbally aggressive behavior was a way to showcase their power. Most representations were "nagging wives who flippantly insult and verbally batter their husbands" or use commands and threats "to get frequently errant children to behave" (Glascock and Preston-Schreck 2004: 428–9). In a series of three studies published in ten-year increments from 1976–97, Brabant and Mooney investigated sex role stereotyping in Sunday comics and noted similar findings as other studies focusing on gender roles. In 1976, they noted female characters played traditional stereotypical roles (Brabant 1976). In 1986, similar findings were seen, including women present more often in the home, providing childcare, less likely to be working or more likely to be seen in the dual role of working and conducting household duties (Brabant and Mooney 1986). In 1997, the researchers concluded women had gone "not very far at all" in terms of progress within the comic arena (Brabant and Mooney 1997: 148). Brabant and Mooney's (1997) study noted females were more likely to be portrayed as passive onlookers, less likely than men to be present in comic strips, more likely than men to be shown in the homes and performing childcare activities, and still remained in stereotyped roles.

In 1997, White and Fuentez were responsible for one of the few studies to focus on Black representations in comics. Though many of the comics they noted contained Black characters, including *Curtis*, *Wee Pals*, *Herb and*

Jamaal, *Jumpstart* and *The Griots*, these did not appear in the study's final sample, for some are no longer produced. Nonetheless, the study provided many key observations about the presence of Blacks in comic strips. First, they noted Black readers would be hard pressed to find reflections of themselves in the comic strips. Secondly, they found Blacks to be grossly underrepresented in daily newspaper comic strips, with representations never reaching more than 3 percent. During the final year of comics included in their study, which spanned an 80-year period, most strips did not contain Blacks. Thirdly, they noted some progress in the appearance of Blacks in a broader range of social settings and occupations. Fourthly, while there was a decline in the presence of stereotypes, 98 images consistent with Bogle's traditional negative Black stereotypes were seen during the study (White and Fuentez 1997).

Methodology

A textual analysis of 13 newspaper comics was completed. In total, 767 newspaper cartoon strips were analyzed during January and February 2011. Textual analysis allowed for an in-depth investigation of not only the quantity of appearances of Black females, but for a greater understanding of what was said and what was done during those appearances. Texts are communicative artifacts by which culture is experienced, and by examining how the author constructs the message, researchers can determine how texts create meaning (Hallahan 1997). While the content analysis method is often utilized in comic strip studies, textual analysis is used for its advantages, including its ability to determine meaning within idiomatic expressions, individual words and other phrases (Fairclough 2003), as well as takes into consideration how meaning can be gleamed through the analysis of the producer of the text (Lindkvist 1981). Further, this approach allowed for analysis of words, as well as movements, actions and facial expressions of the characters. Abraham and Appiah (2006) posit that text analysis attempting to understand linguistic and visual representations provides a better opportunity to uncover the potential coherent meanings within them.

The cartoons in the final sample were *Between Friends*, *Café con Leche*, *Crankshaft*, *Curtis*, *Flo & Friends*, *Funky Winkerbean*, *Herb and Jamaal*, *Out of the Gene Pool*, *Stone Soup*, *Six Chix*, *The Boondocks*, *The Middletons*, and *Wee Pals*. With the noted scarcity of Black characters in comic strips, it was important for this study to include comic strips with the highest potential of including Black female characters. Therefore, unlike many past studies, this study's sample did not include the observation of a single newspaper, because the observation of a single paper may not have provided a rich enough sample for investigation. Instead, cartoons were selected because they were noted in past research for having the presence of Black characters (Glascock and Preston-Schreck 2004; White and Fuentez 1997; Tyree and Krishnasamy 2011), as well as from a 60-day observation period of popular websites showcasing syndicated newspaper comics, including *The Funny Cartoon* website, *Daily Ink*, *GoComics* and *Creators Syndicate*.

In an effort to ensure this study's findings built upon past gender and race centered comic strip studies, key characteristics, behaviors, stereotypes and plot information included in both Glascock and Preston-Schreck (2004) and White and Fuentez (1997) were utilized. For each comic strip, the author's race and gender were analyzed, as well as if the comic strip had a majority White, majority Black or integrated cast. Each character was noted as a primary, secondary or background character. Similar to Glascock and Preston-Schreck (2004), if a character was in five or more comic strips, then she was considered a major character. Physical appearance and characteristics were observed, including age (child, teenager, adult, elder), hair (short, medium, long), hair style (up, down, ponytail, barrettes), height (short, average, tall), clothing and accessories (pants, shirt, short dress, long dress, coat, necklace, glasses, apron, scarf, headwrap) and body type (slim, average, curvy, overweight). Both height and body type were in comparison to other characters in the same comic strip. Occupation was also recorded as law enforcement (judge, police, detectives, spies, military), white-collar (business owners, professionals, managers, supervisory job), pink-collar (beautician, teacher, maid, clerical worker, sales clerk, librarian, secretary, waitress, telephone operator, medical worker, florist, meter maid, nurse), blue-collar (mechanics, laborers, drivers, mechanics, any semi-skilled worker), criminals or no occupation. Each Black female character was also analyzed for the presence or absence of stereotypical behavior, including any physical attributes or language used by the character or other characters in the comic strip about the Black female character. A Black female character needed to exhibit one or more characteristic of a stereotype or reinforce a single characteristic in half or more of her appearances to be classified as a specific stereotype.

The context in which the Black female appears is also important. Therefore, her physical setting, as well as how she was situated within her comics milieu, was noted, including whether she was primarily seen in the role of mother, wife or homemaker. Similar to White and Fuentez (1997), the social situation categories used were alone, background (character), segregated social, integrated social, segregated nonsocial or integrated nonsocial situation. They described the situations as follows: "a social situation was one where the characters were interacting voluntarily whether at home, at play or in the workplace or street. A non-social situation was one where the characters were interacting because they had to in order to accomplish some goal" (White and Fuentez 1997: 77). Finally, the storyline of each comic strip was analyzed as race-dependent or race- independent. For a character to be in a race-dependent storyline, it meant the character's portrayal as African American was essential to either understand or enjoy the comic strip. In contrast, within race-independent storylines, the character could be replaced with one of another race and the understanding or enjoyment of the comic strip would not be changed (White and Fuentez 1997: 77).

Findings and discussion

In total, 33 Black female characters were present in the sample, which included children, teens, adults and elders. There were representations in all except one of the cartoons in the sample. *The Boondock*'s character, Jazmine Dubois, a mulatto friend of the main character Huey Freeman, did not appear during the two-month analysis period, nor did any other female. Similar to the findings of past studies, Black females in this study were presented in stereotypical ways and were largely not depicted as being a part of the workforce. They were more likely to be positioned as background or minor characters, utilized to set up jokes for major or star characters, and the primary parent to discipline children, provide childcare and perform household chores.

The 33 Black females represent 7 per cent of the total sample of 464 characters. This percentage is close to the US Black female population of 6.4 per cent (US Census Bureau, 2009). This figure is significant, because prior studies have noted the nonexistence or scarcity of Black characters. Using an observation period designed to target Black females, as well as a reliance on past studies noting depictions of Blacks, this study's sample specifically targeted comics with the highest probability of having Black female representations. Prior researchers attempting to analyze race or gender often depended on the analysis of comics in one to three newspapers. Yet, the selection of comics within a single or small newspaper sample could reflect the location, biases or targeted audiences of the newspapers. Therefore, they might not give a proper reflection of how Black females are represented in the comics industry, but rather how they are presented in the newspaper(s) under study. In turn, this method provided richer data by which to analyze how Black females were presented, for it drew on syndicated newspaper comics, regardless of which newspapers they appeared across the country.

Black females appeared in diverse social settings, with integrated social settings being the most prominent setting. In total, 190 social situations were categorized, including 53 segregated social situations, 73 integrated social situations, 7 segregated social situations and 36 integrated social situations. A key finding was that Black females were only the sole character in a comic strip six times, which is 3 per cent. Four of the depictions were characters in *Between Friends*, which was illustrated by a White female. Three of those representations were of Kim who was represented equally with the other two main characters of the comic strip and therefore, in the context of this comic strip, the sole appearances were in line with the treatment of the other main characters. The two other representations were in strips created by Black men. Mikki, from *Wee Pals*, was depicted as Baby New Year sucking her thumb and wearing a diaper and 2011 sash. The last depiction was Miss Eula from *Herb and Jamaal* who was practicing her "look," which is a stereotypical reference to how Black mothers can simply peer at their offspring and command respect, attention or fear.

Similar to past studies, appearance did seem to play a role in the portrayal of Black females. The following observations were made:

- Black females did not dress inappropriately, proactively or outside of the norms of the comics in which they appeared.

- There was a pattern of Black women wearing either hoop earrings or round stud earrings, while most White women were not seen with earrings.

- Children were consistently portrayed with up styles and barrettes.

- Older Black females were portrayed as short, overweight or both.

- Black females often had rounded noses and intentionally drawn lips.

- Hairstyles and textures were very diverse for Black females. Cartoonists drew crocked, wavy or curly lines to denote Black females' hair.

- Besides the shading of skin, hair and lips were the two other most distinct signifiers of Black female characters.

With Black females, gender inequality was a major issue. All of the elder and adult Black women in minor and major roles were found primarily in their homes occupying the roles of mother and wife. In contrast, representations of Black mothers in comics by White women had them primarily in the role of friend to the main White character and not in the home. Ruthie from *Flo & Friends* spoke of being a mother, but was not seen with her offspring. In *Between Friends*, Kim was only seen with her son once, and Helen, who is a married mother of two children, was also not pictured with her children.

Black mothers were seen in traditional roles such as cooking, childrearing and baking, and similar to the findings of Brabant and Mooney (1997), the apron had all but disappeared from use by female characters. However, Black female characters in roles as mothers were the most stereotyped group. Of the 11 stereotyped characters, seven were Black mothers. Five angry Black women and one matriarch were noted, and another character was classified as a baby mama and hoochie.

The five characters to be classified as angry Black women were Mrs Garvin from *Café Con Leche*, Diane from *Curtis*, Sarah from *Herb and Jamaal*, Helen from *Between Friends* and Peg Wade from *The Middletons*. As a group, mothers were more likely than not to be seen placing their hands on their hips, pointing at others, frowning and screaming at their children, even in circumstances that did not require this type of verbally aggressive behavior. Examples of angry Black mothers include Mrs Garvin who challenged her daughter-in-law to a fistfight, called her a "heffa" four times and consistently berated her. In *Between Friends*, Kim's single representation had her entering a home screaming "LISTEN UP, EVERYONE – I've come to a decision! I'm tired of always accommodating everyone! Do you hear me?! I've had ENOUGH! From now on, I'm running my life on MY Schedule! ME-ME-ME-ME-ME!" No one was home. She vowed to tell them later. (See Figure 3.1.) Peg Wade was seen with her hands on her hips, frowning and yelling at her son in the comic strips in which she appeared.[1]

In both circumstances, she wanted him to discontinue his current behavior of playing on the computer and watching an "awful movie." In both cases, she was made the butt of the strips' jokes. What is most problematic about this stereotype classification is the small number of times Black females are represented versus the number of times they are seen being verbally aggressive. When a Black woman is seen once or twice, such as Helen and Peg, and all of their representatives have them screaming at their children than it is hard to read these characters as simply having a "bad" day or acting outside of their character. Instead, they are read as another angry Black woman in this mass media.

As a baby mama and hoochie, Jackie from *Out of the Gene Pool* was a self-centered, single mother who cared about her looks, television watching and men. When her son confesses that his father has a girlfriend, she is visibly distraught and discusses her frustration about her "ex" having a girlfriend in the next two strips. However, most of her narrative involved conversations about her dating and consequently being "dumped" by Dante, a "garbage man." She did find some solace in a new television show featuring Taye Diggs, a Black actor. When she mentions that Diggs will be in her home each week to "mend" her broken heart, her friend notes she is not sure it is her heart that needs fixing. When the television show premieres, she "appreciates" when her son tells her "I'll make sure I won't need any motherly love during that time." She also imagines herself in a small pool with three Black men as she screams, "Come on in, boys! There's room for everyone if we squeeze together." When the second panel depicts the "reality" of the situation, it is only a small child and a pig attempting to enter. She was called "trash" by one White character and a "freak" by another one. As a hoochie who is both "sexually assertive" and looking for a man with money, assuming this is her major issue with her garbage man boyfriend, she fits both the "plan hoochie" and "gold-digging hoochie" (Collins 1990: 81). With the strip's cartoonist being a White male, the overall sexual script of Jackie and her subsequent treatment by other White characters lends credence to Collins' (1990) belief that the Jezebel or hoochie is a gendered sign of divergent female sexuality, and it is juxtaposed to the "cult of true White womanhood" that typifies "the hot mammas" of Black womanhood as deviant (p. 83).

In total, eight Black female children and one teenager occupied either minor or major roles in the sample. Of these, three stereotypes were noted. Michelle from *Curtis* was classified as a BAP, Susie from *Rugrats* was classified as a pickinniny and Mikki from *Wee Pals* was labeled a coon. Mikki's character was the most problematic for she consistently showcased her unintelligence in the comic strips, including misspelling a word; noting a taco was the "biggest potato chip" she'd ever seen; and replying she loved French after hearing "this little piggie cried wee, wee, wee." In contrast, *Wee Pals's* Sybil was one of the elder children and was often educating others, setting ground rules for the neighborhood children and being nurturing. Uhura in *Herb and Jamaal*, Keisha Williams in *Funky Winkerbean* and Chutney in *Curtis* were also portrayed as positive characters in the comics.

In total, only four of the 33 Black females had a discernable profession. Two were pink-collar, one was white-collar and one was blue-collar. In *Curtis*, Mrs Wilson was a teacher. Helen from *Between Friends* entered her home with a briefcase and is described as a coworker of Maeve, but she was never shown at work. In *Herb and Jamaal*, Jamaal courts one of his coworkers, Yolanda, who is seen in a firefighter's uniform. She was the only major Black female character to have a job. Finally, in *Out of the Gene Pool*, a character takes a pig to "Great Kuts" for a hair cut. The beautician is a Black female who responded "Um...Okay...This is going to cost more than eight bucks." According to the US Census Bureau, in 2009, 60.7 per cent of Black females were in the civilian labor force (US Census Bureau 2009). Therefore, the rate of 12 per cent noted in this study is five times below the actual Black female rate.

Similar to other studies, overtly racial jokes or storylines were not a major issue. Eighty-nine per cent of strips were racially independent, meaning the Black character could have been replaced with a character of another race and the meaning remained the same. Of those dependent comic strips, there were several positive storylines deserving enumerations, including *Wee Pals'* "Soul Circle" designed to teach readers about prominent Black individuals. The other racially dependent storylines involved neutral and negative depictions of Blacks. For example, neutral representations included Sybil defining racial prejudice, a general reference to Black history month by Mrs Wilson from *Curtis*, as well as an exchange Curtis had with his mother about a Kwanzaa book. The negative racially dependent storylines capitalized on stereotypes. For example, Mrs Garvin offered her daughter-in-law Kool-Aid as a peace offering; Jackie was seen yelling at the screen at the movie theater, and Diz, a Black boy from *Wee Pals*, asks if slaves were purchased using a "massa card." Perhaps, the leading reason storylines were depicted as racially dependent was the use of language. In these instances, Black female characters were the only ones to use improper English, thus it appeared intentional by the cartoonists. For example, in one of only three Black female representations in *Six Chix*, a comic strip was titled "scarf tying 101." Each woman displayed a unique style along with a caption, including "loop & pull through hipster chic," "tied in front classic" and "the I'm French and was born wearing one look." The caption for the Black female was "down the back super woman stylin.'" Superwoman is an emerging negative stereotype that depicts Black woman as overachiever, intelligent, articulate, professional and assertive (Reynolds-Dobbs, Thomas and Harrison 2008).

Of the 13 comic strips under review, there was a cross section of authorship. Four comic strips were developed by White males, five were developed by Black males, three were developed by White females, and no comic strips were authored by Black females. *The Rugrats* was a collaborative effort by numerous Nickelodeon writers and cartoonists whose race and genders were difficult to establish. Three of the five Black male comic strips featured majority Black casts, while the other two were integrated casts. Two of the three strips created by White females had majority White casts, and three of the four White males created integrated casts. No individuals created comic strips with casts primarily of a race other than their own.

The Black female representations were nearly evenly split between the Black cartoonists and the White cartoonists. Black cartoonists had 17 representations, and White cartoonists and the various cartoonists of Nickelodeon had 16 representations. Black cartoonists had the most major Black female characters, while White cartoonists had most Black female representations in the background. They were nearly equal in their minor character representations with four and five characters, respectively. The majority of the racially dependent situations were present in the cartoons created by Black males, and two-thirds of the stereotypical characters were in Black male comics. None of the majority White comic strips contained stereotypical representations. However, two of the three majority White comic strips did have Black females as background characters. In these depictions, Blacks were mainly present in integrated nonsocial situations, such as a public bathrooms and an airport.

Conclusion

Similar to past studies analyzing women and minorities, the Black female representations in comics is both troubling and encouraging. While Black women are portrayed in a variety of social settings and appear in a majority of racially-independent plotlines, the common message is Black female adults belong in the home, do not have jobs, berate their children and are angry. They are also more likely to be present in majority Black casts as well as comics produced by Black males. Yet, within these settings, the Black female has a higher chance of being stereotyped than within comics created by White females and males. This is largely because White cartoonists keep the Black female image in the background or in minor roles.

This work is critical to the continued investigation of the racialized hatred and sexism that often occurs against Black women, which is rooted in myths used to stereotype and subjugate them (Adams and Fuller 2006). Similar to what Young (1994) insists, it is the hope that this critique will work to expose relations of power and domination in our mass media culture and offer another critical reading of how rules, relations and race play a role in the cultivation of gender inferiority and the maintenance of racial stereotypes. The findings suggest Black female characters can be sisters, wives, mothers, grandmothers, friends, coworkers, mother-in-laws, but not star characters in a comic strip. As supporting characters, they helped to set up jokes, tell the stories for others, but seldom was the narrative about them. Considering only 3 per cent of the comic strips featured a Black female character by herself, it makes one ponder if cartoonists believe the Black female character is worthy.

This study supports Glascock and Preston-Schreck's observation that the "behind the scenes" representations might explain the gender and racial representations that manifest themselves in the comics (2004: 430). The noticeable absence of authorship by Black females is troubling to the future of the comics industry, as well as Blacks and women. There is no other person better suited to tell the story on the comics pages of Black females than themselves. There is no one better suited to speak of the Black experience within America in the comics pages than Black females. Currently, the Black female story is being told by others, which has largely left the Black female stereotyped, marginalized and silently operating in the background. The comics industry and US media system are dominated by White males and there must be a concentrated effort to have the voice and representations of the Black female present and rightfully representative of whom they are in reality.

References

Abraham, L. and Appiah, O. (2006), "Framing news stories: The role of visual imagery in priming racial stereotypes." *Howard Journal of Communications*, 17, 183–203.

Adams, T. and Fuller, D. (2006), "The words have changed but the ideology remains the same: Misogynistic lyrics in rap music." *Journal of Black Studies*, 36, (6), 938–57.

Alley, P. (1991), "Hokinson and Hollander: Female cartoonists in American culture", in J. Sochen (ed.), *Women's Comic Visions*. Detroit, MI: Wayne State University Press, pp. 115–40.

Astor, D. (1998, December 5), "Diversity push makes the comics a little less White." *Editor & Publisher*, 131, (49), 34–5.

—(2000, January 10), "King features six women in one cartoon package." *Editor & Publisher*, 133, (2), 34.

Berry, G. (1998), "Black family life on television and the socialization of the African American child: Images of marginality." *Journal of Comparative Family Studies*, 29, (2), 233–42.

Bobo, L. (2001), "Racial attitudes and relations at the close of the twentieth century", in N. J. Smelser, W. J. Wilson, and F. Mitchell (eds), *America Becoming: Racial Trends and their Consequences*. Washington, DC: National Academic Press, pp. 264–301.

Bogle, D. (2001), *Toms, Coons, Mulattoes, Mammies, and Bucks: An Interpretive History of Blacks in American Films* (4th edn). New York, NY: Continuum.

Bond, P. and Perry, P. (1970), "Is the Black male castrated?", in T. Cade (ed.), *The Black Woman: An Anthology*. New York: Signet.

Bowles, S. and Gintis, H. (1976), *Schooling in Capitalist America: Educational Reform and the Contradictions of Economic Life*. New York: Basic Books.

Brabant, S. (1976), "Sex role stereotyping in the Sunday comics." *Sex Roles*, 2, (4), 331–7.

Brabant, S. and Mooney, L. (1986), "Sex role stereotyping in the Sunday comics: Ten years later". *Sex Roles*, 14, (3–4) 141–8.

—(1997), "Sex role stereotyping in the Sunday comics: A twenty year update". *Sex Roles*, 37, (3–4), 269–81

Bristor, J., Lee, R., and Hunt, M. (1995), "Race and ideology: African American images in television advertising". *Journal of Public Policy & Marketing*, 14, (1), 48–59.

Browne, D. R., Firestone, C. M., and Mickiewicz, E. (1994), *Television/radio news & minorities*. Queenstown, MD: Aspen Institute.

Chafetz, J. (1978), *Masculine, Feminine or Human?: An Overview of the Sociology of the Gender Roles*. Itasca, IL: F. E. Peacock Publishers.

Chavez, D. (1985), "Perpetuation of gender inequality: A content analysis of comic strips". *Sex Roles*, 13, (1–2), 93–102.

Cleage, P. (1993), *Fatal Floozies: Deals With the Devil and Other Reasons to Riot*. New York: Ballantine Books.

Collins, P. H. (1990), *Black Feminist Thought: Knowledge, Consciousness, and the Politics of Empowerment*. Boston: Unwin Hyman.

Fairclough, N. (2003), *Analysing Discourse: Textual Analysis for Social Research*. Oxford: Routledge.

George, N. (1992), *Buppies, B-Boys, Baps & Bohos: Notes on Post-Soul Black Culture*. New York: HarperCollins.

Gerbner, G., Gross, L., Morgan, M. and Signorelli, N. (1994), "Growing up with television: The cultivation perspective", in J. Bryant and D. Zillmann (eds), *Media Effects: Advances in Theory and Research*. Hillsdale, NJ: Lawrence Erlbaum Associates, pp. 17–41.

Gibson, L. R. (1988), "Beyond the apron: Archetypes, stereotypes, and alternative portrayals of mothers". *Children's Literature*, 13, (4), 177–81.

Glascock, J. and Preston-Schreck, C. (2004), "Gender and racial stereotypes in daily newspaper comics: A time-honored tradition?". *Sex Roles*, 51, (7–8), 423–31.

Gordon, I. (1998), *Comic Strips and Consumer Culture, 1890–1945*: Washington, DC: Smithsonian Institution Press.

Grant, C. D. (1985), *Afro-American Music: One Form of Ethnic Identification* [microfiche]. ERIC Document: ED 268192.

Graves, S. B. (1996), "Diversity on television", in T. M. MacBeth (ed.), *Tuning in to Young Viewers: Social Science Perspectives on Television*. Thousand Oaks, CA: Sage, pp. 61–86.

Hall, S. (1996), "The after-life of Frantz Fanon: Why Fanon? Why now? Why *Black Skin, White Masks?*", in A. Read (ed.), *The Fact of Blackness: Frantz Fanon and Visual Representation*. Seattle, WA: Bay Press, pp. 12–38.

Hallahan, K. (1997), *The Consequences of Mass Communication. Cultural and Critical Perspectives on Mass Communication*. New York: McGraw-Hill Primus.

Hampton, D. (June–July 2000), "Flick: Girls interrupted". *Vibe*, 169–70.

Hardin, M., Dodd, J. E., Chance, J. and Walsdorf, K. (2004), "Sporting images in black and white: Race in newspaper coverage of the 2000 Olympic Games". *The Howard Journal of Communication*, 15, 211–27.

Harrison, K. and Frederickson, B. L. (2003), "Women's sports media, self-objectification, and mental health in Black and White adolescent females." *Journal of Communication*, 53, (2), 216–32.

Hilton, J. L. and von Hippel, W. (1996), "Stereotypes". *Annual Review of Psychology*, 47, 237–71.

Klein, H. and Shiffman, K. (2006), "Race-related content of animated cartoons". *The Howard Journal of Communications*, 17, (3), 163–82.

Lee, E. B. and Browne, L. A. (1995), "Effects of television advertising on African American teenagers". *Journal of Black Studies*, 25, (5), 523–36.

Lichter, S. R., Lichter, L. S., Rothman, S. and Amundson, D. (1987, July–August), "Prime-time prejudice: TV's images of Blacks and Hispanics". *Public Opinion*, 13–6.

Lindkvist, K. (1981), "Approaches to textual analysis", in K. E. Rosengren (ed.), *Advances in Content Analysis*. Thousand Oaks, CA: Sage Publications, pp. 23–42.

Mastro, D. E. and Greenberg, B. S. (2000), "The portrayal of racial minorities on prime time television". *Journal of Broadcasting & Electronic Media*, 44, (4), 690–703.

McAllister, M. P., Sewell, Jr, E. H. and Gordon, I. (eds) (2001), *Comics & Ideology*. New York: Peter Lang.

Merritt, B. and Stroman, C. A. (1993), "Black family imagery and interactions on television". *Journal of Black Studies*, 23, 492–9.

Mitchell, G. (1999), "Missy Elliott's on top of her World". *Billboard*, 111, (25), 11.

Morgan, M. (1982), "Television and adolescents' sex-role stereotypes: A longitudinal study". *Journal of Personality and Social Psychology*, 43, (5), 947–55.

Morton, P. (1991), *Disfigured Images: The Historical Assault on Afro-American Women*. New York: Praeger.

Myers, M. and Dean, S. (2005), "Why there's no Uncle Tom in Cincinnati's Freedom Center: The uses of slavery in marketing" [abstract], in Neilson, L. C., *The Future of Marketing's Past: Proceedings of the 12th Conference on Historical Analysis & Research in Marketing (CHARM), 2005, Long Beach, CA, 28 April–1 May 2005*, p. 239.

Nabi, R. L. and Kremar, M. (2004), "Conceptualizing media enjoyment as attitude: Implications for mass media effects research". *Communication Theory*, 14, (4), 288–310.

Nachbar, J. and Lause, K. (1992), "Songs of the unseen road: Myths, beliefs and values in popular culture", in J. Nachbar and K. Lause (eds), *Popular Culture: An Introductory Text*. Madison, WI: The University of Wisconsin Press, pp. 82–109.

Nelson, A. (2005). "*Swing Papa* and *Barry Jordan*: Comic strips and Black newspapers in postwar Toledo", in *Proceedings of the Ohio Academy of History, Muskingum College, New Concord, 7–8 April 2005*, pp. 61–74.

Oliver, M. B. (1994), "Portrayals of crime, race, and aggression in 'reality based' police shows: A content analysis". *Journal of Broadcasting & Electronic Media*, 38, (2), 179–92.

Ransby, B. and Matthews, T. (1995), "Black popular culture and the transcendence of patriarchal illusions", in B. Guy-Sheftall (ed.), *Words of Fire: An Anthology of African American Feminist Thought*. New York: The New Press, pp. 526–36.

Reitberger, R. and Fuchs, W. (1971), *Comics: An Anatomy of a Mass Medium*. London: Studio Vista Publishers.

Reynolds-Dobbs, W., Thomas, K. and Harrison, M. (2008), "From mammy to superwoman: Images that hinder Black women's career development". *Journal of Career Development*, 35, (2), 129–50.

Ridgeway, C. (2006), "Gender as an organizing force in social relations: Implications for the future of inequality", in F. D. Blau, M. B. Brinton and D. G. Grusky (eds), *The Declining Significance of Gender?* New York: Russell Sage, pp. 265–87.

Saenger, G. (1963), "Male and female relations in the American comic strip", in D. M. White and R. H. Abel (eds), *The Funnies: An American Idiom*. New York: The Free Press of Glencoe, pp. 219–31.

Sailes, G. A. (1991), "The myth of Black sports supremacy". Journal of Black Studies, 21, (4), 480–7.

Sheppard, A. (1991), "Social cognition, gender roles, and women's humor", ni. J. Sochen (ed.), *Women's Comic Visions*. Detroit, MI: Wayne State University Press, pp. 33–56.

Shrum, L. J. (1996), "Psychological processes underlying cultivation effects: Further tests of construct accessibility". *Human Communication Research*, 22, (4), 482–509.

Sklar, H. (1995), "The upperclass and mothers n the hood", in M. L. Andersen and P. H. Collins (eds), *Race, Class, and Gender: An Anthology* (2nd edn). Belmont, CA: Wadsworth Publishing Company, pp. 123–34.

Steele, C. (1997), "A threat in the air: How stereotypes shape the intellectual identities and performance". *American Psychologist*, 52, (6), 613–29.

Stephens, D. P. and Few, A. L. (2007), "Hip hop honey or video ho: African American preadolescents' understanding of female sexual scripts in hip hop culture". *Sexuality & Culture*, 11, (4), 48–69.

Stephens, D. P. and Phillips, L. D. (2003), "Freaks, gold diggers, divas, and dykes: The sociohistorical development of adolescent African American women's sexual scripts". *Sexuality & Culture*, 7, (1), 3–49.

—(2005), "Integrating Black feminist thought into conceptual frameworks of African American adolescent women's sexual scripting processes". *Sexualities, Evolution and Gender*, 7, (1), 37–55.

Stroman, C. A. (1991), "Television's role in the socialization of African American children and adolescents". *Journal of Negro Education*, 60, (3), 314–27.

Swim, J. K. and Stangor, C. (1998). *Prejudice: The Target's Perspective*. New York: New YorkAcademic Press.

Tasker, Y. and Negra, D. (2007), *Interrogating Postfeminism: Gender and the Politics of Popular Culture*. Durham, NC: Duke University Press.

Tyree, T. C. M. and Krishnasamy, A. (2011), "Bringing Afrocentricity to the funnies: An analysis of Afrocentricity within Aaron McGruder's *The Boondocks*". *Journal of Black Studies*, 42, (1), 23–42.

US Census Bureau (2009), "Current population survey, annual social and economic supplement".

Volgy, T. J. and Schwarz, J. E. (1980), "TV entertainment programming and sociopolitical attitudes". *Journalism Quarterly*, 57, (1), 150–5.

Walker, N. (1991), "Toward solidarity: Women's humor and group identity", in J. Sochen (ed.), *Women's Comic Visions*. Detroit, MI: Wayne State University Press, pp. 57–81.

Wallace, M. (1978), *Black Macho and the Myth of the Superwoman*. New York: The Dial Press.

Ward, L. (2004), "Wading through the stereotypes: Positive and negative associations between media use and Black adolescents' conceptions of self". *Developmental Psychology*, 40, (2), 284–94.

White, D. M. and Abel, R. H. (1963), *The Funnies: An American Idiom*. New York: The Free Press of Glencoe.

White, E. S. and Fuentez, T. (1997), "Analysis of black images in comic strips, 1915–1995". *Newspaper Research Journal*, 18, (1–2), 72–85.

Witek, J. (1999), "Comics criticism in the United States: A brief historical survey". *International Journal of Comic Art*, 1, (1), 4–16.

Wong, W. S. and Cuklanz, L. (2002), "Critiques of gender ideology in Hong Kong comic arts, 1966–1999". *Journal of Gender Studies*, 11, (3), 253–66.

Wyatt, G. (1997), *Stolen Women: Reclaiming Our Sexuality, Taking Back Our Lives*. New York: Wiley Books.

Young, I. M. (1994), "Gender as seriality: Thinking about women as a social collective". *Signs*, 19, (3), 713–38.

Note

1 © 2011 King Features Syndicate Inc. Reprinted with permission.

4

Black comics and social media economics: New media, new production models

Derek Lackaff
SUNY Buffalo

and Michael Sales
Elon University

"There are more of us involved in this business than many people think, doing more than just superhero books," posted journalist and comic creator Rich Watson to a new blog in 2005. "It's my objective to invite people from all walks of life here to learn about our favorite black characters and titles, as well as the people of color who make them" (Watson 2005). Watson's blog *Glyphs*, which focused on comics created by and for people of color, evolved from an email list of the same name, which was in turn inspired by Watson's first visit to the East Coast Black Age of Comics (ECBAAC) Convention.

> I was quite impressed by what I saw. Despite its diminutive size, there was a strong sense of camaraderie and support amongst the creators and fans. I appreciated that, and I also saw within it an opportunity (Noles 2008).

Over the last few years, Watson and others have taken advantage of the new social media to cultivate relationships and communities, inform and educate comics readers, and explore new models for developing Black comic art.

Blackness in the comics industry has been approached from various perspectives by cultural critics. The most prominent approach has been the textual exploration of race as represented in comic books (e.g. Foster 2005; Singer 2002; Strömberg 2003). This important context encompasses the largest arena for discussion, as these conversations currently play out among fans and critics and across blogs, discussion forums, and scholarly journals. A second approach has examined the experience of Black comic writers and artists, and the challenges they face in an industry where both creators and audiences are overwhelmingly White (Brown 2001). A third approach examines "Black comics" as a domain operating outside the "mainstream," often as one of many "alternative" comics scenes created and maintained by a community of creators and fans (Duffy and Jennings 2010; Rifas 2004). This chapter contributes to each of these discussions by providing an overview of the contemporary economic context of Black comics production and distribution, with special focus placed on the contributions of social media. For our purposes, "comics" refers broadly to sequential art that juxtaposes images and text, in formats ranging from comic books to newspaper comic strips to online webcomics. We seek to provide an overview of the economic structures of the comics industry, show the intersections of this industry with the culture of Black comics production, and argue that social web media have strongly impacted the production and distribution of comic art and supported fan community development. We position this argument in relation to the two approaches mentioned previously: the experiences of Black creators, and Black comics as an alternative cultural community.

This chapter's argument is divided into three sections. First, we present a brief sociocultural overview of Black comics as a specific artistic context, and the evolving relationship among creators and audiences. Next, we present a discussion of several recent industrial and technological changes that are reconfiguring the economic structures of comics. Finally, we present and critique the development of fan communities and argue that new digital communication technologies present significant new opportunities for Black comics.

As is the case for many emerging domains of popular culture study, important debate plays out across multiple forums, both popular and scholarly. This chapter, thus, draws upon a range of sources, including articles from traditional scholarly venues, essays posted online by scholars and critics, and posts by journalists and fans to blogs and web forums. We also received comments and perspectives from several Black comics creators and promoters. This chapter does not seek to present a comprehensive analysis of the economics of Black comics, nor to develop generalizable knowledge about topics such as marketing or networking, but to explore emerging practices and perspectives in the Black comics domain and highlight interesting impacts of social media. The following section presents a brief overview of Black comics and their relation to the mainstream of the comics industry.

Black comics and superhero masculinity

Superhero comic books are often perceived as fanciful tales of action, adventure and science fiction. Looking deeper, they can be understood to represent something more, especially for the young men who are the largest consumers of the product. In many ways, these pieces of art represent the ultimate male fantasy. Classical comic book depictions of masculinity are perhaps the quintessential expression of mainstream cultural beliefs about what it means to be a man (Brown 1999). Iconic superheroes—especially the classic characters like Superman and Batman—operate in a world that gives them incredible power and resources. The only restraints on that power are self-imposed. Often, these heroes have no biological families and no "real-life" responsibilities to contend with, and usually test their power and resources against powerful antagonists. Superhero comic books give the male id an unbridled place to be free and play like a child.

Why then do so few ethnic minorities show up in these comics (Foster 2005)? Even in a post-integration America, the number of Black characters in the average mainstream comics lags far behind the number of Black people in the average American workplace. Comic books are a symbolic playground where we let our idealized versions romp; yet relatively few characters of color take part in the fun. Racism or prejudice, while obvious suspects, is not necessarily the answer. When societies create mythical narratives to express a worldview and a belief system, they tend to be extremely personal. Comics compete in an economic as well as cultural marketplace, and alignment with majority, mainstream perspectives might be expected.

Regardless of the cause, Black readers often still feel "left out" (Foster 2005). The comics remain popular among the fanbase despite the lack of diversity and, therefore, force the Black fan to question his or her place in not only the economic landscape of the industry, but also in the reality of everyday life. For some, this feeling of dislocation demands a response, a way to assert their existence artistically and culturally. Creators have indeed attempted to introduce new Black faces into the mainstream comics arena, yet concerns remain that these efforts reflect a sort of tokenism, rather than real attempts to engage (Singer 2002). Other creators have decided to change their focus from the mainstream comics industry and seek alternative modes for communicating their stories to audiences. Both approaches have contributed to the contemporary environment for the "Black comic book."

Mainstream publishers have attempted to engage with Black audiences (or at least Black characters) over recent decades. Marvel and DC, the largest two comics publishers, have developed Black characters like The Black Panther, Power Man and The Black Racer. In some cases, these characters have even periodically helmed their own titles. In the 1970s, these attempts to introduce Black faces left many Black comic book readers unsatisfied. Black characters were often given a heavy-handed stigma that immediately marked them as the "racial" character, especially with their names. Black Panther, Black Lightning, The Black Racer, Brother Voodoo, Black Goliath, Black Vulcan, Black Spider—many of these heroes wore the same stigma new Black employees brought into the corporate world. Integrating comics, it seemed, was very similar to integrating the American workforce—African Americans were "marked" as the "new Black person" as soon as they stepped through the door. Consequently, readers felt pride seeing an African king like Black Panther portrayed as a superhero. But when the sovereign Black monarch of a high-tech civilization is rarely allowed to exercise that power and authority over his White counterparts, the pride is undercut. Black Panther had the high-tech gadgetry and financial resources of a Tony Stark, the regal imminence of Doctor Doom and the international cache of James Bond, but never took center stage in any major Marvel storyline and had no impact on the overall literary narrative. In the real arena where it mattered, his "power" was fake and over time felt more like a token appointment to appease the times, not a real addition to the comic book landscape. Very few of these characters had any lasting appeal, because their depiction came too close to the stereotypical blaxploitation films of that era (Brown 1999). The limits of power placed on the Black characters in Marvel and DC comics left many Black fans artistically and emotionally unfulfilled. That dissatisfaction extended to Luke Cage and other popular characters as well, eventually becoming the primary impulse that impelled the modern "Black Age of Comics" movement.

By the 1990s, a new breed of Black comic book creators began producing work. Titles such as *Brotherman* or those launched by the Black-owned Milestone Comics publishing company came closer to satisfying the artistic, cultural and emotional needs of the audience and, therefore, better fit the definition of a Black comic book. If the comic book is a power fantasy realized with words and pictures, then the Black comics is one that creates that same unfettered sense of escapism and exploration for lack people, depicting a world with limitless possibilities. Black superheroes such as Icon, Static or Brotherman can exert the same power, with the same freedom and the same self-created rules that are given to Captain America or Thor. In this way, a "Black comics" is defined not necessarily by the skin color of the protagonist, but by the agency and dominance of the protagonist operating in this fiction-alized, fantasy world. It is not enough for the character to have superpowers and cutting-edge technology. He (or she) must use them to exert just as much power and have just as much effect on the outcome of their world as any other character in the comic landscape. That equality of power for African

Americans in the comic world is what makes a comic book more fully a "Black comics."

Structure of the comics industry

The mainstream comics industry has evolved into a production and distribution model that is distinct from other forms of contemporary print media. This section provides an overview of the printed comics format and associated economic structures. McCloud (1993) defines comics as "juxtaposed pictorial and other images in deliberate sequence, intended to convey information and/or to produce an aesthetic response in the viewer" (p. 9). The media used for the expression of the comics format include the newspaper *comic strip*, the magazine-format *comic book*, and the book format *trade paperback* or *graphic novel*.

Comic strips

The *comic strip* was an original format for comics art, and many current structural and thematic conventions of contemporary American comics emerged in this format. Newspapers began printing comic art in the later part of the nineteenth century (Harvey 1996), and comic art (and artists) became one of several key issues in the New York "newspaper wars" between William Randolph Hearst and Joseph Pulitzer at the end of the nineteenth century. Even "yellow journalism" (a derogatory term used by critics to deride the perceived low quality and sensationalism of newspapers at the time) was a reference to the *Yellow Kid*, a popular comic strip published by both Hearst and Pulitzer (Campbell 2001). By the early twentieth century, comic strips consisting of a few panels were being regularly published by newspapers, and the sequential art format, with ongoing narratives, had become well-established. Although few regarded comics as a format for exploring "serious" narratives, both creators and audiences were learning to understand the aesthetics and potential of the medium.

Contemporary comic strips are generally distributed to newspapers through content syndicates such as King Features, Universal Press Syndicate, and United Media in a manner similar to editorial, advice, and humor columns. Syndicated strips have a standard format (which may vary between a smaller weekday format and a larger Sunday format). Given the audience structure of newspapers, syndicated comic strips generally require a very broad level of demographic appeal. Entering into a contract with a major syndicate can earn a creator between $20,000 and $1,000,000 per year, depending on how popular the strip becomes (King Features, n.d.). Gaining such a contract is extremely competitive however—King Features notes that while over 5,000 comic strip submissions are received per year, only three are chosen for syndication. Although strips that engage with complex and controversial topics have emerged in mainstream circulation (including notable examples such as Garry Trudeau's *Doonesbury* and Aaron McGruder's *The Boondocks*), the syndicated comic strip in mainstream newspapers has not emerged as a particularly vibrant platform for exploring issues related to diversity.

As of 2008, approximately 15 of the 200 nationally-syndicated comic strips were produced by minority creators (Deggans 2008). Among the most popular strips by Black creators are Robb Armstrong's *Jump Start*, Ray Billingsley's *Curtis*, Stephen Bentley's *Herb and Jamaal*, Jerry Craft's *Mama's Boyz*, and Aaron McGruder's *The Boondocks* (Tyree and Krishnasamy 2011). Aaron Bell, the creator of the syndicated strip *Candorville,* suggests that an approach to the comics page that results in token representation for minority creators contributes to the industrial challenges for strips featuring minority characters. "I dread hearing what strip I've replaced when I'm added to a newspaper, because more often it's *Curtis* or one of the other comics which encouraged me to get into the business" (Deggans 2008).

Outside of the mainstream newspapers, the comic strip has been a more colorful format for expressing challenging ideas. College newspapers provide a venue for young creators to explore and practice their craft. Alternative city newspapers, aimed at urban, adult audiences, attract an audience that can support content that is more provocative, including comics. Distribution of such newspapers is generally limited, however, and creators negotiate specific terms with the newspapers that will carry their strip.

Comic books

The *comic book*, a staple-bound magazine, emerged as a publishing format in the United States shortly after the newspaper comic strip became popular (Harvey 1996). Comic books collected and republished comic strips in black-and-white and in color. Although the first comic book to focus on sequential narrative comics was F. M. Howarth's *Funny Folks* in 1899 (Harvey, 1996), the "modern" color comic book emerged in the early 1930s. Pulling character and story prototypes from the popular pulp adventure stories of the time, creators experimented with multiple types of narratives throughout the 1930s, until the first breakthrough hit of the medium emerged: the superhero. Jerry Siegel and Joe Shuster's *Superman* character first appeared in 1938, and by 1940 the character was selling 1,250,000 comic books per month (Harvey 1996). An explosion of other superhero comics naturally followed. Harvey

(1996) argues that the superhero was the perfect subject for the fledgling medium, as these stories were perfectly suited to the comic book's unique aesthetics. Although ostensibly oriented towards younger readers, superhero comic books were propelled into a mature industry over the course of a few years by demand from soldiers during World War II (Harvey 1996).

Throughout most of their history, comic books were distributed like other magazines, and could be found on the shelves of any retail outlet that stocked magazines. Comic books were purchased in bulk lots, and retailers (newsstands, grocery stores, dime stores, etc.) received from distributors a somewhat random assortment of the comic books that had been released that month. A comics fan who was collecting a particular comic book title (such as *Superman* or *Batman*) might have to visit several retail outlets to find a particular issue. The comic books that went unsold were either returned to the publisher or destroyed, and the retailer received a refund from the distributor, who was in turn reimbursed by the publisher. This system placed most of the economic risk on the shoulders of the publisher, and provided distributors and retailers with no major incentive to actually ensure that the comic books were sold (Depply 2006).

This inconsistency of distribution became increasingly problematic as comics fandom increased, and retailers and fans alike sought a more reliable method for ordering and selling comic books. In the early 1970s, the so-called "direct market" emerged (Depply 2006). With this model, retailers ordered a specific allotment of comic books each month, determined by what they knew they could sell effectively. In return for this opportunity, retailers agreed to purchase the comic books outright, and gave up the right to return those books that did not sell. This approach was welcomed by the distributers and publishers, and worked to the benefit of comic book audiences who could now expect to find their favorite comics easily. Over time, retail specialty shops focused on comic books emerged across the US. Initially, the development of the direct market resulted in a boom of new publishers in the comic book market, which had traditionally been limited to a few major players such as DC (which produced titles such as *Superman* and *Batman*) and Marvel (*Spider-Man*, *X-Men*, and many others). The overwhelming demand for new content provided the potential for new perspectives on the medium and new types of stories. "New comics publishing companies had been rare things since the early 1950s, and as recently as 1974 they were problematic [...] as the Direct Market blossomed, however, there was, seemingly, all the room in the world" (Depply 2006: 7)

In the early 1990s, multiple comic book publishing organizations were started with the explicit goal of producing comics content for Black audiences. One such publisher was Milestone Media, a Black-owned company that signed a distribution deal with DC in 1993 and launched four new superhero titles. Milestone's four titles, *Static*, *Icon*, *Hardware*, and *Blood Syndicate*, featured a coherent universe centered on a fictional American city called Dakota (much like Superman's Metropolis or Batman's Gotham City) where superpowered characters explored issues of inner-city life, race, class, and socioeconomics. The comics received critical and popular acclaim for their examination of serious issues. "The reality it speaks to is a genuine reality," notes Harvey (1996: 259) of a *Hardware* storyline, "The emotional undercurrents here are real, springing from a long history of racism and oppression."

Ultimately, the comics boom that began in the 1970s and 1980s came down with a crash. Critics such as *Fantagraphic*'s Gary Groth (1987) suggest that the direct market became a "juggernaut of stupidity and vacuousness" in the 1990s. Although a handful of high-quality, innovative new projects such as the Milestone line were launched, the market was also increasingly saturated with lower-quality content that was explicitly created to cash in on the boom. The success of the direct market in isolating comic books in specialty shops (and away from newsstands) made it difficult to attract new audiences, not only for new titles but also for the medium itself.

> [T]he audience comics shops had cultivated had become a micro-world unto itself—a world that some have called a superhero ghetto. If you weren't the kind of loyal reader who made regular trips to comics shops, you rarely even saw comic books, let alone talked about them over the water-cooler (Depply 2006).

The Milestone line of comics was just one casualty of the mid 1990s crash, with these comics ceasing publication in 1997. By the time this economic turbulence had passed, many comics shops had gone out of business, and the industry had restructured itself into its current form, which supports a handful of major publishers such as DC and Marvel, which combined command approximately 75 per cent of the total overall comics market (Diamond Comics Distributors 2011).

Graphic novels

The most recently developed printed format for comics is referred to as the *trade paperback* or *graphic novel*. This format typically contains 64 pages or more of comics content bound as a paperback or hardback book. Some graphic novels are conceived of as longer-form narratives, and appear in this format upon their initial release. Other graphic novels are collected editions of a narrative that has been serialized across multiple comic books (or even collections of multiple narratives from multiple comic books). The exact nature and connotation of the term graphic novel is subject to rather intense debate within the comics and comics studies community. For the purposes of this chapter, however, the important factor is that the comics is bound as a book, rather than a magazine. This has important implications for how the printed product can be produced and distributed.

Unlike the comic book, the graphic novel is easily stocked and distributed by retailers other than comic book shops, primarily booksellers. While one would have to visit a specialty store to pick up the latest issue of a major superhero comics, a compilation edition comprising four or more volumes of the comic book can be purchased at a general-audience bookstore or easily ordered from an online bookseller. The industry's move to this format has expanded the audience for comic art and increased demand: libraries and educational institutions have become major purchasers of the format. A second impact has been a broader critical and popular embrace of the comics format as a serious literary medium, and a popular demand for stories beyond the superhero genre.

Black comics, new communities, and new media

At the same time that the medium had attracted a new generation of artists and writers, an important new communication platform was emerging and radically restructuring everything from major industries to intimate social relationships. The world wide web was launched as a user-friendly interface to the underlying internet in the early 1990s. The development of the web coincided with the evolution of the internet from a relatively exclusive domain for academics and engineers to a public and commercial environment supporting many types of social exchange. An online comics culture had been established by this time across newsgroups and discussion boards, but the scope of comics conversations expanded dramatically as new websites were launched and more fans found their way online. The asynchronous communication found in former Marvel editor-in-chief Stan Lee's "Bullpen Bulletins" and readers' letter sections was now supplemented by instantaneous communication online and a new, more symbiotic relationship between creator and fan was established. The internet presented significant new opportunities for the development of fan communities and new distribution channels, ranging from mail order of printed material to webcomics. This section addresses the rise and evolution of the contemporary Black comics community, the impact of "Black age" comics and culture conventions, and looks to the future potential of social media to promote Black comics.

"Alternative" comics communities with some level of cultural and political importance have emerged, grown, and declined multiple times in recent decades. In contrast to the sanitized mainstream of comics, the "underground comix" scene of the late 1960s and early 1970s addressed controversial and politically-charged topics, and often featured graphic depictions of drug use, sex, and violence. A unifying feature of the underground comix movement was its distain for the comics industry's self-censorship code, the Comics Code Authority (Rifas 2004). Although many creators identified with the political Left of the era, Rifas (2004: n.p.) argues that these artists also railed against the standards of the emerging political norms: "Comix artists often tried to outdo each other in violating the hated Code's restrictions [... some] used extreme racial stereotypes in their comix as further demonstrations of this freedom of expression." While engagement with issues of race was far from universally positive, underground comix introduced a venue for more serious examination of the topic. Strömberg (2003: 229) notes "it wasn't until the boom of adult comics that the medium was being taken seriously, both by cartoonists and readers – and [...] this made it possible to break free from the ingrained simplifications that comics up until then had had to live with."

Black comics conventions, pioneered by "Black age of comics" creator Turtel Onli, have been foundational in establishing an active community around Black comics. Annual conventions for creators and fans, already an accepted cultural practice of the mainstream comics world (San Diego's Comic-Con attracts an annual audience of more than 130,000) have become an important mainstay of the Black comics community. Onli organized the first Black Age of Comics convention in Chicago in 1993. Onli's annual Chicago event has since been joined by the ECBAAC Convention (Philadelphia, since 2002), Motor City Black Age of Comics Convention (Detroit, since 2009) and ONYXCON (Atlanta, since 2009).

The Black comic book scene that developed in the 1990s and 2000s was also broadly supported by the lowering costs of communication. At least three benefits have been realized within the Black comics community through social media use, including the creation and consolidation of supportive fan communities, the ability to refine and develop new economic approaches to producing and distributing comics, and the ability to reach increasingly larger audiences with lower financial investment.

As with other relatively small and dispersed communities, the internet helped Black comics creators and fans find and support one another. Artist Jamar Nicholas (2011) observes "before the internet, it was insanely difficult to find people with the same interests, especially such a difficult, small niche as comics" (personal communication). One hub of this community is the newsblog Blacksuperhero.com and its associated forums (called HEROTALK). The website and forums allow members of the creator and audience communities to share news, announce projects, and discuss aspects of their fandom. Jonathan Gayles, an academic and filmmaker, notes the importance of communities that are at least somewhat independent of the mainstream comics culture:

> While black online communities exist outside of the mainstream, they are not limited by the social forces (in particular, market forces and white supremacy) that construct "mainstream" representations of the genre. The difference then, is that these communities are independent and self-actualized in ways that "the mainstream" cannot sustain (J. Gayles, personal communication, 2011).

Joseph R. Wheeler III, the founder and president of the New Art Order and ONYXCON Convention, concurs:

> On boards that cater to the African Diaspora and its progressive supporters, there is a unique culture. Like any other board, there are the info gurus, fluff talkers, lurkers, and beef instigators. But what makes these culturally unique boards special for me is that people can generally relax in their dialogue and speak from a common group of perspectives on things in entertainment and current issues without having to feel generally afraid that the responses will not be interpreted from a common cultural fabric (J. R. Wheeler, personal communication, 2011).

The synergy between the intimate, in-person experience of the conventions and the persistent, on-going communication via social media channels is seen by many creators as a useful foundation for community support and development. Artist Ashley Woods (personal communication, 2011) suggests that online communities have been vital in discovering fellow creators, noting that "before I had the internet, there were a lot of black creators and works I didn't know about, [but] after joining BSH [Blacksuperhero.com] I made a lot of new artist friends and there was a strong support system." Artist Afua Richardson found that participating online allowed her to make the most of a visit to the Black Age convention in Chicago:

> I was totally blown away at the bonds, the synchronous conversation, the family community that was present. It was an awe-inspiring encounter. Artists who felt like cousins. Fellow women in comics [whom] I'd only met for the first time. I can thank all of those experiences and connections to social media (A. Richardson, personal communication, 2011).

The development of a supportive, accessible, and distributed community for creators encourages new participants and new projects.

This community development presents more benefits than just inter-personal encouragement and support. Blacksuperhero.com, as just one example, also enables new economic structures to develop. Artists and writers connect to pursue creative projects . Illustrators get their work critiqued. Writer Geoffrey Thorne (personal communication, 2011) suggests that this phenomenon is uniquely expressed in Black online communities, and that "helping others improve has never been part of the larger comics creative community, minority or not." New creators interested in the area receive advice from veterans and develop new audiences. Wheeler (2011) admires the potential for creative growth in these spaces: "I have witnessed a sketchbook challenge or a writer's brief idea become a full-fledged comic book, video game, or film concept. It is a beautiful way to see new innovative ideas bloom." Woods (personal communication, 2011) observes, "the people of BSH promote each other all the time and even collaborate on projects. Joining online communities is also a good way to learn a lot of industry infor-mation and get advice about publishing your work."

Finally, social media such as social networking sites (like Facebook), blogs, and microposting sites (like Twitter) can help to level the playing field for marketing and audience access. Thorne (personal communication, 2011) notes that social media can increase visibility by "providing wider access for a considerably less cost to creators who, in the old days, didn't have a prayer of getting seen and building an audience." Artist Keith Knight (personal communication, 2011) goes further, stating "every company and artist should have someone who specializes in social media and search engine optimi-zation for maximum success of their product." The convergence of popular social media, such as increasing cross-site accessibility of Facebook, help to bind communities that are distributed across different technical platforms. Blogs such as GhettoManga and World of Black Heroes, for example, provide updates via Twitter and Facebook, and allow users to connect with mutual friends.

The future of black comics

The ossified direct sales model for comics that shut out many alternative voices is rapidly dissolving in the face of new distribution models. For printed comics media, costs are rapidly declining as technologies like print-on-demand (POD) mature and eliminate the need for retailers to take financial gambles on new concepts and products. While the digital distribution of comics has not yet emerged as a major focus for many Black creators (with a few notable webcomics exceptions such as Knight's *K Chronicles*), the increasing prevalence of smartphones and tablet computers is starting to represent a significant new market. Digital comics distributor *comiXology* sells comics on the iPhone and iPad, and reports that fewer than 20 per cent of its customers were buyers of traditional comics (Forsythe 2011).

The development of a community that expands across geographic distances and persists across time is forming the basis of the current "Black age" comics movement. Highly decentralized, but with several touchstones of community reference, the community is providing opportunities for its members and enriching the broader cultures of comics. The simple fact that fans and creators can begin to understand themselves to possess critical mass supports the production of work of ever-increasing quality and the development of audiences with increasingly sophisticated understanding of the comics medium. Comics has long been an effective medium for telling complex and personal stories, and signs point to increasing opportunity and growth.

This chapter showed how new digital communication technologies are presenting significant new cultural and economic opportunities for Black comics, based on three interrelated analyses. First, the Black comics developed within a specific sociocultural history, interacting with a social and economic context that changed radically in the space of a few decades. Secondly, the broader industries of entertainment and publishing have been forced to reckon with a world that is increasingly digital, which has challenged old industrial models and laid the foundations of entirely new production models. Thirdly, we suggest that online technologies have increased the visibility and viability of fan and artist communities, allowing new social structures to develop that provide support and momentum to a growing Black comics movement.

References

Brown, J. A. (1999), "Comic book masculinity and the new Black superhero". *African American Review*, 33, (1), 25–42.

—(2001), *Black Superheroes, Milestone Comics, and Their Fans*. Jackson, MS: University Press of Mississippi.

Campbell, W. J. (2001), *Yellow Journalism: Puncturing the Myths, Defining the Legacies*. Westport, CT: Praeger.

Deggans, E. (2008, January 14), "Minority cartoonists: Don't lump us together". *St. Petersburg Times*. Retrieved from: http://www.sptimes.com/2008/01/14/Entertainment/Minority_cartoonists_.shtml.

Depply, D. (2006), "Fine young cannibals: How Phil Seuling and a generation of teenage entrepreneurs created the direct market and changed the face of comics". *The Comics Journal*, 277. Retrieved from: http://classic.tcj.com/history/a-comics-journal-history-of-the-direct-market-part-one/.

Diamond Comics Distributors. (2011, March), "Publisher market shares: February 2011". Retrieved from: http://www.diamondcomics.com/public/default.asp?t=1&m=1&c=3&s=237&ai=106262.

Duffy, D. and Jennings, J. (2010), *Black Comix: African American Independent Comics, Art and Culture*. Brooklyn, NY: Mark Batty Publisher.

Forsythe, E. (2011, January 24), "Digital comics pioneer comiXology discusses its past and future". *tfaw.com*. Retrieved from: http://www.tfaw.com/blog/2011/01/24/digital-comics-comixology/?qt=ea_wiki_comixology.

Foster, W. H. (2005), *Looking for a Face Like Mine*. Waterbury, CT: Fine Tooth Press.

Groth, G. (1987), "Black and white and dead all over". *The Comics Journal*, 116. Retrieved from: http://classic.tcj.com/history/a-comics-journal-history-of-the-direct-market-part-two/.

Harvey, R. C. (1996), *The Art of the Comic Book: An Aesthetic History*. Jackson, MS: University Press of Mississippi.

King Features (n.d.), "Submissions guidelines". Retrieved from: http://kingfeatures.com/contact-us/submission-guidelines/.

McCloud, S. (1993), *Understanding Comics: The Invisible Art*. Northampton, MA: Kitchen Sink Press.

Noles, P. (2008, January 7), "Talking all things Glyphs with Rich Watson". *And We Shall March*. Retrieved from: http://andweshallmarch.typepad.com/and_we_shall_march/2008/01/rich-watson.html.

Rifas, L. (2004), "Racial imagery, racism, individualism, and underground comix". *ImageTexT: Interdisciplinary Comics Studies*, 1, (1). Retrieved from: http://www.english.ufl.edu/imagetext/archives/v1_1/rifas/.

Singer, M. (2002), "'Black skins' and White masks: Comic books and the secret of race". *African American Review*, 36, (1), 107–19.

Strömberg, F. (2003), *Black Images in the Comics: A Visual History*. Seattle, WA: Fantagraphics.

Tyree, T. C. M. and Krishnasamy, A. (2011), "Bringing Afrocentricity to the funnies: An analysis of Afrocentricity within Aaron McGruder's *The Boondocks*". *Journal of Black Studies*, 42, (1), 23–42.

Watson, R. (2005, May 31), "Salutations". *Glyphs: The Language of Black Comics Community*. Retrieved from: http://web.archive.org/web/20101017083124/http://glyphsonline.blogspot.com/2005/05/salutations.html.

5

Beyond b&w? The global manga of Felipe Smith

Casey Brienza
University of Cambridge

Halfway through the third and final volume of Felipe Smith's Japanese manga series *Peepo Choo*, the author provides a seven-page, thirty-three panel synopsis of an episode of the fictionalized animated television show that lends the manga its title. It begins with two tribes of clown-nosed cartoon creatures who are at war with each other. On one side are black creatures with plus signs on their bellies. The creatures on the other side are near identical in shape, but are white instead of black, and have minus signs on their bellies instead of pluses. Clouds of smoke and raucous sound effects indicate that the two tribes are well on their way to annihilating each other in violent battle … until Peepo Choo steps in to intervene. A whirlwind of positive energy, he vomits and defecates comically upon two unlucky combatants, stopping them dead in their tracks with disgust and nearly getting them killed by their one-time allies. But when the icky stuff has finally been inhaled back down Peepo Choo's mouth, the two tribes realize that they have *all* been transformed into gray creatures with equal signs on their bellies. There is no difference between them to fight about anymore. Peace has been achieved!

Precisely the same shade of gray screen tone used to flesh out these newly incarnated creatures is also used for the skin color of Jody, one of *Peepo Choo*'s main characters, and Omario, the protagonist of Smith's debut work, *MBQ*. (The title *MBQ* stands for "McBurger Queen," a fictionalized burger and fries chain.) With their exaggerated range of facial expressions and distinctively upswept dreadlocks, they are virtual dead ringers of each other—and they, more than any other characters in these two manga series, resemble the artist himself. Yet Smith is anything but a piece of cartoon fiction; he is easily the most prominent rising star in international manga publishing and the first American ever to have had an original series published in Japan in all of modern manga's 60-odd year history. Both *MBQ*, published by Tokyopop from 2005 to 2007, and *Peepo Choo*, which began serialization in 2008 in the Kodansha *seinen manga* magazine *Morning 2* and was published in three complete volumes in English by Vertical in 2010, are sometimes satirical, sometimes sentimental stories of hybridity. The gray tone in these black-and-white manga is an apt metaphor for both the artist and his creative project. Smith is without question fiercely talented—but he was also at the right place at the right time. His diverse background and globe-trotting career trajectory would seem to make him the perfect *mangaka* [manga artist] to hail the transnational audience for manga in the twenty-first century that, while dreaming of moving beyond simple black and white, nevertheless remains woefully—even ridiculously—ignorant of the other.

In this chapter, I will begin by explaining the word "manga" and providing a brief historical overview of the medium in Japan and the United States. Then, I will outline a theory of comics and communication based upon the medium theory of Marshall McLuhan and Scott McCloud, which accounts for the medium's utility as a forum to grapple with issues of race, ethnicity, nationality, and culture. I will also provide a short biography of Felipe Smith himself, concentrating upon his unique background and self-identification. I will then provide in-depth textual and visual analyses of the *MBQ* and *Peepo Choo* manga series respectively, suggesting that both works promote simple messages grounded in orthodox American values about human equality and hard work. I will conclude this chapter with a careful discussion of the moral valance of these sorts of messages from a creator of fast-growing importance in the field with a readership in the United States, Japan, and beyond.

A brief history of manga

Before proceeding, a brief digression into the definition of "manga" and its place in the global cultural industries is in order. The word manga, typically written in Japanese as either マンガ or 漫画 and pronounced MAHN-gah, is a compound of two Chinese characters meaning "irresponsible pictures." It is Japanese for the medium of the comic strip, of sequential art, and in the United States has come to refer specifically both to Japanese and Japanese-influenced comic books. Although the first recorded use of the word is attributed to Hokusai Katsushika, the woodblock print artist best known for his classic nineteenth century image of Mt Fuji (Schodt 1983), what is now known as manga is not descended directly from the work of Hokusai. After the forced opening of Japan in 1853, Western culture—including comics— soon followed. Political cartoons and short comic strips were common by the 1920s, and in the 1930s chapter length comics called "story manga" were being pioneered (Gravett 2004; Schodt 1983). Post-World War II, Osamu Tezuka, nicknamed *manga no kamisama* [God of Manga], pioneered the cinematic visual narrative style of story manga now widely considered synonymous around the world with the word "manga" (Gravett 2004, Schodt 1983). The manga publishing industry as it now exists in Japan dates to this postwar period of reconstruction and has since become mature, large, and lucrative, accounting for approximately 25 per cent of all book sales and 20 percent of all magazine sales in 2006 according to the Japan External Trade Organization (JETRO 2006 cited in Lee, 2009). Manga genres are typically defined in terms of their target readership; *shounen manga*, for example, means comics for boys, while *shoujo manga* means comics for girls. Smith's works are *seinen manga*, comics for young men. As is the case in Western fiction, however, in practice female-oriented titles are read solely by other girls and women, whereas male-oriented titles, particularly *shounen manga*, are read equally by both genders. Examples of titles currently popular worldwide include *Naruto*, *Hetalia*, *Bakuman*, and *One Piece*.

Owing to its migration from the field of comics publishing to that of trade book publishing, manga has also become an increasingly important category in North American publishing, with the research firm ICv2 estimating that US manga sales grew an unprecedented 350 per cent from 2002 to 2007 (Brienza 2009a). The most recent figures put annual sales in the United States at approximately $150 million, with well over 1,000 new volumes released each year (Brienza 2010). Due to this success, competition between US publishers over the best licenses from Japan, and the ease with which books can now be classified as "manga" in the bookstores, many publishers now release comics which they refer to as "manga" even though they have not been produced by Japanese people in Japan (Brienza 2009b; Johnson-Woods 2010). There are numerous terms used to refer to this medium: The earliest appears to be "amerimanga," short for "American manga" (Schodt 1996). Others such as "OEL manga" (OEL is an acronym for "original English-language") and "world manga" became common in the first few years of the twenty-firstst century to accommodate *mangaka* who are neither Japanese nor English-speaking, but the term that currently appears to have the most currency is "global manga" ("Tokyopop To Move Away from OEL and World Manga Labels" 2006). I too prefer this term over the alternatives and consider it the most appropriate to refer to Smith's creative work.

Comics as communication

The mechanism by which comics communicate meaning is grossly under-theorized, perhaps owing to their historic lack of cultural legitimacy both within and without the academy (Groensteen 2009; Lent 2010; Lopes 2009). Among the few to write about how comics work and ground it within a broader theory of the media is Marshall McLuhan. In *Understanding Media* (1964), he defines media as anything that extends the senses. This concept is further divided into a "hot" and "cool" binary. Hot media, because they are data-rich, do not require the audience to bring anything of themselves to the experience. Cool media, by contrast, require that the audience actively fill in a lot of information because so much sensory information has been left out. If they do not, they will not understand what is being communicated. Comics are an example of a cool medium; they are, according to McLuhan, "a highly participational form of expression" (p. 179), "simply because very little visual information is provided" (p. 24). However, while readers of manga such as Smith's must bring a high level of cultural and linguistic competency to their reading experience, precisely *how* comics reading is accomplished by the reader—or, for that matter, facilitated by the comics creator—is left unexplained.

Veteran comics artist and theorist Scott McCloud (2000) draws heavily upon McLuhan's concept of hot versus cool media in his similarly titled comics treatise, *Understanding Comics*, in order to explore that very question. Starting from the premise that comics are intensely fascinating and compelling to so many people, he then asks why this might be so. He argues that the answer is the "amplification through simplification" of the cartoon drawing (p. 30). According to McCloud, people see another's face in "vivid detail" (p. 35), but they apprehend their own face only in vague sensations of the general placement of their most prominent facial features, the eyes, nose, and mouth. Therefore, people experience the lived existence of their own bodies in space and time as if they were comic book characters themselves, and it is through their own bodies that people come to understand the meaning of a comics. This is how he explains his theory of cartoons: "Thus, when you look at the photo or realistic drawing of a face, you see it as the face of *another*. But when you enter the world of the cartoon, you see *yourself*" (p. 36). This, he asserts, is why his own persona in the book is so simply drawn: "*Who* I am is irrelevant. I'm just a little piece of *you*. But if who I am matters *less*, maybe what I *say* will matter *more*" (p. 37). By simplifying the mechanism of delivery in this manner, the message is made all the clearer and more urgent. And why would this be the case? Because, when confronted by the cartoon, it is as if the cartoon's message is coming at a person not from without but rather from within, not from another but rather from oneself.

Naturally, comic art can exist at multiple points on four axes between complex and simple, realistic and iconic, objective and subjective, specific and universal (McCloud 2000: 46). In contrast to scholars such as Iwabuchi (2002), who attributes the global success of Japanese popular culture to the absence of distinctively Japanese traits that he calls "odor," I would argue that mainstream Japanese manga tends to fall somewhere in the middle range of these four axes. Thus, individual manga characters are complex enough not to be taken for just anybody or each other, but they are nevertheless iconic enough for Westerners to want to know why they always seem to look "white" (Thorn 2004). Put differently, race must be marked in manga, either by features distinguishable from other characters, by language, or by the story itself; otherwise, readers will be inclined to see them as members of the unmarked majority: Japanese people see Japanese characters, while Americans see White characters. Incidentally, because Whiteness in American culture is the most universal, unmarked category with other non-White races requiring a relatively higher degree of specificity, even non-White Americans also typically see White characters when reading manga or watching anime. Manga characters can only ever become "Black" when their skin is specially screen toned, and because this screen tone constitutes a significant amount of extra labor for the artist, it is never done without specific signifying intent. This issue is particularly important in the context of *MBQ* and *Peepo Choo* because Smith is a *mangaka* who consciously resists simple, iconic self-definition while attempting to represent multiple races, nationalities, and cultures in manga form.

About the author

Felipe Smith was born in the United States to a Jamaican father and an Argentine mother and raised in Argentina. He returned to America to attend college at the School of the Art Institute of Chicago and lived for several years in Los Angeles working odd jobs before moving across the Pacific to Japan. On Japanese television, however, Smith simplifies this complex personal history at the intersections of multiple ethnic, racial, and national affiliations and tells his interviewers, *"Amerikajin desu* [I'm American]" ("PEEPO CHOO: Felipe Smith in Japan" 2010). This declaration, among the first learned in Japanese language classes throughout the United States, is one that does not require further explication in Japan. Although in Japan as elsewhere the stereotypical American is blond-haired and blue-eyed, the Japanese do readily accept the premise that Americans are phenotypically diverse. He is thus acting strategically to forestall further compli-cated questions about the nature of his ethno-racial self-identification.

When interviewing in English, Smith's resistance to being categorized at all becomes increasingly transparent. For example, he tells Deb Aoki of *About. com* that the sort of creative work he produces "has nothing to do with where I'm from. It's just what you want to do, what you set out to do and how hard you work for those things" (Aoki 2010). Indeed, like an increasing number of young Americans today (Saulny 2011), he chooses not to self-identify as any one particular race, Black *or* White. He does not place particular emphasis upon a Latino identity either, although this is commonly done in the United States as an alternative to Blackness (Itzigsohn 2005; Rodríguez 2000). Nevertheless, one of the characteristics of any minority status is involuntary membership, and in a global society where the son of a White American mother and a Black Kenyan father can still be called "America's first black president" (MacAskill et al. 2008), it is hard not to conclude that Smith will be regarded by many around the world as the first Black *mangaka*. Indeed, he has already become an inspiration and role model of achievement for Blacks and African Americans; one anonymous online commenter writes (text as original): "This guy really inspired me. I'm a african american living in america and I now know I have at least a standing chance at becoming a manga-ka. Ever since the days of DBZ I have been fascinated by Manga. Now I know that it is possible! Thank You Felipe Smith!!! My dreams have been reattached after countlessly being shattered" ("PEEPO CHOO: Felipe Smith in Japan" 2010).

This tension between how Smith views himself and his work and how he and his work are viewed by others must be of central concern in any analysis of his corpus, and it is an issue to which I will return later in some considerable depth. Of course, Smith's intention might not be what is communicated to his readers (Fiske 1987; Hall 1980; Jenkins 1992), but even if the text were to ever achieve its creator's communicative aims fully, it would be hard to accept at face value the claim of any writer that one's work has nothing to do with one's background, particularly when the subject matter draws upon the author's own experience. Therefore, in order to know *why* Smith has succeeded as Japan's first American *mangaka*, I would argue it is important not to read these manga as if they simply arrived magically onto bookstore shelves and forget the real person who produced them. In the next two sections, I will provide an in-depth textual and visual analysis of Smith's two manga series *MBQ* and *Peepo Choo*, respectively. My analysis will focus upon these three questions: First, how is difference portrayed in these manga? Secondly, how does Smith's own biography inform these portrayals? And thirdly, what, precisely, is being communicated to the reader?

MBQ: Work hard for what you want

Smith, like other now-established artists M. Alice LeGrow (*Bizenghast*), Mike Schwark and Ron Kaulfersch (*Van Von Hunter*), Amy Kim Ganter (*Sorcerers & Secretaries*) and Christy Lijewski (*Next Exit*; *RE:Play*), got his professional start in global manga through Tokyopop's Rising Stars of Manga contest. A semi-annual (later annual) contest run from 2002 to 2008, the Rising Stars of Manga was inspired by similar contests held by manga publishers in Japan and used to scout new, locally sourced talent. The contests were necessitated by the increasing domestic competition for the best-licenced manga, competition which increasingly was shutting Tokyopop out. Although controversy surrounding the terms of the contracts offered to the winners later darkened the contest's reputation, it was the only competition of its sort for global manga artists in the United States and attracted a good amount of attention from aspiring young creators. Smith won second place for his entry "Manga" in the third Rising Stars contest and was offered a contract by Tokyopop to publish the three-volume series that would become *MBQ*. The first graphic novel volume was released in 2005; the subsequent two volumes were published in yearly intervals, the third and final installment released at the end of 2007. Due to adult content, many bookstores did not carry it, but it was critically well received, and *Publisher's Weekly* nevertheless named *MBQ* one of its best new comics for 2005.

    MBQ is set in West Los Angeles. Characters include LAPD cops Finch and O'Malley, gangster and electronics thief Dee, full-time karaoke bar manager and part-time hip-hop artist Brian, and the mild-mannered fast food restaurant employee Jeff. And at the center of this ensemble cast of characters is Omario, whose single-minded pursuit of his dream of becoming a manga artist is done mostly in his bed in the small apartment he shares with Jeff. Omario, you see, is above menial labor, and because he cannot work in the comics industry without compromising what he views to be his creative ideals, he does not do much in the way of working at all.

    Several events in quick succession change Omario's mind. The first are remarks from his friend Dee, who despite the tattoos, musculature, demonic hairdo and life of violent crime, has some rock solid advice for his young friend: "Doing what you want may be one of the most rewarding things in life. That's what we should all aim for. [...] You're going to have to fight for it if you want it. It's always a fight" (Smith 2006: 197). The second is a chance encounter with Hisao, a fellow alumnus from the School of the Art Institute of Chicago (Smith's own alma mater as well). The man, in spite of his Japanese name, is the epitome of Euro-chic, sitting outside a café, smoking and working on his sketching. Omario is greatly impressed by the quality of

Hisao's drawing and figures that clients must be beating his door down, but when he asks what he is working on now, the reply is, "Oh. Not much really. Just developing some projects of my own; trying to get things off the ground. I'm still planning things out, you know?" (Smith 2007: 132). As it turns out, he actually works as a barista at the café Omario had previously assumed he had been patronizing! The final straw is seeing his friend Brian, the long suffering manager of a karaoke bar, onstage and performing a hip-hop routine to the adulation of devoted fans. So, in order to start paying for the $5,000 worth of water damage he causes to the apartment when the bathtub overflows, he begs Jeff to get him a job at McBurger Queen. The story ends with Omario working the register at MBQ.

The races of most the characters in this work are quite difficult to separate from their basic character descriptions and the stereotypes which accompany them. Officers Finch and O'Malley are White, as is Brian, McBurger Queen's most reliable, beloved employee and soon-to-be manager. The two art-oriented characters who are most admirably committed to the furtherance of their creative work, Brian and Hisao, are both Asian. (Brian's last name "Shin" sounds more Korean than Japanese, but the manga states that he is Japanese. Either way, the "model minority" stereotype holds.) Dee, the gangster, is Black, and his hairline is partially shaved so that he looks like he has horns ... just to hammer home the "Black devil" stereotype in the visual space. Other criminal elements in *MBQ* also tend to be Black, and although there is a Korean mafia presence as well, Dee, as Omario's confidant, appears the most frequently and is by far the best-developed Black supporting character. To summarize, then, the face of law, order, and authority is a White one; the face of the hard-working, aspiring immigrant is Asian, and the face of crime and violence is Black.

What then, about Omario himself? He is, as noted previously, the most transparently autobiographical of Smith's characters in *MBQ*. He attends Smith's alma mater, the School of the Art Institute of Chicago, and he espouses a creative philosophy near identical to the one expressed by Smith in interviews: "I draw, I tell stories. Graphic novelist, comic book artist, manga-ka ... call it what you like. It's just a title ... I tell stories with pictures" (Smith 2005: 194). In other words, he rejects easy labels for his professional persona and draws genre- and category-busting sequential art. Yet his name evokes that of Omari Ismael Grandberry, better known as Omarion, the R&B artist from Los Angeles, and without any other references to Omario's personal history, he is meant to be read as Black. In fact, the first clear image of Omario is of him bruised and bleeding, wearing a tracksuit and headphones around his neck—and grimacing with menace at the gun in his hand. He starts out, in short, fitting the Black gangster stereotype; a part of the comedy of the story is finding out otherwise later.

Where, finally, does *MBQ*'s message lead? What does it tell its readers to believe? Smith himself admits at the end of the third volume that his own struggle to draw comics nobody in the industry thought would be marketable informed the story's conclusion; if he could not compromise his creative aspirations to draw "family-friendly, kid-safe material, [he was told that he] would never work" (Smith 2007: 215). He continues, "If I were to look only at sales figures for [*MBQ*], or measure the lack of impact it's had on the comic-book industry, I'd have to admit that they were right and that I was in fact wrong to go against the grain and do what I wanted" (Smith 2007: 215). Even so, he refuses to let sales figures—and his inability to make a living off of manga from the get-go—deter him: "But being hardheaded as I am, I refuse to admit that I was wrong. [I]f you really want something, you have to fight for it; even if it means sometimes doing something completely unrelated" (Smith 2007: 215). This is *MBQ*'s message: It says that hard work is worth it. Who cares if you have to take some lousy job in the meantime? Your effort will pay off someday, as long as you never stop working hard for what you want.

The virtue of hard work in order to get ahead is a familiar component of the so-called American Dream, one that characterizes the United States both to its own citizens and to people from all over the world. Wayne Baker and Gail Campbell (2011) describe this key American value for W. W. Norton's *Everyday Sociology Blog*:

American society is unique in the emphasis placed on achievement and success. Three of four Americans agree that getting ahead is important to them. Those who fail to get ahead suffer a defect of will, a lack of persistence, verve, or some other personal shortcoming. Most Americans recognize that forces larger than the individual affect our fates, yet this doesn't change our strong-held faith in self-made achievement and success.

This is precisely what Smith himself believes and what he attempted to say through *MBQ*. Clearly, while the characters of this global manga might be multiracial and multiethnic, the moral of its story is all-American.

Peepo Choo: No difference between me and you

Peepo Choo, by contrast, does not immediately strike one as being "all-American," either in the context of its publication or in the context of its plot. The seed that would eventually become this manga was first planted at the San Diego Comic-Con, the largest event of its kind in the United States. Smith had been approached by an editor for the Japanese publishing house Kodansha at the convention about doing a manga for Japanese audiences. Smith admits that he was not initially keen on the idea of writing for Japanese audiences per se: "I told him I wasn't really interested in writing for a Japanese audience, I wanted to write for a **global** audience. I wanted to write something that a Japanese person, as well as American, as well as Argentine, Jamaican, or **anybody** could pick up and get something from this story and enjoy it. And I think he liked that idea" (Aoki 2010). After a period of collaboration, both long-distance from Los Angeles to Tokyo and in Tokyo, the two men reached an agreement and *Peepo Choo* began its run in Kodansha's *seinen manga* magazine *Morning 2* in June 2008, the first Japanese manga series ever to be penned by an American. It ran for a total of three volumes and as befitting its global orientation has subsequently been published in English translation by Vertical, a US-based affiliate of Kodansha.

The story of *Peepo Choo* begins with Milton, a 16 year old Black boy from Chicago who looks much younger than his real age and harbors a secret passion for the Japanese anime also called "Peepo Choo." He spends as much free time as possible at his local comic book store in front of the television with other anime fans, called "otaku," and learning its special language, which he assumes must be Japanese. So needless to say Milton is thrilled when the store holds a contest that will take the winner to Japan, little suspecting that the store owner is secretly an assassin who has been hired by a Japanese yakuza family to take down a member who has recently become an inconvenience. Store manager Jody, who had heard that Japan is chock-full of sexually available women, decides that Milton would be the best person to help him to communicate with the locals, rigs the contest, and hands Milton the prize.

Upon arriving in Japan, Milton is horrified to discover that the language he had learned from "Peepo Choo" is not proper Japanese at all and that using it does nothing but baffle and horrify the people he meets there. If it were not for a chance encounter with Miki, an otaku herself, he would have surely have been lost. Miki in turn introduces Milton to her friend Reiko, a beautiful young woman who, despite impeccable English language skills, has nothing but contempt for foreigners—all of whom take one look at her ample breasts and never bother trying to see the person behind them. Jody, meanwhile, encounters Morimoto, the very person his boss was sent to assassinate, and mistakes him for some sort of local celebrity. Morimoto, for his part, is obsessed with American gangster culture—it is that obsession that has made him a liability to his yakuza family—and assumes that Jody, in his Blackness and American-style clothing (purchased in Japan), must be a *real* gangster.

All of the characters in *Peepo Choo* have deep misconceptions about "the other," and some are transformed by their encounters with the real thing, but for the purposes of this chapter I will focus upon three: Milton, Jody, and Morimoto. What unites them all, in spite of their considerable differences, are fundamental misconceptions about cultures other than their own and an identification, either self-identified or ascribed, with Blackness. Morimoto, the young organized crime kingpin, wishes that he could be Black. He introduces himself, in poorly accented English, "Mai neimu izu, mazza fakkin' rokkustaa [My name is motherfucking Rockstar]," a sentence which is not necessarily improved by being written in standard English spelling (Smith, 2010a). His hair is dyed white, his skin is tanned extra dark, and he wears a huge piece of jewelry around his neck, which says "Brick Said," a misspelling of "Brick Side," the title of an obscure gangster flick he adores and watches over and over. He has also learned gang signs on YouTube. Jody, upon seeing this, observes, "That's my hood's victory walk! Ha ha! Morimoto ... You could get shot for doing that in the wrong place, homie" (Smith 2010c: 144). But he does not always get them right; Jody also soon notices, "But you're throwing the wrong hand signs ... And some of those steps are off, dogg" (Smith, 2010c: 144). He believes that these gang accoutrements are the outward aesthetic of a particular way of life, which involves loyalty to one's comrades and violent retribution against any slight, the gang life portrayed in "Brick Side."

Jody, for his part, has no illusions about what life is like in Chicago and although he pretends to be the sort of Black man that Morimoto imagines he must be, in reality he would prefer to stay out of trouble and would "never do any of this on the street back at home" (Smith 2010c: 145). He happens to be one of the most important sources of recurring comic relief throughout the series; besides an oft-thwarted sex drive, he also discovers that he has a doppelgänger in Japan. The doppelgänger is a celebrity, the so-called "Beauty Judy," loosely based upon real Japanese "talents," such as Masaki Sumitani, aka "Hard Gay," who perform a faux brand of homosexuality for television (Smith 2010b: 30). Jody also bears a striking physical resemblance to Omario, the protagonist of *MBQ*, but—perhaps a sign of Smith's own maturing relationship to his art—Jody is for the most part only a witness to the cross-cultural caper in mutual misunderstanding that is *Peepo Choo*. He is not the real hero of this story.

That particular honor goes to Milton, one member of a large African American family living in the South Side of Chicago. The first chapter of the manga provides a poignant portrayal of an ordinary day for Milton. He leaves home, careful to wear the sort of tough kid clothing that allows him to fit in with his tough neighborhood, even though he hates it. Instead of going to school, however, he ducks into a public restroom and changes into a homemade Peepo Choo costume and heads to the comic book store. There, he feels, he can be himself—and being in Japan would be even better: "If I lived in Japan, I could be **me**, the real Milton! Life in the States sucks. I should have been born in Japan" (Smith 2010a: 38). It is worth noting that identifying with the popular culture of a non-White, non-Western for a Black youth like Milton can be viewed as a less problematic alternative to both American culture, Black or White, from which he feels alienated. On the one hand, he can feel allegiance to Japan as a fellow non-Caucasian, but as the citizen of a Western country relating to a non-Western one on the other, he can also simultaneously enjoy the vicarious pleasures of geo-political dominance. But once he actually arrives in Tokyo, though, Milton quickly realizes that he does not fit in any better there: "They're laughing at me," he muses as he walks down the street at night. "It's like … I'm back in Chicago" (Smith 2010a: 240). Fortunately he runs into the *otaku* subculture in Japan and begins to hang out with people with whom he has more in common.

The lesson that Milton learns in Japan is the moral of *Peepo Choo*'s story, and it is not one conveyed with subtlety. At the end of the third volume, with the widest of smiles, he tells Gill, comic book store owner and part-time assassin, what he has discovered:

> I was unhappy, 'cause I felt like in the States I couldn't fit in. But after coming to Japan I realized that what I was looking for … isn't found in any one place or country. It's found in the friendship of good, like-minded people! The perfect place for us isn't determined by country or culture. It's determined by *us* … the way we choose to live and those we surround ourselves with! (Smith 2010c: 230).

The prose used here is admittedly clunky and perhaps not entirely convincing coming out of the mouth of a 16 year old. Yet, it is easy to see why Milton's Blackness is so effective here; he is a member of a minority group as well as an *otaku*, a sort of double jeopardy that makes him an outsider in more ways than one. Thus, the message of this manga series is equally applicable to either category of identification; the point is not to be resigned to the particular family, culture, or nationality in which one finds oneself. It is within everyone's basic ability to find their bliss as they choose, to seek a set of like-minded people. In other words, difference whether racial or affiliational is overstated, the possibility of connection is immanent, and the pursuit of happiness really is an inalienable right.

Beyond black and white?

Smith's manga surely cannot be divorced from the particular period of history in which they were first published. That period was the beginning of public interest in Barack Obama, from his election to the US Senate in 2005 to the first term of his presidency beginning in 2009. The phrase "post-racial America" became the media buzzword, the most optimistic interpretations hoping that the United States has begun at last to transcend the old divisions between Black and White that have distorted its society for so long (Tesler and Sears 2010). Matt Bai (2010) opines for the *New York Times*, "This blurring of racial and ethnic lines is, for the most part, deeply inspiring, the manifestation of hard-won progress." Even Obama himself reports being acutely aware of the complexity of his biracial identity and multi-national upbringing—while believing it possible to embrace all of these aspects of himself simultaneously (Fraser, 2009). Smith, then, due to his diverse personal background, is a sort of Obama of the manga world, his career that crosses national boundaries riding the wave of global sentiment emanating from and surrounding Obama's presidential campaign and victory.

And he is more than just the Obama of the manga world. Stories are not just stories, after all; underpinning their narratives are particular moral valences (Fisher 1989). Through the sequential art medium, Smith also performs this post-racial moment—and he does so, despite protestations otherwise, for a particularly American audience. As noted by Miyoshi (1994), Americans typically believe that people everywhere are fundamentally the same, with the same sorts of hopes, dreams, and desires, while Japanese people believe themselves to be culturally different from everyone else and different in different ways from everyone else—"uniquely unique," to put it most succinctly. The semi-autobiographical character in *MBQ* learns that hard work is rewarded; the semi-autobiographical character in *Peepo Choo* observes two countries on opposite sides of the Pacific which have many misconceptions about the other while also being home to people who are not all that different from each other. These are emphatically *not* universally held values; they are *American* values, and Smith, like the very Americans he identifies himself with, mistakes them for universal, global values.

Taken together, what do these misrecognized messages in manga form imply? Do their precise moral valence truly provide a challenge to America's racialized orthodoxy, or do they inadvertently reinforce it? Unfortunately, I must conclude the latter. *Peepo Choo* and *MBQ* lack what C. Wright Mills terms the "sociological imagination" (Mills 1959). To quote his most succinct statement on the subject: "[T]he individual cannot understand his own experience or gauge his own fate without locating himself within the trends of his epoch and the life-chances of all the individuals of his social layer" (Mills 1951: xx). By refusing to acknowledge the importance of difference, of persistent social structures of inequality, which mean that hard work is not equally rewarded across groups, Smith reduces black and white to mere aesthetic choices of screen tone. He fails to locate himself within the broader sociocultural processes within which he is embedded and instead presumes to believe that he as an individual is an embodiment of his imagined global society. To conclude that because your hard work is rewarded, that hard work is always rewarded no matter the circumstances is a common fallacy leading to a blame-the-victim mentality.

Arguably worse, however, is Smith's decision to make his protagonists Black. Although he would prefer not to be Black or White himself, comics is a medium which lend itself to simplification and exaggeration, so in the backgrounds of the characters Milton, Omario, and Jody, there is no indication of any ambiguity in their self-identification. They are not even White by cartoon default. They are *Black*, born and raised in the United States. Given, as discussed earlier in the chapter, that comics such as Smith's manga are especially good at communicating meaning through the reading of the characters as oneself, this is—in a racialized, unequal society—a particularly pernicious media effect. The manga series are not merely about another person who finds friends in a non-Western country or who believes in the virtues of hard work to get ahead; rather, they are about the Black *self* who does and believes those things. So although Smith is a pioneer of global manga, he has not yet, I must conclude, been able to transcend the rhetorical boundaries between Black and White.

References

Aoki, D. (2010), "Interview: Felipe Smith—Creator of *Peepo Choo* and *MBQ*". *About.com: Manga*. Retrieved from: http://manga.about.com/od/mangaartistinterviews/a/Interview-Felipe-Smith.htm.

Bai, M. (2010, June 29), "Ethnic distinctions, no longer so distinctive". *The New York Times*. Retrieved from: http://www.nytimes.com/2010/06/30/us/politics/30bai.html?_r=1&ref=politics.

Baker, W. and Campbell, G. (2011, March 21), "American values: Are we really divided? " *Everyday Sociology Blog*. Retrieved from: http://nortonbooks.typepad.com/everydaysociology/2011/03/american-values-are-we-really-divided.html.

Brienza, C. (2009a), "Books, not comics: Publishing fields, globalization, and Japanese manga in the United States". *Publishing Research Quarterly*, 25, (2), 101–17.

—(2009b), "Paratexts in translation: reinterpreting 'manga' for the United States". *The International Journal of the Book*, 6, (2), 13–20.

—(2010), "Producing comics culture: A sociological approach to the study of comics". *Journal of Graphic Novels and Comics*, 1, (2), 105–19.

Fisher, W. R. (1989), *Human Communication as Narration: Toward a Philosophy of Reason, Value, and Action*. Columbia, SC: University of South Carolina Press.

Fiske, J. (1987), *Television Culture*. London: Routledge.

Fraser, C. (2009), "Race, postblack politics, and the democratic presidential candidacy of Barack Obama", in M. Marable and K. Clarke (eds), *Barack Obama and African American Empowerment: The Rise of Black America's New Leadership*. London: Macmillan, pp. 169–82.

Gravett, P. (2004), *Manga: Sixty Years of Japanese Comics*. New York: Harper.

Groensteen, T. (2009), "Why are comics still in search of cultural legitimization?", in J. Heer and K. Worcester (eds), *A Comics Studies Reader*. Jackson, MI: University Press of Mississippi, pp. 3–11.

Hall, S. (1980), "Encoding/Decoding", in S. Hall, D. Hobson, A. Lowe, and P. Willis (eds), *Culture, Media, Language: Working Papers in Cultural Studies, 1972–79*. London: Routledge, pp. 128–38.

Itzigsohn, J. (2005), "The formation of Latino and Latina panethnic identities", in N. Foner and G. M. Fredrickson (eds), *Not Just Black and White: Historical and Contemporary Perspectives on Immigration, Race, and Ethnicity in the United States*. New York: Russell Sage Foundation, pp. 197–216.

Iwabuchi, K. (2002), *Recentering Globalization: Popular Culture and Japanese Transnationalism*. Durham, NC: Duke University Press.

Jenkins, H. (1992), *Textual Poachers: Television Fans & Participatory Culture*. London: Routledge.

Johnson-Woods, T. (2010), *Manga: An Anthology of Global and Cultural Perspectives*. New York: Continuum.

Lee, H. (2009), "Between fan culture and copyright infringement: Manga scanlation". *Media, Culture & Society*, 31, (6), 1011–22.

Lent, J. A. (2010), "The winding, pot-holed road of comic art scholarship". *Studies in Comics*, 1, (1), 7–33.

Lopes, P. (2009), *Demanding Respect: The Evolution of the American Comic Book*. Philadelphia, PA: Temple University Press.

MacAskill, E., Goldenberg, S. and Schor, E. (2008, November 5). "Barack Obama to be America's first black president". *The Guardian*. Retrieved from: http://www.guardian.co.uk/world/2008/nov/05/uselections20084.

McCloud, S. (2000), *Reinventing Comics: How Imagination and Technology are Revolutionizing an Art Form*. New York: Perennial.

McLuhan, M. (1964), *Understanding Media: The Extensions of Man*. London: Routledge.

Mills, C. W. (1951), *White Collar: The American Middle Classes*. New York: Oxford University Press.

—(1959), *The Sociological Imagination*. New York, NY: Oxford University Press.

Miyoshi, M. (1994), *Off Center: Power and Culture Relations Between Japan and the United States*. Cambridge, MA: Harvard University Press.

"PEEPO CHOO: Felipe Smith in Japan". (2010, June 16). *YouTube*. Retrieved from: http://www.youtube.com/watch?v=0G8h02U1-1o.

Rodríguez, C. E. (2000), *Changing Race: Latinos, the Census, and the History of Ethnicity in the United States*. New York, NY: New York University Press.

Saulny, S. (2011, January 29), "Black? White? Asian? More young Americans choose all of the above". *The New York Times*. Retrieved from: http://www.nytimes.com/2011/01/30/us/30mixed.html?ref=us.

Schodt, F. L. (1983), *Manga! Manga! The World of Japanese Comics*. Tokyo: Kodansha International.

—(1996), *Dreamland Japan: Writings on Modern Manga*. Berkeley, CA: Stone Bridge Press.

Smith, F. (2005), *MBQ (Vols. 1–3, Vol. 1)*. Los Angeles, CA: Tokyopop.

—(2006), *MBQ (Vols. 1–3, Vol. 2)*. Los Angeles, CA: Tokyopop.

—(2007), *MBQ (Vols. 1–3, Vol. 3)*. Los Angeles, CA: Tokyopop.

—(2010a), *Peepo Choo (Vols. 1–3, Vol. 1)*. New York: Vertical.

—(2010b), *Peepo Choo (Vols. 1–3, Vol. 2)*. New York: Vertical.

—(2010c), *Peepo Choo (Vols. 1–3, Vol. 3)*. New York: Vertical.

Tesler, M. and Sears, D. O. (2010), *Obama's Race: The 2008 Election and the Dream of a Post-Racial America*. Chicago, IL: University of Chicago Press.

Thorn, M. (2004). "The Face of the Other". *matt-thorn.com*. Retrieved from: http://www.matt-thorn.com/mangagaku/faceoftheother.html.

"Tokyopop to move away from OEL and World Manga labels". (2006, May 5). *Anime News Network*. Retrieved from: http://www.animenewsnetwork.com/news/2006-05-05/tokyopop-to-move-away-from-oel-and-world-manga-labels.

PART TWO

Representing race and gender

6

Studying black comic strips: Popular art and discourses of race

Angela M. Nelson

Black comic strips are open-ended dramatic narratives about a recurring set of core characters of African descent, told in a series of drawings, including dialogue in balloons and a narrative text, and published serially in newspapers (Inge 1979: 631). They are primarily authored by people of African descent but have also been authored by people of European descent. For example, White cartoonists Allen Saunders and Alden McWilliams wrote and drew, respectively, *Dateline: Danger!* (1968–74), which was a biracially centered strip about Black reporter and undercover agent Danny Raven (Strömberg 2003: 134–35). Black comic strips amuse or engender pleasure in Black and non-Black audiences and emerge from self-conscious intentions, whether artistic, economic, or political, to illuminate Black characters and/or Black experiences, real or created. There are three types of traditional Black comic strips: comedy (gag), family, and action (e.g. Cripps 1978; Reid 1993).

Ultimately, Black comic strips are products of popular culture that express a Black repertoire and reflect race relations in the United States. This paper will construct a theoretical framework for studying Black comic strips from two perspectives: (1) as popular culture in general and Black popular culture in particular—examining their textures, texts, and contexts, and (2) as illustrative of American racial discourses—segregationist, assimilationist, pluralist, and multiculturalist. These strategies taken together form a unique dynamic paradigm for the analysis of Black comic strips, past and present that promises to reveal their cultural significance.

Popular culture and black comic strips

One framework for examining Black comic strips is to analyze them as a popular art form. Although this is not a new concept, delineating the specific angles in which comic strips can be analyzed as popular culture is a helpful exercise. M. Thomas Inge edited one of the first thorough treatments of comics as popular culture in an in-depth section of the *Journal of Popular Culture* in 1979. He speculated then that the comic strip represents one of "America's major indigenous contribution[s] to world culture" (Inge, 1979, p. 631). Inge went on to describe how comic strips are a "revealing reflector of popular attitudes, tastes and mores" (p. 631) and that they derive "from popular patterns, themes and symbols of Western culture" (p. 632).

Black comic strips are Black popular culture. Generally, Black popular culture consists of artifacts and practices created by people of African descent and based on their beliefs, values, and norms. Black popular culture is related to popular culture in general because it concerns pleasure and good, which is the core belief-value orientation of all popular cultural productions. Although Black popular culture involves all people of African descent internationally, US Black popular culture is often highlighted because it is within US culture and US culture is increasingly exported to the entire world (Hall 2005: 285–6).

Textures

Black popular culture must be interpreted within the context of popular culture in general. A cultural process that includes the elements of texture, text, and context (see Dundes 1964) can help us to understand Black comic strips as popular culture. This articulation of three distinct processes (whose interaction in reality overlaps and intertwines) should be applied to Black comic strips (or any popular culture product) if it is to be adequately studied (du Gay et al. 1997: 3–4). Texture, the first cultural process component, is the crucial element to reading the cultural expressions of Blacks because it involves belief-value systems and beliefs, and values help to make Black popular culture "Black." There are social textures (or social belief-value orientations) and artistic textures (or performative belief-value orientations). Artistic textures are the principles, beliefs, and values governing how people relate to and create the arts and other popular creative expressions. Social textures involve human relations, interactions, and experiences. Social textures are the beliefs and values that govern how people relate to themselves and to others. They include core beliefs and values.

The master, or governing, social belief-value orientation of popular culture and Black popular culture is pleasure and good. Pleasure includes all joy and gladness—all our feeling good, or happy (Katz 2009). David Perry defines pleasure as a concept used to mark "enjoyment" and to indicate that a person is "pleased about a thing" (1967: 214–7). Good is the most general term of approval, both moral and non-moral, whether intrinsic or extrinsic. If a comic strip engenders pleasure and is good to the cartoonist and audience, then it is good based on their terms and perceptions. Newspaper comic strips are unassuming, unobtrusive collaborations of words and images that are approved by audiences of comic strips because they engender pleasure from the repetitive personas and rituals of popular culture found in them.

Several core beliefs and values are unique to Blacks beginning with the African worldview, which serves as a historical foundation for the beliefs and values of all dispersed African people. Social textures often found in Black popular cultural productions include the belief-value orientation of the communal nature of relationships, or collective participation, spirit-soul-body perspective; and an "in time" rather than "on time" time perspective, as well as Black religious beliefs that include the supremacy of God; providence of God; justice of God; equality of persons; and heaven as transcendent reality. In the ground-breaking study *Black Metropolis: The Study of Negro Life in a Northern City*, St. Clair Drake and Horace Cayton (1945/1993) listed five "dominating interests" or "centers of orientation" of Blacks in "Bronzeville" (Chicago, Illinois's South Side) following World War II. These key belief-value orientations extracted from a mass of research conducted by Works Progress Administration field workers in the late 1930s include: (1) staying alive, (2) having a good time, (3) praising God, (4) getting ahead, and (5) advancing the race (p. 385).

Middle-class ideology is a core belief-value orientation found in Black comic strips and in several Black (and other) American popular art forms. The middle-class ideology in popular arts is represented with affluence, unlimited consumerism, conspicuous consumption, individualism, social and economic mobility, heterosexual love relationship and/or marriage, and nuclear family. The significance of middle-class ideology in Black popular culture production is that it exalts, celebrates, and centers Black urban life rather than Black rural or religious life. The strips also speak to the urban Black middle class, expressing a vision of urban Black life in America that is equal to Whites' socially, culturally, educationally, economically, and (implicitly) politically. A Black middle-class orientation, therefore, becomes synonymous with racial integration, peace, harmony, and equality, a recipe that complements the rhetoric of equal Civil Rights evinced in the activities of the NAACP (National Association for the Advancement of Coloured People) and similar organizations, and suppresses social contradictions of inequality, racism, discrimination that exist in society.

The performative belief-value orientation, or artistic textures, of Black popular culture are best understood through the concept of repertoire.

Black comic strips are products of popular culture that are drawn from a Black cultural repertoire. In "What is this 'Black' in Black popular culture?," Hall (1992/2005) describes three "Black repertoires" from which Black popular culture draws: style, music, and the use of the body as a canvas of representation.

> First, I ask you to note how, within the Black repertoire, *style*—which mainstream cultural critics often believe to be the mere husk, the wrapping, the sugar coating on the pill—has become *itself* the subject of what is going on. Second, mark how, displaced from a logocentric world—where the direct mastery of cultural modes meant the mastery of writing, and hence, both of the criticism of writing (logocentric criticism) and the deconstruction of writing—the people of the Black diaspora have, in opposition to all of that, found the deep form, the deep structure of their cultural life in music. Third, think of how these cultures have used the body—as if it was, and it often was, the only cultural capital we had. We have worked on ourselves as the canvases of representation (Hall 1992/2005: 289–90).

Together these repertoires form a Black aesthetic, which Hall (1992/2005) defines as the "distinctive cultural repertoires out of which popular representations" of diaspora Blacks are made (p. 290). I define Hall's concept of Black cultural repertoire as the specific devices, techniques, ideologies, expressive art forms, or products of people of African descent that form part of their culture (whether as context, texture, or text), that are often derived from the folk tradition (see Soitos 1996: 37) and dominant culture, that form a foundation of a Black aesthetic, and that are used to create Black popular cultural products.

I identify 11 components of the Black repertoire: religion and spirituality; middle-class ideology; orature and auriture; music; dance and gesture; city; church and nightclub; food and cuisine; heroes; worship service and party; and the Black body. While all eleven components of the repertoire do not appear in all Black comic strips or all Black popular art forms, the inclusion of at least three or four components in one Black popular cultural product simultaneously forms a holistic construct imbued with cultural meaning, symbolism, and significance. In two Black postwar comic strip series, *Toledo Sepia City Press*'s *Swing Papa* (1948) and *Toledo Bronze Raven*'s *Barry Jordan* (1954–5), the main characters are both musicians and bandleaders representing the music repertoire component. Bret Harvey in *Swing Papa* and Barry Jordan emphasized the Black body component of the Black repertoire. Barry Jordan, in particular, was shaded brown, had well groomed hair (natural, not processed), clear muscular features, full but not oversized nose and lips; a firm, square jaw, and he wore fashionable, tailored suits (17 July 1954, 4/2; 31 July 1954, 4/3–4; and 11 Sept. 1954, 4/3, 6). The iconic imagery of *Swing Papa* and *Barry Jordan* also stressed the "urban landscape" with all of its trappings (Soitos 1996: 23).

Texts

Inge (1979) stated in his essay that comic strips are a "form of creative expression apart from their relationship to other forms of art" (Inge, 1979, p. 637). This creative expression is made tangible through the texts of popular culture, the second cultural process component. The texts of popular culture are the actual visible, audible, and performative artifacts and practices that people experience. The artifacts of popular culture are popular objects, or icons, and popular people, or personas. Popular practices are activities, events, and experiences, the art forms and rituals surrounding popular people and objects. These components of the texts of popular culture—icons, personas, arts, and rituals—are the products toward which people experience the social belief-value orientation of pleasure and good.

Two components of the texts of popular culture are significant to comic strips, indeed for all narrative-based popular art: personas and rituals. A single comic strip series relies upon a set of recurring characters (personas) and a particular narrative strategy (ritual), which is initiated through some type of "disruption"—whether moral, ethical, physical, emotional, or social—that is resolved (Woollacott 1986: 199). The characters, or heroes, in Black comic strips represent the primary beliefs, values, and goals of the cartoonist of the strip. These fictional people have "narrative power" simply because the installments are written from their point of view, are based on their values, and literally revolve around them. For example, the Black comic strip hero's narrative importance is rendered (1) in the flow and content of familial conversations, (2) in their position at the center of the narrative, and (3) in their visual and oral dominance within the frames of the strip (Leibman 1995: 118, 129).

There are two narrative strategies, or rituals, often found in Black comic strips: integration and order. Many comic strips provide rituals of integration whereby "individuals are initiated into proper social behavior and shown wrong ... behavior." Family and comedy, or gag, strips such as *Bungleton Green* (1923–3), *Curtis* (1988–present), and *Little Magnolia* (January 15, 1949 to May 7, 1949, *Sepia City Press*) utilize integration rituals. For example, *Little Magnolia* revolved around a precocious "tweener" named Magnolia. A traditional gag strip with four panels that included a punch line in the final panel, jokes were based on misunderstandings often encountered by children.

Other comic strip series provide rituals of exclusion, which "mock and attack deviants who are outside the social order" (Kellner 1982: 145). Action-adventure strips such as *Dateline: Danger!* and *Jive Gray* (1943–51) utilize exclusion rituals. In the action-adventure strip series *Barry Jordan*, this Black bandleader and amateur detective solved crimes and captured "deviants" involved in an "infidelity racket" at the interracial Island Casino Club in Toledo, Ohio, and an arson ring targeting area nightclubs.

Contexts

The contexts of Black popular culture, the third and final cultural process component, concern social organizations, institutions, groups, and the people who experience, participate in, live, and consume popular culture. Three types of contextual social organizations, institutions, and groups that relate to popular culture in general and Black popular culture in particular are: (1) individuals and audiences, (2) producers and disseminators, and (3) controllers and regulators. I will focus on the production and dissemination of Black comic strips. In general, the production, dissemination, circulation, and exhibition of popular culture is situated into five levels or spheres: personal peripheral; local-urban-regional peripheral; national peripheral; national core; and global core-peripheral (Crane 1992: 5–9; Nachbar and Lause 1992: 172–4). Although Blacks are represented and participate in all spheres of production and dissemination, profitable and successful forms of Black popular culture created for and by Blacks often appear in the local-urban-regional peripheral and national peripheral spheres. The national peripheral sphere is produced and disseminated by organizations on a national basis but to distinct micro-groups based on age, race, sex, class, and lifestyle (Crane 1992: 5, 8). The local-urban-regional peripheral sphere includes products that are produced and/or given meaning by individuals or organizations in a distinct region (smaller than a country or nation) such as a school, town, city, college, or state to audiences who are fairly homogenous in terms of either age, social class, ethnic or racial background, or education (Crane 1992: 109).

Black comic strips are also located within the national peripheral and local-urban-regional peripheral spheres of production and dissemination. Although the earliest Black comic strip lead characters appeared in mainstream illustrated humor journals and newspaper comic strip supplements in the late nineteenth century (Gordon 1998: 60), significant Black comic strip series and characters appearing after World War I were in Black newspapers that, depending upon circulation, were within the national peripheral and local-urban-regional peripheral spheres of production and dissemination. Cities with a significant Black population had Black newspapers and during the 1930s, 1940s, 1950s and 1960s, Black comic strips were included in them. Targeting a fairly homogenous group of Blacks in such cities as Chicago, Norfolk, Harlem, Pittsburgh, Baltimore (Squires 2009: 44), and Toledo, Black newspapers concentrated on increasing their circulation and found the inclusion of comic strips as one way to increase and maintain their readership. Excellent examples of these strips that operated within the local-urban-regional sphere of production and dissemination are Ollie Harrington's *Jive Gray* (1943–51) and Jackie Ormes's *Torchy Brown* (1937–40; 1950–4), both in the *Pittsburgh Courier* and Leslie Rogers's *Bungleton Green* (1920–63) in the *Chicago Defender*.

Examining Black comic strips as a popular art form can reveal the hopes and intents of the Black cartoonist and the Black people he/she sought to represent. The relationship between Blacks and Whites in the United States also will reveal information about the condition of race relations. I will elaborate on this aspect of the analysis next when I discuss racial discourses in Black comic strips.

Racial discourses and black comic strips

In *Watching Race: Television and the Struggle for "Blackness,"* Herman Gray (1995) posits that the contemporary images of African Americans are anchored by three kinds of discursive practices: assimilationist/invisibility, pluralist/separate-but-equal, and multiculturalist/diversity (p. 84). He states earlier in the chapter that contemporary representations of Blackness were shaped by the formative period of television, which he in general confines to the 1950s. Gray (1995: 74) suggests that this formative period is:

> a defining discursive and aesthetic moment that enabled and shaped the adjustments that Black representations continue to make. It remains the moment against which all other television representations of Blackness have reacted. And it is the defining moment with which subsequent representations, including those in the 1980s and beyond, remain in dialogue.

The formative period of television involves a fourth discursive practice which I call "segregationist," or "separate-but-unequal." Together, I label all of these practices, "racial discourses." The dominance of a particular set of images and representations of Blackness are contingent on the social, cultural, and institutional conditions in which they are situated. How the strategies of signification employed in representative Black comic strips construct, frame, and narrate general issues of race and Black (objectivity and) subjectivity in US society can (or should) be one important question answered by researchers of Black comic strips (Gray 1995: 75–6).

Gray's argument is relatable to comic strips because of the similarities between comic strips and situation comedy. Key points of connection between situation comedies and comic strips are their narratives, characters, settings, and rituals, as well as the impact of certain controls and regulations and production and dissemination processes on these art forms. Both art forms are self-contained episodes and installments with a regular core cast of characters. Many but not all comic strips and situation comedies deal with family life, child-rearing, and middle-classness. In both art forms, Blackness is mediated similarly through home life, family, middle-classness, character, orature/auriture, and gesture. Family is mediated through home life, Whiteness, heterosexual love, middle-classness, material consumption, success, and traditional gender roles. Just as Gray found with Black situation comedies, Black comic strips series and Black lead characters also include a dominance of images and representations from 1897 to the present, which construct issues of race and Black objectivity and subjectivity. I will now explore the operation of these discourses in representative Black comic strips as a third framework useful for studying Black comic strips.

Segregationist (separate-but-unequal) discourses and black objectivity (1897–1966)

Segregationist discourses presented Blacks in stereotypical and subservient roles, thereby making them socially, culturally, and politically "separate and unequal" to Whites. Black sitcoms appearing on television from 1948 to 1965 illustrated explicit social and cultural rules of race relations between Blacks and Whites. Specifically, Black otherness (or Black objectivity) was required for White subjectivity; Blacks and Whites occupied separate and unequal worlds; Black labor was always in the service of White domesticity; and Black humor was necessary for the amusement of Whites (Gray 1995: 75). In Black comic strips, White cartoonists initially established this discourse with Black comic strip characters operating in segregationist discourses from 1897 to 1966. However, a few Black cartoonists, E. Simms Campbell, creator of *Hoiman* (1937), and Wilbert Holloway, creator of *Sunny Boy Sam* (1929–50), were also known for displaying segregationist discourses especially in relationship to the images of their Black lead characters.

Representations of Blackness in comic art date back as early as 1897 with Thomas Worth's *Darktown Comics* and Edward Kemble's *The Ragtown Polo Team Walks Away with the Blackberries* (Appel 1992: 34).

The earliest attempts to develop a Black comic strip character were Richard Outcault's *Here's the New Bully* in 1898, Outcault's series *Shakespeare in Possumville* in 1901, which carried grotesque African American caricatures to extremes (Gordon 1998: 63–4; Appel 1992: 34), and *Gallus Coon* in Joseph Pulitzer's *New York World* newspaper (Goulart 1995: 2–3). The title character, New Bully, was a tough Black boy who led an all-White gang. "Gallus Coon" was about a Black child. The title including "Coon" in it (as if that was the child's last name) is telling of American race relations in that time period.

Long-running Black comic strip series *Sunny Boy Sam* appeared in the *Pittsburgh Courier* from 1929 to about 1950 (Stevens 1974: 122–4; Wolseley 1990: 209–10). *Sunny Boy Sam* was a comedy/gag strip created by Wilbert Holloway that, at first, depicted Sunny Boy with heavy dialect, minstrel features, and an intense preoccupation with playing the numbers. However, by 1947, John Stevens notes that Sunny Boy was speaking like a college graduate (Inge 1993: viii; Stevens 1976: 239, 241–2).

Interestingly, this racial discourse ended approximately in 1970, the year Kenneth Kling, the cartoonist of the horse racing-themed series *Joe and Asbestos* (1925–6, 1928–66), died. Asbestos was a stable boy whose facial features were drawn like most Black adults, male or female, of the period with an "eightball" head with white, round, bulging eyes; thick, white, clown-shaped lips; odd-shaped hairstyles (if headgear was not drawn); totally black skin; and nondescript clothing or a uniform of some sort to denote the character's occupation as a servant or domestic (Gordon 1998: 61–2, 72; Jones 1986: 21; Sheridan 1971: 41, 205). Although other grotesquely stereotyped images of African Americans in comic strips were abandoned long before the late 1960s, Kling did not change Asbestos because he had very little incentive to do so. In fact, even though *Joe and Asbestos* only appeared in a few newspapers, it continued to be very profitable until Kling's death (Don Markstein's Toonopedia).

Pluralist (separate-but-equal) discourses and black subjectivity (1920–present)

Black comic strips from 1920 to the present show Black characters who are just like White characters except for minor differences of habit and racial perspective and show that Blacks face the same experiences, situations, and conflicts as Whites, except that Blacks live in separate communities. In these strips, Black individuals or families are isolated and living in separate but equal worlds (Gray 1995: 87). The same discourses appeared in television situation comedies from 1972 to the present.

Another post-World War I and pre-World War II Black comic strip series, *Bungleton Green*, appeared in the *Chicago Defender* newspaper from 1920 to 1963 and is an example of pluralist discourses (Stevens 1974: 122–4; Wolseley 1990: 209–10). *Bungleton Green*, drawn by four artists over 43 years (first drawn by Leslie Rogers), portrayed the ironies and vicissitudes of Black life in Chicago and American society in and around World War II, as well as the effects of racial discrimination through the eyes of African American Bungleton Green (Stevens 1976: 241; Stevens 1974: 122). Bungleton, who was representative of the traditional "fall guy" or *schlemiel*, had a wife and one son named Cabbage. Although *Bungleton Green* began as a comedy/ gag strip, it switched to an action-adventure format in the early 1930s and again during the mid 1940s (Inge 1993: viii; Stevens 1976: 239, 241–2). Another separate-but-equal racial discourse strip, *Swing Papa*, was published in the *Toledo Sepia City Press* in 1948. Drawn by Harold Quinn and written by O'Wendell Shaw, *Swing Papa* featured Bret Harvey, an unmarried African American bandleader of the Swingsters Sweet Orchestra. In this two-month series, Bret becomes involved with the rich, socialite Marta Gray and has adventurous, romantic encounters in Toledo, Ohio. Contemporary Black comic strips such as Robb Armstrong's *Jumpstart* (1989–present) and Ray Billingsley's *Curtis* (1988–present) present African American life as normal and natural but still primarily separate-but-equal.

Assimilationist (invisibility) discourses and black subjectivity (1954–74)

Comic strips operating within assimilationist discourses were created between 1954 and 1974 and they treat the social and political issues of the Black presence in American society in particular and racism in general as individual problems. Television situation comedies featured this racial discourse from 1961 to 1973. Although Black characters are SUBJECTS (rather than objects of the segregationist discourses), especially in terms of their visual representations, these strips are assimilationist to the extent that the worlds they construct are distinguished by the complete elimination or, at best, marginalization of social and cultural difference in the interest of shared and universal similarity.

Jimmy Dixon's *Barry Jordan* (1954–5), published in Toledo's *Bronze Raven*, is an example of invisibility discourses in Black comic strips. Barry Jordan is the bandleader and "ace tenor sax man" of his trio who also doubles as an amateur detective. Jordan represents assimilationism in this strip because he is a Black man shown moving in and out of White and Black circles with equal ease, his world is racially integrated, he possesses an intellectual, mental, moral, ethical, and artistic capacity superior to the other characters, and he is depicted as intelligent and rational because of his amazing ability to escape life-and-death situations with criminals and to solve crimes. *Barry Jordan* was devoid of significant African American traditions (except that he was a musician), social struggle, racial conflicts, and cultural difference. Rather, the focus was on racial integration, peace, harmony, and equality (Gray 1995: 85). *Dateline: Danger!*, *Friday Foster* (1970–4) and *The Badge Guys* (1971–2) also operate within assimilationist discourses.

Multicultural (diverse) discourses and black subjectivity (1965–present)

The diversity racial discourse in Black comic strips began in 1965 with Morrie Turner's *Wee Pals*. The discourse of multiculturalism/diversity shows African Americans as SUBJECTS who are fully integrated in American society, who are fully seen with viewpoints and perspectives that are voiced and heard, and who interrogate and critique "differences of Blackness with other Blacks" (Gray 1995: 90). Many Black sitcoms appearing after 1984 operated within this discourse and featured innovative approaches to the artistic form of the situation comedy. A significant moment for Black comic strips, all strips within this racial discourse are found in mainstream newspapers holding distribution agreements with mainstream features syndicates such as King Features Syndicates and Universal Press Syndicate. Other Black comic strips such as Jerry Craft's *Mama's Boyz* (1990–present) are available on the internet and are self-syndicated by the cartoonist. *The Boondocks* (1999–present) by Aaron McGruder is one example of the use of innovative approaches in Black comic strips. When his series appeared in almost 200 newspapers in April 1999, McGruder's employment of Japanese manga-style art and representations of hip-hop culture illustrated some of the most cutting-edge, innovative practices in American comic strip art in general.

Series early in this time period including Morrie Turner's *Wee Pals* (1965–present), Brumsic Brandon, Jr's *Luther* (1969–86), and Ted Shearer's *Quincy* (1970–86), dealt with the universal human aspects of childhood from a child's perspective and made political statements commensurate with the events of the Civil Rights struggle in particular and Black self-awareness and activism in general. All continuing Black lead characters were of equal social status to their White counterparts (Jones 1986: 27).

In terms of race relations, pre- and post-World War II Black comic art anticipated television images of Blacks by several decades and this relationship is instructive about genres and how similar narrative and ideological outcomes are achieved. While their characters, themes, settings, and rituals are relatively the same, Black images in comic art and sitcoms differ in terms of racial discourses. For example, Black comic strips that emerged in the 1920s were pluralist while television did not progress into this stage until the 1970s with *Sanford and Son* (NBC 1972–7), *Good Times* (CBS 1974–9), and *What's Happening!* (ABC 1976–9). However, just like Black sitcoms (1965–73), there was a small window of time open for assimilationist discourses in comic strips (1954–74). What can account for this similarity and difference? I believe it is the art forms involved. Television program production and dissemination is located at the national core sphere which is dominated by conglomerates that disseminate cultural products to national and international audiences and to which all members of the population are exposed to some extent (Crane 1992: 5) The conglomerates producing television programs are less likely to innovate and more likely to adapt superficial aspects of their programs in response to market demands (Crane 1992: 49–50). Several people are involved in the production of a situation comedy including writers, creators, producers, directors, and actors among many other support personnel.

The newspaper industry is commodified as well and comic strips are reliant on being published in a newspaper facilitated by the syndication process. However, few people are involved in the creative process of the comic strip. Most comic strips are authored by one person who both draws and writes. However, drawing and writing tasks are sometimes divided between two people such as was the case with *Dateline: Danger!* and *Swing Papa*. With newspapers in general and Black American newspapers in particular, production and dissemination is in the local-urban-regional peripheral and national peripheral spheres, with audiences in the thousands. As such, African American values are permitted to go directly to print with little to no editorial interruptions. In other words, even though Black cartoonists had to, for the most part, harmonize with the political goals of the Black editors of the newspapers that included their strips, they still had more freedom to express their thoughts about the social, political and economic conditions of African Americans between 1920 and 1975. The television industry simply does not (or will not) provide this kind of creative freedom with *any* type of programming it offers. True Black popular art expresses Black beliefs, values, norms, and behaviors. Black comic strip artists in unique ways express their interpretation of Black beliefs and values through the combination of words and images.

Conclusion

Two perspectives—popular culture and racial discourses—have been described as potential, productive theoretical strategies for scholars to engage in researching and studying Black comic strips. Joseph Nuttin finds that "in the human context, different types of rewards and pleasures—and probably the most important ones—are created by man himself, and that they can be made out of practically any material, i.e. any object, real or imagined, within his world" (1973: 254). Popular culture is created and/or embued with significance and symbolic meaning by all people. Analyzing comic strips with the understanding of the cultural process of textures, texts, and contexts provides a systematic order for exploring how they signify as pleasure and good. Determining which racial discourses a Black comic strip series operates within, is a window to the social, technological, and institutional conditions in which they are situated. Black comic strips (indeed, all American comic strips) demonstrate that popular art is never far from the culture in which it originated.

References

Appel, J. J. (1992), "Ethnicity in cartoon art", in *Cartoons and ethnicity*, the 1992 Festival of Cartoon Art. Columbus, OH: The Ohio State University Libraries, pp. 13–48.

Crane, D. (1992), *The Production of Culture: Media and the Urban Arts*. Newbury Park, CA: Sage.

Cripps, T. (1978), *Black Film as Genre*. Bloomington, IN: Indiana University Press.

Don Markstein's *Toonopedia*. Retrieved from: http://www.toonopedia.com/abnslats.htm.

Drake, S. C. and Cayton, H. A. (1993), *Black Metropolis: A Study of Negro Life in a Northern City*. Chicago, IL: University of Chicago Press. (Original work published 1945.)

du Gay, P., Hall, S., Janes, L., Mackay, H., and Negus, K. (eds) (1997), *Doing Cultural Studies: The Story of the Sony Walkman*. London: Sage Publications.

Dundes, A. (1964), "Texture, text, and context". *Southern Folklore Quarterly*, 28, 251–65.

Gordon, I. (1998), *Comic Strips and Consumer Culture, 1890–1945*. Washington, DC: Smithsonian Institution Press.

Goulart, R. (1995), *The Funnies: 100 Years of American Comic Strips*. Holbrook, MA: Adams Publishing.

Gray, H. S. (1995), *Watching Race: Television and the Struggle for "Blackness"*. Minneapolis, MN: University of Minnesota Press.

Hall, S. (2005), "What is this 'Black' in Black popular culture?", in R. Guins and O. Z. Cruz (eds), *Popular Culture: A Reader*. London, ENG: Sage, pp. 285–93. (Reprinted from Dent, G (ed) (1992), *Black Popular Culture: A Project by Michele Wallace*. Seattle, WA: Bay Press, pp. 21–33.)

Inge, M. T. (1979), "Introduction: The comics as culture". *Journal of Popular Culture*, 12, (4), 631–9.

—(1993), "Introduction", in M. T. Inge (ed.), *Dark Laughter: The Satiric Art of Oliver W. Harrington*. Jackson, MS: University Press of Mississippi, pp. vii–xliii.

Jones, S. L. (1986), "From 'under cork' to overcoming: Black images in the
    comics", in C. Hardy and G. F. Stern (eds), *Ethnic Images in the Comics:
    An Exhibition in the Museum of the Balch Institute for Ethnic Studies*.
    Philadelphia, PA: Balch Institute for Ethnic Studies, pp. 21–30.
Katz, L. D. (2009), "Pleasure", in E. N. Zalta (ed.), *The Stanford Encyclopedia of
    Philosophy (Fall 2009 Edition)*. Retrieved from: The Metaphysics Research
    Lab.
Kellner, D. (1982), "Television, mythology and ritual". *Praxis*, 6, 132–55.
Leibman, N. C. (1995), *Living Room Lectures: The Fifties Family in Film and
    Television*. Austin, TX: University of Texas Press.
Nachbar, J. and Lause, K. (1992), *Popular Culture: An Introductory Text*. Bowling
    Green, OH: Popular Press.
Nelson, A. M. (2005), "*Swing Papa* and *Barry Jordan*: Comic strips and Black
    newspapers in postwar Toledo", in *Proceedings of the Ohio Academy of
    History, Muskingum College, New Concord, 7–8 April 2005*, pp. 61–74.
Nuttin, J. R. (1973), "Pleasure and reward in human motivation and learning", in
    D. E. Berlyne and K. B. Madsen (eds), *Pleasure, Reward, Preference: Their
    Nature, Determinants, and Role in Behavior*. New York: Academic Press, pp.
    243–74.
Perry, D. L. (1967), The Concept of Pleasure. The Hague/Paris: Mouton &
    Company.
Reid, M. A. (1993), *Redefining Black Film*. Berkeley, CA: University of California
    Press.
Sheridan, M. (1971), *Comics and Their Creators*. Westport, CT: Hyperion.
Soitos, S. F. (1996), *The Blues Detective: A Study of African American Detective
    Fiction*. Amherst, MA: University of Massachusetts Press.
Squires, C. R. (2009), *African Americans and the Media*. Malden, MA: Polity
    Press.
Stevens, J. D. (1974), "*Bungleton Green*: Black comic strip ran 43 years".
    Journalism Quarterly, 51, (1), 122–4.
—(1976), "Reflections in a dark mirror: Comic strips in Black newspapers".
    Journal of Popular Culture, 10, (1), 239–44.
Strömberg, F. (2003), *Black Images in the Comics: A Visual History*. Seatte, WA:
    Fantagraphics.
Wolseley, R. E. (1990), *The Black Press, U.S.A.* (2nd edn). Ames, IA: Iowa State
    University Press.
Woollacott, J. (1986), "Fictions and ideologies: The case of situation comedy",
    in T. Bennett, C. Mercer and J. Woollacott (eds), *Popular Culture and Social
    Relations*. Milton Keynes: Open University Press, pp. 196–218.

7

Blowing flames into the souls of black folk[1]: Ollie Harrington and his bombs from Berlin to Harlem

Christian Davenport

It is said that the devil is in the details. If this is the case, however, then those among us who are the most aware, the most astute of the horrors done by some against others are the closest to hell. Whatever we might think about what it is like to be near the darkest of places (with the heat, the damned, the depression and the hatred), the one thing that we can probably agree upon is that the proximity likely takes a toll on those unfortunate enough to get a glimpse. We, as the recipients of the insights provided, are better informed and perhaps a bit unsettled from the receipt, but we do not take the full brunt of the hits that accompany the initial vision. For engaging in this treacherous enterprise of gazing into hell and blowing flames into the souls of Black folk in order to educate as well as incite, we owe political cartoonist like Ollie Harrington a debt that cannot be repaid easily. Nevertheless, I will attempt to contribute to such an effort.

By the time Ollie Harrington (the cartoonist, war correspondent and satirist/social critic) joined this world in 1912 within the sleepy town of Valhalla (in upstate New York), it was already clear that hell was all around him—having burned for several hundred years. Up to this date, African Americans had lived through mass abduction, the "middle passage," forced slavery, the American Civil War, the hope and the betrayal of Reconstruction and the harsh repressiveness of lynching. This was to be quickly followed with more lynching,

Jim Crow (the unofficial slavery), mass migration, limited opportunities and a new version of racism that was found in the urban North. Those present during the latter period (the 1920s and 1930s) beheld a world that strained comprehension. And in this space, individuals attempted to keep themselves grounded. These individuals wanted to stay aware but not *too* aware, hopeful but not too delusional. To do this, they relied upon news journalists, teachers, blues singers and, yes, political cartoonists—in the case of Harrington.

In this essay, I will argue that Harrington epitomized the brilliance as well as the problems of one with keen insight into the complexities and outright brutality of the situation for Black Americans in the early through mid 1900s. To understand Harrington and his work, one has to think in part as journalist and chronicler; compassionate therapist; storyteller; and, even or especially as provocateur. His insights appear to be partly for himself (revealing that he was not crazy through self-revelation) but also for an ever-increasing but now largely forgotten audience (reveling in their sanity at seeing the insane). To understand Harrington and his work, one also has to think about the Black middle class itself, the role of Black newspapers in this community that largely served as the primary vehicle through which his work was distributed, and the weight carried by one who was very much aware and astute. As I will detail below, Harrington reveled in blowing flames into the souls of black folk but it is clear that every blow probably enlivened as well as depleted him. How could it not?

Below, I will discuss a bit of the political, economic, as well as cultural, situation into which Harrington was born (The Context) and the seemingly complex but largely charmed/fortuitous existence that he led (The Life). I will then address the importance of Black cartoons, cartooning and satire (The Medium), as well as some of the themes of this work (The Message). In particular, I wish to situate Black cartoons into the broader repertoire of sociopolitical and sociocultural products used by oppressed people to both educate and incite. I conclude with a discussion about the connection of Harrington with a broader field of social-political criticism (The Ending). Here, I will make comparisons to others who serve(d) in a similar capacity and invite us to engage this work in a deeper historical purview.

The context

The world for African Americans in the early 1900s was something of a living horror. One after the other (with some overlap) they lived through slavery, Civil War, Reconstruction, lynching and Jim Crow. The last is especially poignant for in many ways it established the parameters for Black existence that came after it. There was some variation in this situation illustrated within the figure provided below by Pauli Murray (1997). This becomes important because, although highly discussed, it was possible to navigate around some of the worst of what was done against the Black community. Quite frequently, this involved leaving everything that one owned/was familiar with and moving from the South to the North, which was done by Ollie Harrington's father who ended up in upstate New York.

As discussed by many, the move North came with new as well as older problems but also with some opportunities. The key for much of this era— especially for the Black middle class but also for those who strove to improve their lot, involved integrating into the US, attaining full citizenship and making democracy "work." Many were quite eloquent on this point. For example, Ralph Bunche (1973) argued that democracy as a concept and by implication the US nation had to open up for African Americans or else fail and, again by implication, be replaced with something else. As he says:

If democracy is to survive the severe trials and buffetings to which it is being subjected in the modern world, it will do so only because it can demonstrate to the world that it is a practical, living philosophy under which all people can live the good life most abundantly. It must prove itself in practice or be discredited as a theory. Democratic nations such as our own have an obligation to all mankind to prove that democracy, as a form of government, as a practical means of human relationships, as a way of life, is a working and workable concept. This America can do only by making democracy work, by abandoning the shallow, vulgar pretense of limited democracy—under which some are free and privileged and others are permanently fettered. The Negro, and especially the Negro in the South, already has had too vivid an experience with embryonic fascism in the very shadow of democracy. Within our own gates are found intense racial hatreds, racial differentials which saturate the political, economic and social life of the nation, racial ghettoes—all the racial raw materials for a virulent American fascism (Bunche 1973: 106).

He continues that Blacks have a right to be skeptical but should not give up completely. As he states:

Negroes are all too familiar with the many and serious shortcomings of American Democracy; but they know, though they do not always recall, that democracy as a concept, as a way of life, had afforded them the sole basis for whatever progress they have made as a group since slavery, for the heroic struggle they have incessantly waged, for their aspirations in the future. Democracy, even imperfect democracy, has been the ideological foundation upon which Negro life has been based; it has been the spiritual lifeblood for Negroes. As an ideal, it has not progressed very rapidly in the world we know. But what else has the world to offer the Negro? (Bunche 1973: 110).

With the history of American violence discussed as backdrop, African Americans of the 1920s and 1930s attempted to make good on American promises of incorporation (again[2]) but, of course, only some made such overtures. While in some places laws were being passed and discussions being had, in other places knives were being sharpened, assassin's bullets aimed, placards drawn and hostile mobs formed. While part of America tried to open, another America tried to close the lid altogether. Into this situation, Harrington was born and raised.

The life

Like many, Ollie Harrington's creativity emerged from a simple act of racism. In Junior High School, Harrington moved to the South Bronx from upstate and into the classroom of a Miss McCoy. McCoy is memorable because he maintained that she

> used to call me and the other black pupil in the school—a great, big guy by the name of Prince Anderson—to the front of the room and present us to the class. She'd say, "these two, being black, belong in the waste basket (Inge 1993: 98).

Unable to strike back directly, Harrington did what James Scott (1985) and later Robin Kelley (1994) would call "everyday forms of resistance." He did something that would simultaneously allow him to address the abuse in some manner that would not result in injury and at the same time maintain some level of dignity. Harrington's approach was to draw cartoons of her. As for the type of drawing, he is clear: "they were much more violent than anything you can find in the present day so-called comics. I did her up fine" (Inge 1993: 98).

As an African American attempting to navigate through the US educational system, I immediately associated with the situation but there were some differences. My McCoy was a male teacher—Block (complete with evil-curly mustache at the tips and deep Southern accent) and my environment was not a public school in New York but an elite(st) preparatory school in Greenfield, Massachusetts called Northfield Mt Hermon. My Block did not beckon me and the other Black person in the class (Arthur Scott) to come to front of the class—at least not physically. Additionally, reflective of the day (the early 1980s) Block's comment was not as obviously uttered to set us apart and belittle us but the effect was nevertheless the same. After an especially nigger-laden section of Huckleberry Finn, Block queried aloud: "I wonder what the Black man felt." We (Arthur and I) knew what was coming next (as do many of you who have been there) but we were naively hopeful that it would not come. Of course, it did. Attempting to "move the conversation along," Block quickly followed up the reading with: "Christian? Arthur? Would you care to contribute anything?" Our silence at this request was matched by the silence of the class. You could not hear Block or any of the students laugh or us physically shrink (or more appropriately disappear) but both happened. In a matter of seconds, we were gone from that class, from that place—never to return (in our different ways Arthur and I withdrew from each other, as well as our classmates).

Unfortunately, neither Arthur or myself had any artistic skills to speak of to seek our virtual vengeance on Block. Like Malcolm X after being told that law was not really for him and that carpentry might be preferred, we sat there with our worlds somehow being defined for us with very little agency. Instead of striking or drawing back—as it were, we languished all semester long hoping that there would be no other explorations of Black culture. Both of us searched for our ways. Mine led to the written word and a strong appreciation for satire, wit and cartooning.

Although difficult, Harrington's life was full of McCoy-like experiences, which he seemed to meet with equal levels of success. Repeatedly and with enough economic benefit to sustain a career, he was able to find outlets for his artistic abilities. After Junior High, Harrington attended DeWitt Clinton High School (in 1929) and/or Textile High School (in 1927)—depending upon whom you read.[3] Here, he received accolades for his artistic skills and founded a club of other artists (Art Young, Denys Wortman and Daniel Fitzpatrick). Following graduation, Harrington moved/escaped to Harlem and began studying at the National Academy of Design.

It was in this location that he interacted with Charles Hinton, Leon Kroll and Gifford Beal—artists and teachers. Always ambitious and multitasking, it was also during this period (1932) that he got his first break with some of his political cartoons (e.g. Razzberry Salad), publishing in the National News (until it folded four months after he joined) and the New York State Contender. This later extended to the other newspapers, including the New York Amsterdam News, the Baltimore Afro-American and the Pittsburgh Courier, as well as an organization that represented a collection of papers called The Harlem Newspaper Club (where he met Bessye Bearden of the Chicago Defender and her son Romare Bearden—the soon to be famous artist). This exposure later allowed him to begin a comic strip *Boop/Scoop* in 1933, as well as the highly popular *Dark Laughter* introducing the character Bootsie (which later took over the name of the work) that would propel him into the spotlight in 1935. In addition to this activity, Harrington taught at a WPA (Work Projects Administration) art program—a highly prestigious position at the time. Present during one of the most creative explosions up to that time in the midst of the Harlem Renaissance and with the complexity of everyday life in the most-populous, as well as important, Black community in the US at the time, all Harrington said that he did was allow the city to provide his material.

Despite all this, Harrington managed to attend New York University's School of Art with Romare Bearden for a few years and later graduated from the Yale University School of Fine Arts, finishing in 1940. Both were major achievements experienced by few African Americans at the time (and perhaps since). Degrees in hand, Harrington got his first full-time job as the art director at the *People's Voice*—a weekly put out by then political entre-peneur, religious leader and social advocate, Adam Clayton Powell Jr. This began a deeper immersion into politics.

In 1944, Harrington was sent to Italy as a correspondent with the all-Black 332nd Fighter Squadron in order to detail what they went through. In part, because of what he saw while abroad concerning positive as well as negative treatment of African Americans and the injustices taking place at home regarding race relations, in 1944 he also decided to join the NAACP and help them to create their public relations department. This position lasted for three years when he felt he wanted to get back to his primary passion—cartooning.

After having been away for several years, Harrington was rather quickly able to return consistently putting out his cartoons and strips, as well as a few other projects. Having acquired the political "bug" and unable to turn it off, it was around this time that he became involved in various overt political campaigns (e.g. committees in support of the American Labor Party and Communists in violation of the Smith Act). While biographers play down his political orientation and affiliations, it is clear that he simply knew a great number of individuals active in politics, broadly supported social justice and that during this period a great many of them were viewed as political threat-ening to the US political economy. In 1950, Harrington became more overtly affiliated with the left as he began to edit *Freedom*, a weekly put out by Louis Burnham and Paul Robeson (who was frequently pursued for his political beliefs), and he taught art at the Jefferson School of Social Sciences (which was identified by the FBI as a "subversive" institution).

Given his high profile through his popular drawings, connections throughout the Black artistic elite, and increasingly critical tone regarding the lack of political reform regarding African Americans, in the heated context of anti-communism, Harrington was prompted to leave the United States or face potential investigation for radical activities. Between being told that he should leave in 1949, it was another two years before he followed through.

Once abroad, Harrington threw himself into the life of the local culture of France—joining Richard Wright (who would become one of his best friends), as well as numerous others. This did not slow down his work too much. From abroad, Harrington continued to blow flames into the souls of Black folk, publishing cartoons and an occasional article. He had seen enough to have a lifetime of material by that point and did not physically need to be in the US.

After some scandal, the mysterious death of his friend (Wright) and a new opportunity to illustrate a book series in German, Harrington traveled to East Berlin in 1961. What happened next was pretty outstanding. As he tells it:

> I heard a very sinister sound in the streets. I looked out of my tiny hotel window and down below there was a stream of tanks going along. They were Soviet tanks. That gave me a bad feeling because I'd seen that before.
>
> I went down out of my room and walked in the direction the tanks were going for about a mile. On the edge of a place which has since become known as Checkpoint Charlie there was a line of US tanks. I knew I was right in the middle of World War III. I went back to my hotel, but found that I couldn't leave because I didn't have the proper visas. The bureaucracy, the Cold War bureaucracy had really set in at that point. I was a virtual prisoner. I couldn't leave there. I lost my French apartment. I lost everything. I had to stay there (Inge 1993b: xxxvii).

Now, if this was not strange enough, it turns out that the East Germans liked having Harrington there and he was essentially able to continue as a political cartoonist from behind the iron curtain. During this period, he had his work published in *Eulenspiegel* and *Das Magazine*, as well as garnered a bit of what is described as a "cult" following. Also, during this period, he married Helma Richter (his third and last wife) and in 1968 got invited to submit to the *Daily World*, where he would continue to publish for quite a number of years with work that increasingly became more and more critical of US domestic as well as foreign policy.

In 1972, Harrington returned to the US for his 60th birthday as well as for the publication by the *Daily World* of a collection of his work called *Soul Shots*. After the event, he returned back to East Berlin where he remained until he died in 1995. He did visit the US again in 1991 and returned more frequently up until his death.

The medium

Why did Ollie Harrington draw cartoons? It is not quite clear other than this was his method of expression and where his talent lay. Indeed, there is a good line in the film *Good Will Hunting* that describes the phenomena well: "When it came to stuff like that [math in the film for the Matt Damon character and drawing in Harrington's case], I could always just play." I have never read anything that discussed why he drew nor even how. I also found nothing on whether he preferred single images or comic strips; he did both but his most famous work involves single images.

Of course, there is somewhat of a long history of parody in African American culture but most of this is associated with more performative arts (e.g. the blues [Jones 1963/1999]). Most Blacks simply do not have the opportunity to use as well as develop the artistic skills that were required to illustrate—especially during the period that he was drawing and publishing. Regardless, we see that Harrington was able to do so and continuously.

It is also important to identify that especially in the time period relevant to Harrington, cartoons themselves were intricately connected with the Black press, which merits some discussion as it is partly connected with communication, as well as class.

By most accounts the Black press had an interesting history in the US— in particular between the 1930s and 1970s (Wolseley 1971). One of the important characteristics of this has been its speaking directly to the needs and interests of African Americans but at the same time navigating the context of a frequently violent society that could seemingly turn on Blacks at any moment. In many respects, this reality made political cartooning so important. Here, an artist could with minimal elements highlight a particular point of observation and let the internal dialog within a community take it from there. Indeed, as Harrington blew flames in the souls of Black folk, the African American community took them and set their imaginations ablaze— with laughter but most likely with some fury and tears as well.

The message

As for what Harrington illustrated and how to understand it, one needs to think of James Scott's (1985) idea of "everyday resistance" but also Albert Hirchman's (1970) work on engaging in "voice," as well as Charles Tilly's (2008) idea of "performance." Harrington's work addressed them all. At once, he is creating a symbolic representation of a shared but potentially unstated understanding of a world which is set within a communal setting that is read/experienced anew at each viewing—sometimes individually/alone and sometimes collectively. His objective seems to be entertainment to sooth, education to guide, and information to incite. While all three appear to be present in the work, I would say that the earlier pieces combined all three but the latter work became more concerned with the last.

Essentially, I would argue that Harrington (like all good political cartoonists) employed juxtaposition to generally communicate his point. Quite frequently the background is the chaotic but completely comprehensible circus that was Black life in America. In the midst of it all sits Harrington's character, who substitutes for the conscious observer and perhaps Harrington himself. This being is frequently dazed, a bit aware but not quite, overwhelmed to the point of numbness and seemingly calm. What are the elements of the context? Well, initially they concern the paradoxical nature of Blacks trying to enter a social, economic and political structure that maintains that it would like them to enter but at every turn sets up roadblocks, restrictions, as well as death squads to prevent it.

Regardless of the hardships involved, the aspirations are clearly middle-class in orientation—the dominant one present during the Harlem Renaissance where Harrington acquired something of his political awakening, as well as formative friendships and alliances that would carry him into the future. As Leroi Jones (1963/1999: 134) notes in *Blues People*:

The rising middle class-spawned intelligentsia invented the term *New Negro* and the idea of the Negro renaissance to convey to *the white world* that there had been a change of tactics as to how to climb onto the bandwagon of mainstream American life. The point here is that this *was* to be conveyed to white America; it was another conscious reaction to what white America and another adaptation of the middle-class Negro's self-conscious performance for his ever appreciative white audience.

This ideological orientation held sway even when other alternatives were present. As he continues:

The middle class reacted to the growing "nationalism" among poorer Negroes and the intelligentsia by adopting a milder kind of nationalism themselves. And even though most were startled at first by the kind of radicalism that the Niagara Movement, which led to the eventual establishment of the NAACP, and people like W. E. B. DuBois represented, they did begin to protest in earnest about "Jim Crow," and "the brotherhood of man." They eventually took over such organizations as the NAACP, aided by the dependence of such organizations on the philanthropies of white liberals, and molded them to their own purposes.

But from the beginning, when the black middle class began to *realign* itself toward an America from which they could ask "equality" instead of privilege, they had oriented themselves as would-be *citizens*, rather than freedmen, or ex-slaves [...] The middle class accepts the space, the openness and/or "liberalism" of twentieth-century America as the essential factor of its existence in this country as citizens. But when the recognized barriers to such "citizenship" are reached, when all their claims to equality with the rest of America, on the one hand, and superiority, on the other, to their own black brothers seem a useless and not wholly ideal-istic delusion because in the end they are still regarded by this society as "only Negroes," they are content with the name "second-class citizens" (Jones 1963: 135–6).

Such an orientation was important because:

The middle-class black man, whether he wanted to be a writer, or a painter, or a doctor, developed an emotional allegiance to the middle class (middle-brow) culture of America that obscured, or actually made hideous, any influence or psychological awareness that seemed to come from outside what was generally acceptable to a middle-class white man, especially if those influences were identifiable as coming from the most despised group in the country. The black middle class wanted no subculture, nothing that could connect them with the poor black man or the slave (Jones 1963: 132).

Thus, one finds in Harrington's work up until the very end a consistent effort to confront the idea of attaining citizenship (gaining voice), which is a function of the time, with the reality of its achievement (overcoming repression and hatred), which is also a function of the time. At every turn, however, there seemed to be something else that was not thought of and at every turn there were Whites who were seemingly in opposition to what was taking place.

Nowhere is this situation clearer than in the illustration where several individuals from the US military contemplate trying to get a little Black child (Little Luther) to school. The piece always strikes me for what quickly becomes acknowledged as Harrington's canvas. Front, slightly right of center and below the Whites you have Little Luther who is all but oblivious to all that is around him: tanks, different military units and a strategic meeting hidden in the hills near Lynchville.

Above Luther are three members of the US military strategizing on what is to be done next in order to make school integration a reality. Clearly the members of the military are intent on accomplishing their objective and by the end of the text, they have a plan.

What will they do once they get Little Luther to school? What will he learn once there? What could he learn? How will he be treated? What (if he gets through) will Luther do next? They do not discuss it and, in all likelihood, they do not know and that is part of Harrington's point. The effort was ill-conceived. Short-sighted. Other questions also arise from the cartoon. For example, it is clear that the scene takes place in Lynchville because it is mentioned but which Lynchville; the one in Tennessee, Virginia, South Carolina or Georgia? One does not know this either and frankly it is not important. They all presumably had problems and that is part of the cartoons strength—its simplicity and quick generalizability. The image works because it problematizes what is perhaps one of the most commonly thought of concerns of integration: getting little Black children into school with little White ones. What is often left unaddressed, however, is the issue of exactly how this was supposed to get done, as well as what impact this process would have on those being integrated.

With the one image, Harrington takes us into a world filled with the best of intentions, as well as one with the most horrific of obstacles—all for such a simple task: getting a Black child into school. That a complex, multidimensional military operation is necessary for such a basic accomplishment is both an indictment of the ludicrous nature of American racism, as well as the types of responses that were put in place to overcome it. One questions the existence and validity of both.

Bringing the details, complexities and contradictions of this historical period is Harrington's gift. For example, the illustration concerning the lecture of Prof Jenkins on "interstellar gravitational tensions in thermo-nuclear propulsion" brings many of these elements together. There you have a Black professor (complete with three-piece suit, glasses, balding and aged) prepared to give his talk at some university before a collection of his peers; indeed, he holds the papers in hand for said lecture. As he is a professor, it is assumed that this person had to go through everything professors do: examinations, classes, theses and so forth to the level of some institutions satisfaction. Additionally, he must be decent at his craft because he was invited to lecture to the university. Before he begins though, Prof Jenkins is asked to lead the all-White faculty sitting at the large conference table in a "good old spiritual" (one hears the word Negro in the text between "old" and "spiritual" in Block's accent but it does not actually appear). Again, Jenkins stands there as Little Luther—slightly dazed and to right of center, but in this image he is standing above the table, as well as above the globe. The ridiculousness of the situation again emerges along with the reality that another simple task cannot be accomplished without racism: giving a talk.

Of course, not all of Harrington's characters are without agency and having things done to them. In one *Bootsie/Dark Laughter* cartoon (Harrington,

"General Blotchit, you take your tanks and feint at Lynchville. General Pannick, you move into the county seat. And then in the confusion, my infantry will try to take little Luther to school!"

1958), the lead character is sitting in the White section of some bus adorned in a native American headdress. The White bus driver is speaking with another White person who seemingly just came on the bus and asked why the nigger was in his seat (the N-word and Block's voice are implied, of course— Harrington would not curse and he did not know my Block). One can faintly see in the back the sign ("Colored Passengers: Rear Seats Only"). Defusing the situation, the bus driver tells the White man that the interloper is not Black but Red and that he has no ability to tell without a blood test. The rest of the passengers have seemingly already bought the ruse, looking out the window and conversing with each other.

Of course, we know that Red is probably only slightly better than Black in terms of how individuals were treated but it does show that despite oppressive as well as repressive circumstances, there is some wiggle room for resistance; passing as Red or White, playing 'ol massa with some performance that avoids punishment and facilitates rebellion is/was crucial for daily survival at the time and all of that was necessary to trick Whites into giving what they would not otherwise give: humanity and rights. Again, the task addressed by Harrington was a simple one: riding the bus, but again racism shows the complexity of this. In this context, however, the character is not overwhelmed and dazed. Rather, they have played/gamed it; overly aware of the risks and giving the finger as they take a ride. Racism itself is not undermined in this single activity—how could it be? But, a Black man gets a ride, a little dignity and shows their intelligence. What more could one want from a 30-second viewing of a cartoon?

Similarly, Harrington shows more "everyday resistance" when he has an elevator operator, in an apparently all-White building, stop between floors and force the White passenger(s) to crawl out. Although working for Whites, the operator is literally free to elevate or de-elevate whites to whatever level he deemed appropriate—compelling the Whites to deal with what the Black operator had delivered and uncomfortably get out. Here, the Black operator seemed a bit dazed but in the angry White man's response, we know that he is in complete control of the elevator and, thus, the context. The juxtaposition is stark. The Black operator seems almost lifeless, without affect, while the White passenger seems furious, on the verge of a stroke. Despite the difference, as a Black viewer, one's sense of emotions is almost completely reversed. The African American knows exactly what the operator feels and the White emotion is irrelevant.

As Dunbar[4] noted of Blacks, "we wear the mask that grins and lies." We also wear the mask that feigns awareness and agency; fewer repercussions that way. This was the path to survival and resistance during the period of interest to Harrington. There was a narrow space for African American navigation at this point in time. One needed work but one needed humanity at the same time.

Somewhat later (into the 1960s), Harrington shifted his interests and became a bit less concerned with the particularities of Black–White integration and began to highlight the persistent underdevelopment of the Black community, as well as the strong sense of desperation felt there. This makes sense because with age and across diverse sections of African Americans, the myth of integration gave way to the reality of separate as well as unequal lives.

"... He says he's from some tribe called the Hockway-Gibblits. So whut kin Ah do ... Give 'im a blood test?"

For example, in one illustration Harrington identifies that Blacks have been running their whole lives. From panel to panel, he shows that they have run from rats in their own houses, the White thugs on their block, from racist policemen trying to gun them down, as well as the Klan. When this same individual ends up winning races (later in life), Harrington seems to suggest that we should not be surprised. Blacks are bred for this but not in some biologically constructed super-athlete kind of way but because of social,

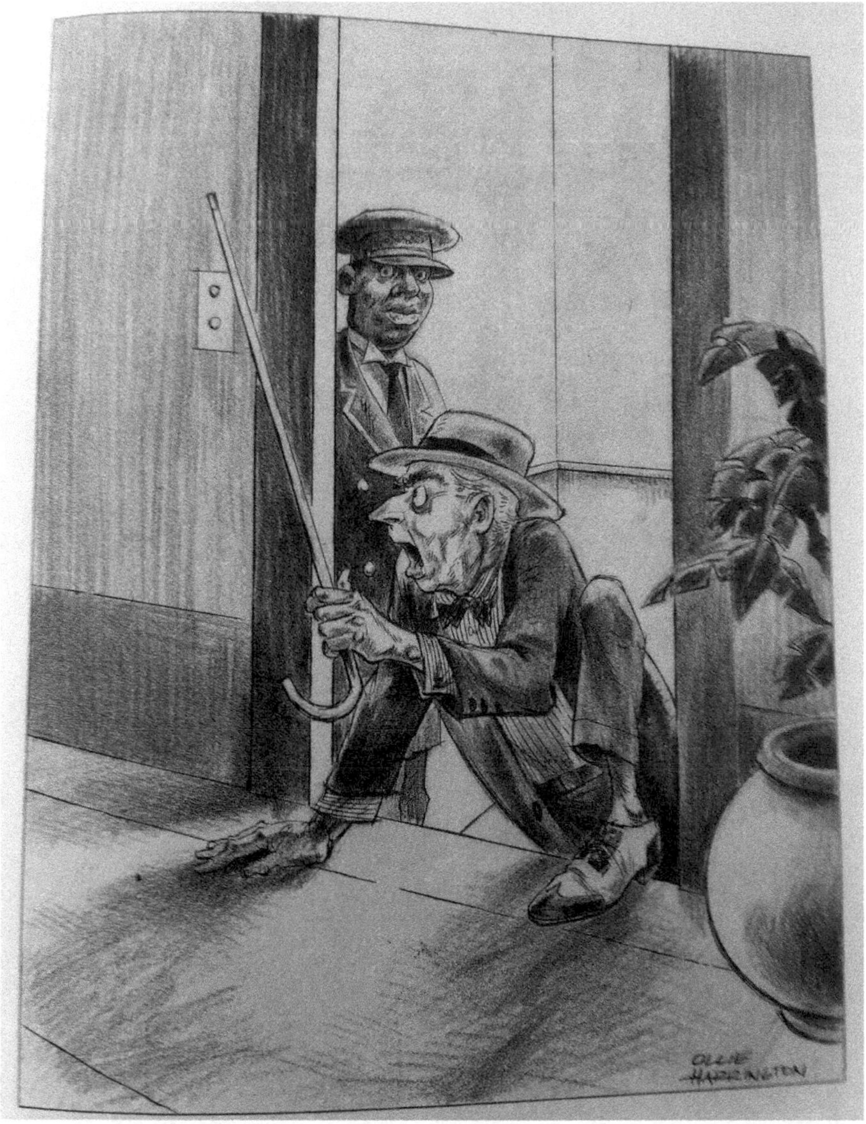
OLLIE HARRINGTON

"I don't care what the hell the NAACP thinks about it but I'm gettin' fed up. You've been doing this to me ever since that Patterson got knocked out!"

economic and political survival. Ghetto-strong (as opposed to Army-strong like in the advertisement). Interestingly, although the Black youth "wins" in the end, you come away without any sense of joy at the achievement. Gazing into the face of the character running across the finish line, you do not see happiness; you see relief that he has outrun those chasing him (yet again).

In one cartoon, Harrington transforms one's understanding of Blacks in sports and changes the way that all the people on the screen are viewed.

This is no life tale as one would find during the Olympics or during some final series where they discuss some aspects of the hard life that led to the Black star and the marvelous athletic contest that the viewer is about to behold. Indeed, now even more meaningful, individuals are expected to enjoy the event more. Rather, this is an anti-life tale where the character has defied the various processes created to exterminate them through sheer will alone, rending the athletic contest irrelevant.

Practice makes perfect!

After years of reflection and new information, Harrington also seemed to become more disenchanted. Indeed, in one image, he no longer envisioned Blacks being lynched individually. Rather, he envisioned a whole bus being strung up by a White mob. The symbolism here is powerful. Through the cartoon, we go back in time to the lynching and show that it is only the target that has changed. Then, Black men; now, young Black children are the ones terrorized, threatened, tortured and sacrificed. The Black youth are not clearly identifiable in the bus. The Whites are spared nothing however. They are shown in all their disglory—angry, shouting, distorted, bestial and from varied walks of life.

As such, the image reverses the sentiments of racist America. Hanging upside down, like the bus, all is reversed. Here, the situation is complex as the earlier work but there is no calm. There is only violence. Perhaps the only calm is seen in the suspended Black child who is about to hit the ground. For them, they are afforded a moment of peace: one after the agonization of being shaken out of the bus (shown in the ghostly and tortured hands of those still remaining) and one before the agonization of being killed by the horde of hatred lying below. In that moment, suspended forever as the image does not move from this point, one gets to reflect on the sequence. Brilliant. Agonizing. Provoking.

Similar, from this later period, there is an image of the CIA cutting loose some genie of anti-Soviet terror that rises ominously from the bottle just rubbed (like Aladdin). This is representative of an important transformation in Harrington's work because these works move past the racist violence of the United States to see these activities in a more global context. It is as if to say that Whites and the US are not just violent against Blacks here but they are violent globally through their support of White South Africans, as well as against those around the globe who challenge them in Europe and Asia (e.g. Vietnam).

With this, Harrington's middle-class aspirations seem to have completely disappeared. Survival is key to the work in this later manifestation, as well as a deeper analysis of violence, colonialism and empire itself. Harrington does not use the words of violence, colonialism and empire; that is not his medium. He does use the images though and of course he does say a great deal with his venues for publishing; toward the later part of his life, he publishes with the *Daily Worker* put out by the Communist Party USA. Like those before him, Harrington's observations of racist hell and a critical mind turned him to the Left but also like Ellison's invisible man, it also turned him both internal (inside himself), as well as external (outside of the United States to somewhere else—anywhere else).

103

The ending

When first approached about this volume on Black comics, I was interested in doing a comparative piece on Ollie Harrington and some more contemporary artist. I am glad that I did not do this for the exclusive attention on Harrington provided me with greater insight into him, his work as well as the context within which he worked. It is simply a completely different animal to be

writing about social, political and economic life in 2011, rather than in 1935. There are clearly still injustices to be discovered, discussed and overcome, but the sheer confluence of factors present when Harrington was producing his cartoons is truly astounding. One can only think that for one who blew so many flames into the souls of Black folk with wit, grace and artistry, that the least we could do is provide some praise and remembrance when given an opportunity.

I hope that this brief essay has prompted your curiousity and that the next time you take a look at *The Boondocks*, you will reflect on the legacy that got us to where we are. Indeed, as one flips through comics, graphic novels, hip-hop and R&B songs featuring rap, as well as even t-shirts that display an awareness of discrimination, it is useful to think that we now take much of this for granted. Our ability to access such information has shifted immensely over time. In short, flames have been blown and we have seen many of them—at least in some form (though they might actually be diminishing in number). The task now lies in us taking it all in, seeing how far we have or have not gone and reflecting on where all of this has taken us. In short, we now need to be warmed as well as moved by the flames blown.

References

Bunche, R. J. (1973), *The Political Status of the Negro in the Age of FDR*. Chicago, IL: University of Chicago Press.

Du Bois, W. E. B. (1992), *Black Reconstruction in America, 1860–1880*. New York: Atheneum.

Gates, H. L. and Higginbotham, E. (2009), *Harlem Renaissance Lives: From the African American National Biography*. New York: Oxford University Press.

Harrington, O. (1958), *Bootsie and Others: A Selection of Cartoons*. New York: Dodd, Mead.

Hirschman, A. (1970), *Exit, Voice, and Loyalty; Responses to Decline in Firms, Organizations, and States*. Cambridge, MA: Harvard University Press.

Inge, M. T. (ed.) (1993a), *Dark Laughter: The Satiric Art of Oliver W. Harrington*. Jackson, MS: University Press of Mississippi.

—(1993b), *Why I left America and Other Essays*. Jackson, MS: University Press of Mississippi.

Jones, L. (1999), *Blues People: Negro Music in White America*. New York: Harper Perennial. (Original work published in 1963.)

Kelley, R. D. G. (1994), *Race Rebels: Culture, Politics, and the Black Working Class*. New York: Free Press.

Murray, P. (1997), *States' Laws on Race and Color*. Athens, GA: University of Georgia Press.

Scott, J. (1985), *Weapons of the Weak: Everyday Forms of Peasant Resistance*. New Haven, CT: Yale University Press.

Tilly, C. (2008), *Contentious Performances*. New York: Cambridge University Press.

Wolseley, R. E. (1971), *The Black Press, U.S.A.* Ames, IA: Iowa State University Press.

Notes

1 This phrase is taken from something that Harrington wrote in 1971 called "Our Beloved Pauli" concerning Paul Robeson.

2 See Du Bois (1992) for discussion of an earlier attempt.

3 What appears below is extracted from *Why I Left America and Other Essays* (Inge 1993b), *Dark Laughter: The Satiric Art of Ollie W. Harrington* (Inge 1993a) and *Harlem Renaissance Lives: From the African American National Biography* (Gates and Higginbotham 2009: 376).

4 "Paul Laurence Dunbar was the first African American to gain prominence as a poet (1872–1906)."

8

Panthers and vixens: Black superheroines, sexuality, and stereotypes in contemporary comic books

Jeffrey A. Brown

Comic book superheroes have been an important part of American popular culture ever since Superman first appeared in 1938. Though the medium of comic books and the genre of superheroes are typically derided as inconsequential and formulaic children's entertainment, the enduring presence of costumed superbeings makes them a useful subject for tracking cultural changes. In fact, it is precisely because superheroes are considered innocuous fantasies that they warrant serious consideration. Everyone knows who Superman, Batman, Spider-Man and Wonder Woman are. Even if we have never read a comic book or seen their movies or watched their television series, we know their basic stories. We also know what they look like, and about their never-ending crusades for justice, and are at least familiar with their unique powers. As omnipresent characters in Western culture, we cannot help but be shaped in part by the ideologies that superheroes embody. Superheroes reveal some of our most basic beliefs about morality and justice, our conceptions of gender and sexuality, and our attitudes towards ethnicity and nationality. The primary focus of this chapter is the depiction of Black superheroines in contemporary comic books and how they are portrayed according to specific racial and sexual stereotypes. Looking specifically at recent stories focused on the Black superheroines Black Panther and Vixen, it becomes apparent that while many of the superficial ingredients may reinforce racial and sexual stereotypes, they can also present tales that move beyond derogatory stereotypes to provide positive and heroic examples of Black women in popular culture.

Background: Gender and ethnicity in comic books

Despite many cultural advances over the last 50 years, Black women in the media, especially within the superhero genre, are still constructed as exotic sexual spectacles, as erotic racial "Others." In contrast to the dominant model of male heroes, and in distinction to non-ethnically identified female characters in the comics, Black superheroines are often presented as hyper-sexual and metaphorically bestial. Moreover, popular Black superheroines like Storm, Vixen, Pantha, and the Black Panther are explicitly associated with exoticized notions of Africa, nature, noble savagery and a variety of Dark Continent themes, including voodoo, mysticism, and animal totemism. While heroic images of Black women challenge the dominant model of superheroes and represent some very real and very positive changes, the continued use of stereotypes reinforces some of our most rudimentary racial conceptions. In the case of Black Panther and Vixen there is a small step forward to representing Black superheroines who are more than just a cluster of racial stereotypes.

The colorful stories of comic book superheroes have always been concerned first and foremost with parables of justice, of basic cultural values about heroism, and of good triumphing over evil. But, as volumes of research over the past two decades has shown, issues of gender and sexuality are also central implicit themes played out in superhero tales. Week after week, new issues hit the stands with depictions of perfectly muscled men, what Anthony Easthope (1988) refers to as "super-masculine ideals," (p. 29) ready to defend America against any array of criminals, terrorists or alien invaders. In addition to teaching lessons about right and wrong, superhero comic books have always provided a clear and rudimentary example of gender ideals. In comic books women have historically been damsels in distress, or at best plucky reporters. But men in superhero stories have always been paragons of masculinity. Male superheroes are depicted as incredibly powerful, smart, confident, and always in control. Moreover, the illustrations emphasize the muscles and the stature of the heroes as perfect male specimens. The Clark Kent and Peter Parker side of the characters may exist, but these wimpy secret identities only stress the exceptional nature of Superman and Spider-Man. Alan Klein argues that: "Comic book depictions of masculinity are so obviously exaggerated that they represent fiction twice over, as genre and as gender representation" (Klein 1993: 267). The conventional superhero is an adolescent fantasy of hegemonic masculinity, either literally or figuratively armored against possible threats. Scott Bukataman points out that in contemporary comics the superhero's body is "hyperbolized into pure, hypermasculine spectacle" (Bukataman 1994: 106). The masculine ideal embodied by heroes such as Superman, Batman, Iron-Man and Captain America play out a reassuring fantasy about the eminence of patriarchal authority for the genre's mostly young and mostly male readership.

The dominant male superheroes embody masculine ideals and serve as a point of identification for readers. Female superheroines, on the other hand, are primarily depicted as scantily clad and erotically posed fetish objects. Despite some major advancement for female characters, and an increasing presence of female writers and illustrators, women in the comics continue to be portrayed primarily as sexual spectacles. In comparing the superheroines from his childhood to more recent ones, Pulitzer Prize winning author Michael Chabon notes that:

[B]oobs were a big part—literally—of the female superhero package. Almost every superwoman apart from explicitly adolescent characters such as the original Supergirl or the X-Men's Kitty Pryde came equipped, as if by the nature of the job, with a superheroic rack. Furthermore, the usual way of a female-superhero costume was to advertise the breasts of its wearer by means of décolletage, a cleavage cutout, a pair of metal Valkyrie cones, a bustier. [...] Today's female costumed characters tend to sport breasts so enormous that their ability simply to get up and walk, let alone kick telekinetic ass, would appear to be their most marvelous and improbable talent (Chabon 2008: 198, 201).

Similarly, in his analysis of comic book mutants and bodily trauma Scott Bukataman argues that:

The spectacle of the female body in these titles is so insistent, and the fetishism of breasts, thighs, and hair is so complete, that the comics seem to dare you to say something about them that isn't just redundant. *Of course*, the female form has absurdly exaggerated sexual characteristics; *of course*, the costumes are skimpier than one could (or should) imagine; *of course*, there's no visible way that these costumes could stay in place; *of course*, these women represent simple adolescent masturbatory fantasies (with a healthy taste of the dominatrix) (Bukataman 1994: 112).

The unequal presentation of gender is certainly not unique to comics. In most forms of popular culture men are depicted as strong and authoritative figures while women are, to borrow Laura Mulvey's (1975) famous phrase, valued for their "to-be-looked-at-ness." That this gender dichotomy is taken to an extreme in comics, where men are crafted as hypermasculine heroic ideals and women as scantily clad and extremely curvaceous sexual objects, may not be surprising given the genre's target audience of young males, but it does perpetuate sexist beliefs and is indicative of the medium's reliance on stereotypes.

Just as superhero comics have always relied on gender stereotypes of the most extreme sort, ethnicity in the comics has predominantly been portrayed according to racial stereotypes. In his discussion of shifting forms of Black identities within superhero stories, Marc Singer notes that: "Comic books, and particularly the dominant genre of superhero comic books, have proven fertile ground for stereotyped depictions of race" (Singer 2002: 123). It is this reliance on stereotypes that makes truly progressive depictions of Black superhero characters difficult within mainstream comics from industry giants like Marvel and DC Comics. Male Black superheroes have come a long way since blaxploitation influenced characters like Luke Cage, Black Panther, Black Lightning and Black Goliath first appeared in the 1960s and 1970s (for a more detailed discussion of Black male superheroes see Brown, 2001; Singer 2002; McWilliams 2009; or Cunningham 2010) In the 1960s and 1970s blaxploitation inspired superheroes were mostly stereotypical "Black male bruts" who focused on street crime in inner-city ghettos. Contemporary Black super-heroes have become far more powerful, diverse and respected. For example, where originally Luke Cage was an ex-convict who fought pimps and drug dealers in Harlem while uttering his trademark expletive "Sweet Christmas!," the current version of Cage is a husband and father, a trusted and revered superhero who fights urban blight in inner cities as well as world-class super-villains and alien invasions, and most significantly he is the newest leader of Marvel's legendary superteam, The Avengers. While Luke Cage may be the most remarkable example of a Black superhero who has risen to prominence within the genre, he is joined by a growing number of other characters that represent a challenge to the traditionally White dominated heroic landscape. Whether part of a team or headlining their own series, there are a substantial number of Black superheroes that currently populate the Marvel and DC universes, including such fan favorites as Cyborg, Steel, Blade, Icon, Static, Bishop, Mister Terrific, War Machine, and Deathlok.

While significant advancements have been made with Black male super-heroes, in both their sheer numbers and the manner in which they are portrayed, the development of Black female superheroines has been slower. There are several notable examples of popular Black superheroines in mainstream comics, including Marvel's new female version of The Black Panther and DC's Vixen, both of whom will be discussed in detail below, but they are often depicted in a manner that is more problematic than portrayals associated with either White superheroines or Black superheroes. Elsewhere (Brown 2011) I contended that ethnically diverse superheroines continue to traffic in orientalist conceptions of exotic fetishism because their portrayal is dictated by the twin burdens of racial and sexual stereotyping. In that earlier piece I was concerned with ethnic superheroines as a general type. I argued "the power of exoticism is still a dominant trope played out on the body of the female Other, especially in visual mediums, in a manner that reduces her to a racially charged sex object and a readily consumable body" (Brown 2011: 170). Here, I want to address how the figure of the Black superheroine reinforces and challenges specific racial markers. Nearly all comic book superheroines who are identified as ethnic minorities are treated as erotic spectacles, as hypersexual "Others." For example, Latina superheroines like Arana (aka Spider Girl), White Tiger, Fire, Feral and Tarantula are routinely depicted as seductive and hot-tempered beauties, often referred to in the comics as "hot tamales." Likewise, Asian superheroines such as Lady Shiva, Katana, Hazmat, Psylocke and Colleen Wing are portrayed as mysterious and alluring Dragon Ladies. By virtue of their ethnicity and their femininity Black superheroines are presented as exotic beauties in a manner similar to other female characters from different minority backgrounds. It is worth noting that, in addition to Black characters, minority representation is restricted in mainstream comics almost exclusively to Asian and Latina (extraterrestrial superheroines may have different skin colors but they are physically depicted as Aryan). In addition to hypersexuality, Black superheroines are also specifically aligned with Afrocentric stereotypes related to nature, mysticism and totemism.

Volumes of research have explored the ways that Black women have been constructed and reproduced in the popular imagination as supremely racialized and sexualized figures (for example see McClintock 1995; Hooks, 1992; Collins 2005; and Negra 2001). Based historically in a colonial logic that sought to contain and marginalize non-Whites, and thus to valorize Whiteness as a cultural category which was personified in the figure of chaste White womanhood, Black women in particular became the locus for a specific set of intertwined racist assumptions. In her treatise on the colonial imagination, Anne McClintock notes the centuries old tradition in Europe of conceptualizing Africans with unbridled sexuality: "popular lore had firmly established Africa as the quintessential zone of sexual aberration and anomaly" (McClintock 1995: 22). Patricia Hill Collins echoes the same sentiments when she argues: "Through colonial eyes, the stigma of biological Blackness and the seeming primitiveness of African cultures marked the borders of extreme abnormality" (Collins 2005: 120). And most importantly, as McClintock clarifies, African "women figured as the epitome of sexual aberration and excess. Folklore saw them, even more than the men, as given to a lascivious venery so promiscuous as to border on the bestial" (Collins 2005: 22). Likewise, in his discussion of nineteenth century depictions of Black women, Sander Gilman noted that they were characterized as "more primitive, and therefore more sexually intensive," than White women and that their bodies and sexuality were described as "animal-like" (Gilman 1992: 177). This colonialist and imperialist worldview allowed White Europeans to accept a system of race-based hierarchy as natural. It also facilitated demeaning and dehumanizing practices whereby Black bodies were seen as available commodities to be bought and sold in systems of slavery and where, especially Black female bodies, could be presented for sexual entertainment or displayed as sexual curiosities.

Contemporary representations of Black women are still haunted by the colonialist conception of African females as "animal-like" hypersexual creatures. Bell Hooks notes that: "Representations of black female bodies in contemporary popular culture rarely subvert or critique images of black female sexuality which were part of the cultural apparatus of nineteenth-century racism and which still shapes perceptions today" (Hooks 1992: 114). These stereotypes still function, at least in part, as a means to sanctify White female sexuality by contrast. In their discussion of women in modern music videos, Railton and Watson argue that depictions of sexuality are intimately grounded in these long-standing conceptions about race and gender:

> These imperial discourses are only one branch of a long tradition of cultural representation which produces white and black womanhood as very different. Much of this difference turns upon a series of binary oppositions, oppositions which both disguise the complexities of lived experience and structure thinking in ways which tend to mask and shore up hierarchies of power. Simply stated, within this tradition of representation, white women are defined by asexuality in direct contrast to the presumed hypersexuality of black women. On the one hand, black women's "hypersexuality" is seen to derive from a series of apparently natural traits that link them to the animal, the primitive and the "dirty." In defining the black woman first and foremost through a series of physical characteristics, her body is not only made available to both white and black men but the buttocks of that body are figured as emblematic of black womanhood generally and the icon of black female sexuality more precisely (Railton and Watson 2005: 56).

The colonial tradition which Railton and Watson, Collins, Hooks, McClintock and countless others have documented clearly still informs media represen-tations of Black women as hypersexual, "bootylicious" and wild. Recent popular performers continue to present the commodifiable image of the wild Black woman, from Grammy-winning singer Beyoncé, and Nicki Minaj, to award-winning actresses like Halle Berry, to tennis champions Venus and Serena Williams, to reality television stars like New York. Likewise, the variations of this stereotype have been explored in dozens of recent academic studies, including such specific examples as music videos (Railton and Watson 2005), but also sports (McKay and Johnson 2008), and even video pornography (Miller-Young 2010).

The modern black superheroine

The depiction of Black women as superheroines in comic books shares many of the same traits associated with Black female representations in other media forms. But the very nature of superheroines facilitates a different type of representation than typically occurs when Black women appear as singers, actresses, models, porn stars, and even as celebrity athletes. Despite the sexual spectacle that is an inherent aspect of contemporary superheroines, they are also undeniably strong and heroic characters. While the compounded hypersexuality of being both costumed superheroines *and* Black women means that Black superheroines run the risk of simply reinforcing racial and gendered stereotypes, they also have the potential to embody progressive and empowering concepts about Black female strength and heroics. After all, the entire narrative purpose of any superhero is to right wrongs, to defend the weak, and to be a champion for justice. Black female characters in popular culture rarely have the potential to be as explicitly and unabashedly heroic as they do in superhero comic books.

Unfortunately, there are still relatively few Black superheroines in mainstream comics. Characters like Marvel's Storm, Misty Knight and Monica Rambeau (aka Captain Marvel), and DC's Thunder, Onyx and Bumble Bee may have a devoted following among serious comic book fans, but none of them are considered popular enough to headline their own monthly series. Most of these characters stay in circulation as minor to middling heroines on various superteams like The Teen Titans, The Outsiders, or Heroes for Hire. Even Storm, who is arguably the most widely recognized Black superheroine of all time thanks to the overwhelming popularity of the X-Men comics, cartoons and movies, remains a character in superteam books with only an occasional one-shot or miniseries of her own. Thus, it was surprising that in 2009 both Marvel and DC chose to feature Black superheroines as title characters. Marvel rebooted the *Black Panther* series with a female character taking over the role that had previously been held only by men. The first six issues of the series where the African princess Shuri assumes the heroic identity from her fallen brother proved very popular and was reprinted in the trade paperback collection *Black Panther: The Deadliest of the Species* (Hudlin and Lashley, 2009). At DC the character of Vixen, who has bounced around the DC universe on various superteams since the early 1980s, was given the opportunity to headline her own miniseries after positive fan reactions to her increased presence as a member of the newly revised Justice League of America. The title won the 2009 Glyph Fan Award (from the East Coast Black Age of Comics Con) for best comic and is available in the trade paperback collection *Vixen: Return of the Lion* (Wilson and Cafu 2009). These two books coincidentally have a lot more in common than just featuring Black superheroines. Both characters are African citizens and the stories take place in fictional African settings. Moreover, both of the adventures are about characters coming into their own as superpowered beings and accepting the truth about themselves and their responsibilities. Both Black Panther's and Vixen's stories involve mysticism and nature as a central plot point, and both have powers closely associated with animals. Though these parallel tales mobilize a range of traditional stereotypes, they each manage to present Black superheroines who are ultimately far more than just wild, bestial, hypersexual spectacles.

Black Panther's and Vixen's stories

The original Black Panther debuted within the pages of Marvel's *Fantastic Four* #52 in 1966 and was the first Black superhero to appear in mainstream American comic books. The Black Panther was part of the comic book industry's initial wave of blaxploitation heroes but was popular enough to remain in circulation well after many of his imitators had perished. His biography, powers and base of operations has been revised many times over the years, but at his core he is T'Challa, the wise ruler of the fictional and technologically advanced African nation Wakanda. The Black Panther has a mystical connection with the Wakandan Panther God that grants him superhuman senses and abilities, including increased strength, speed, agility and stamina. By the mid 2000s the T'Challa version of the Black Panther was firmly established as a top-tier hero and his marriage to Ororo Monroe (aka Storm) was treated as a company-wide event.

The events of *Black Panther: Deadliest of the Species* take place shortly after T'Challa's wedding. During a surprise attack by the villainous Doctor Doom, T'Challa is left comatose and Wakanda is rendered vulnerable to an impending assault by the mystical Morlun—Devourer of Totems. Ororo assumes the role of Wakanda's ruler, and travels to the underworld with the help of an ancient witch doctor in order to bring her husband's soul back to his body. And because Wakanda must have a military leader to survive, T'Challa's sister Shuri undertakes a spiritual test to become the new Black Panther. After some physical trials that pose no real challenge to Shuri, she ingests a magical herb that allows her to commune directly with the Panther God. When Shuri declares herself worthy to be the next Black Panther and demands the magical gifts that go with the position, the Panther God scolds her hubris and rejects her pleas. Shuri is disheartened by her failure but refuses to give up on her people in their hour of need as Morlun destroys Wakanda's army and ravages the city. Despite having no superpowers, Shuri dons the mantle of the Black Panther and sets forth on an apparent suicide mission to battle Morlun. But in the midst of the struggle Shuri's bravery is rewarded and she becomes the one true Black Panther, and destroys Morlun. "The panther god is subtle and wise," explains the witch doctor Zawavari in the final pages, "You threw yourself into the fight … not for glory, but for your people. And in doing so, you *became* the Black Panther." *The Deadliest of the Species* is a typical superheroic story about bravery and self-sacrifice that both utilizes and challenges centuries old stereotypes about Africa and Black women.

In the DC Comics universe, Vixen was one of the first Black superheroines to turn up when she made her initial appearance in the pages of *Action Comics* #521 in 1981. Vixen is really Mari Jiwe McCabe and was raised in a small village in the fictional African nation of Zambesi. After Mari's parents are killed, she moves to America and becomes a successful fashion model, but eventually returns to Africa to take back the magical Tantu Totem that her uncle had murdered her father for. The Tantu Totem is a mystical icon that allows Mari to tap into the Earth's "morphogenetic field" and assume the characteristics of any animal she desires—fly like a hawk, run with the speed of a cheetah, fight with the strength of a bear, etc. For two decades Vixen bounced around the DC universe on various superteams such as Suicide Squad, Birds of Prey, and Checkmate, finally ending up as a core member of the Justice League of America. During his mid-2000s run as the writer of the revamped JLA series, Dwayne McDuffie (one of the cofounders of Milestone Media Inc. and a leader in the development of ethnically diverse superheroes) raised Vixen's profile within the team and paved the way for her own spin-off miniseries *Vixen: Return of the Lion*.

Written by G. Willow Wilson and illustrated by Cafu, *Vixen: Return of the Lion* features a heroine who is initially insecure about her place among such superpowered luminaries as Superman, Batman, and Black Canary. The solo adventure begins when Vixen decides to return on her own to Zambesi when new information about her mother's murder comes to light. She returns to her childhood village to visit friends but finds them living in fear. Vixen is soon wounded and left to die on the African plains after an initial fight with the seemingly superpowered villain, Aku Kwesi, who both murdered her mother and continues to terrorize the village. In her weakened state, Vixen's connection to her magical animal powers begins to fade and she seems near death until a friendly lion finds her and delivers her to the care of Brother Tabo, a monk who helps her to recover both her health and her connection to animal powers. Tabo teaches Vixen that she can have unlimited access to the spirit of the animals, even without the Tantu Totem, if she just frees her mind and soul to accept their mystical gifts. While Vixen was recovering with Brother Tabo, other members of the Justice League discovered that Kwesi was more than just a local warlord and he was helping the organization of super villains known as "Intergang" to gain a foothold on the African continent. Several of the League's top guns travel to Africa but are ambushed by Intergang who manage to poison Superman and Black Canary turning them into mindless zombies who attack their own teammates. Vixen arrives with a newfound confidence and sense of purpose and first fights with and then cures Superman moments before he could kill all of the heroes. Vixen then returns to the village and defeats Kwesi on her own before returning to America a renewed superheroine.

Recurring themes

That both *Black Panther: Deadliest of the Species* and *Vixen: Return of the Lion* are set in Africa is atypical for the superhero genre. Stories are usually set in either real or fictional American cities, thus allowing the heroes to explicitly defend "the American way." When Africa, or any other foreign locale, is utilized the setting characteristically implies an atmosphere of unfamiliar danger. That both Black Panther and Vixen are African lends the setting more authenticity. Africa is not presented in either story as a mysterious or unknowable place for the heroines. They are familiar with the customs, the people, and the landscape. The overall effect, though, does conform to what Edward Said (1979) famously described as Western "Orientalist" notions of Africa as a treacherous Dark Continent. In the colonialist fantasy that Said outlines, the West perceives the East, and in fact all who can be categorized as "Others," as mysterious and exotic mythical places filled with primitive natives, bizarre customs, and dangerous environments. This collective fiction of the "Orient" has long provided a justification for the Western world's domination and subjugation of non-Western nations and people. As conventional adventure stories danger does lurk around every corner in both *Deadliest of the Species* and *Return of the Lion*, and much of it is presented as specifically wild African dangers. For example, the Black Panther has to fight off real panthers and battle African sorcery, and Vixen is attacked by lions and warlords who target her village.

In addition to the omnipresence of dangerous wild panthers and lions, it is the presence of voodoo throughout both of the stories that most stereo-typically aligns Africa and these Black superheroines with ideas of Africa as a mysterious and primitive land. Shuri is granted her Black Panther super-powers by the mystical Panther God and eventually defeats the black magic of Morlun with the aid of an ancient witch doctor. Vixen has to reconnect with the magic powers of her amulet totem and is renewed by the faith and teachings of an African monk. In both stories the people of Africa are depicted as superstitious, resorting to mystical herbs and witch doctors to help save Wakanda, and repeatedly accusing Vixen of being a "voduun" witch for her powers. To their credit, the Black Panther stories also depict Wakanda as a technologically advanced society as well, complete with supercomputers, hi-tech medical equipment and flying motorbikes. But this is a genre where people can fly, shoot laser beams out of their eyes and ice from their fingers, voodoo is an accepted reality in superhero comics. The presence of voodoo is never questioned or treated as out of the ordinary in these stories. More specifically voodoo is not treated as a uniquely African motif. Taken as singular examples these stories might compound stereotypes of Africa as a dark, mysterious and mystical place, but for regular superhero readers it is only part and parcel of the larger genre.

Both Black Panther and Vixen have costumed identities and powers associated with animals. This animalistic association is a clear remnant of colonial stereotypes that characterized African women as the embodiment of an abnormal, voracious and almost beastial sexuality. The trade paperback covers for both *Black Panther: Deadliest of the Species* and *Vixen: Return of the Lion* depict strikingly similar images that clearly suggest a range of stereo-types about Black women as exotic sexual fantasies. The cover illustration for *Deadliest of the Species* shows Shuri in the skin-tight black leather Panther costume that covers her entire body, head and face. With just a thin belt slung low around her hips and a long necklace hanging across her breasts, the costume seems to be, in typical comic book fashion, simply painted on to her body. Every curve is emphasized as this female Black Panther leans back against a jungle tree with one arm entwined with a branch and her head tilted in an inviting pose (it is difficult to imagine Marvel portraying T'Challa's male version of the character in a similar cheesecake pose). Under her other arm is a large, muscular, and snarling black panther. Similarly, the cover for *Return of the Lion* features Vixen splayed out in the tall grass of the African plains in her signature skin-tight, mustard colored body costume complete with clawed gloves and a plunging neckline that shows off much of her chest. Vixen is lying back with one leg flirtatiously pulled up across the other, her head is tilted and her expression is, like Black Panther's, a look that is both confidently challenging and seductive. Accompanying Vixen is a majestic male lion that she is leaning against, with one arm stretched out behind his mane and the other stretched across his torso.

These purely symbolic images (neither depicts a scene that occurs in the stories) are typical of the way that superheroines are portrayed as sexual objects on comic book covers. Where male characters usually strike heroic action poses, superheroines are far more likely to be illustrated as pin-ups or centerfolds. Given the ethnicity of these two specific superheroines and the nature of these adventures, the covers of both *Deadliest of the Species* and *Return of the Lion* symbolically also allude to a level of racial fetishization. The jungle and the plains settings suggest an aura of savage primitivism associated with Africa as The Dark Continent. The costumes, like those of all superheroines, clearly marks the characters as promising the possibility of erotic and/or fetishistic adventures. Or what Bukataman referred to in the earlier quotation as "simple adolescent masturbatory fantasies (with a healthy taste of the dominatrix)" (Bukataman, 1994, p. 112). And the presence of the panther and the lion symbolizes the heroines' powers, but also their affinity with nature and these deadly beasts. That each heroine is posed seductively with an arm around these ferocious African cats further implies that the women's sexuality may be alluring but it is animalistic and threatening as well.

That both Black Panther and Vixen are explicitly associated with big cats is especially noteworthy. Of course Black Panther's powers are based in those of a real panther and are magically bestowed by a Panther God, so her animal association makes sense narratively. But Vixen, whose magical totemic powers grant her access to the abilities of all animals, is repeatedly aligned with lions specifically... as the title, *Return of the Lion*, makes clear. At various points in her story Vixen is ambushed by a lion, saved by one, and has to fight one that has gone mad and attacked a village. When Vixen slays this rogue beast she repeats the mantra: "I *am* the lion. I *am* the lion." The strong association of these heroines with wild African cats is easy to interpret as both racial and sexual in nature. This symbolic alignment of superheroic identities with animals is a common convention in comic books, and is not restricted to women or ethnically identified characters. The genre is ripe with this type of hero: Batman, Spider-Man, Hawkman, Animal-Man, The Blue Beetle, The Falcon, etc. But the overloaded sexual symbolism of cats and their specifically feminine connotations is hard to ignore. Male super-characters associated with cats do exist, such as the original Black Panther or the villain Cat-Man, but they are far fewer and far less sexually charged than female costumed cat characters. The best known may be Catwoman (often described as "the original feline fatale"), but she is joined by the likes of Black Cat, Pantha, Tigra, Cheetah, Hellcat, Shadowcat, Alley Cat, and Feral.

The sexual inference of these various "catwomen" is clearer in some cases than others. Both Tigra and Cheetah, for example, are literally drawn as sexy cats, and some times are even called "pussies" by other characters. They each have ideal female bodies but are covered in actual fur, stripes and all, and have tails. To stress the exoticism of their sexy feline/female bodies, both Tigra and Cheetah wear only the skimpiest of bikinis as their costume. As one adolescent superhero in training says of Tigra in *Avengers Academy* #8: "She walks around practically naked." It is worth noting that both Tigra and Cheetah are Latina characters so their sexual depiction also serves to reinforce their ethnic stereotyping. Other feline costumed characters, like the White women Catwoman and Black Cat, are only symbolically associated with cats through their roles as cat burglars and their cat-themed costumes. Yet Catwoman and Black Cat are both portrayed as eminently erotic, as sex kittens, flirtatiously and shamelessly flaunting their figures in revealing outfits. All of these fictional catwomen in comics are a modern embodiment of the centuries-old conception of cats as feminine, sexual and untrustworthy (see for example Darnton 1984). Black Panther and Vixen also fit into this cat-like sexual iconography, but no more so than any of the other characters. In other words, their identity as Black women who are depicted as cat-like does have racist stereotype implications, but it is also a formulaic convention of the larger superhero genre. Yes, these feline heroines are eroticized, but their sexualization seems to have less to do with their ethnicity than it does with the genre. Black Panther and Vixen may be animal-like but their totemic association is not explicitly linked to their sexuality (as it is with Tigra, Catwoman and Black Cat), it is tethered to their physical strength. At least in *Deadliest of the Species* and *Return of the Lion*, the heroines' animal nature is not explicitly about sex.

To say that the wild animal nature of both Black Panther and Vixen's superheroine identity is not explicitly linked to their sexuality in these stories is not to say that they are exempt from sexualized depictions. They are both illustrated as extremely attractive and fit women in skin-tight costumes. And, as the cover illustrations make clear, they are both positioned and sold as erotic spectacles. Yet, neither story contains romantic subplots or erotic scenes, no one comments on their attractiveness or even makes a sexist remark. And despite the pin-up quality of the covers, the interior artwork does not overtly stress their idealized bodies... certainly no more that any other comic book depiction of women (and far less than most). In these particular stories Black Panther and Vixen are no more sexualized than White superheroines usually are. Given that the superhero genre routinely depicts women visually in a highly fetishistic manner, and that Black women continue to be represented as hypersexual in the media, it would seem logical for these characters to be determined first and foremost by their sexuality. By not over emphasizing Black Panther and Vixen's sexuality according to centuries old racial stereotypes these stories do not contribute to the accumulative and persistent type of characterization that Railton and Watson argue occurs in other media forms like music videos. Railton and Watson conclude: "through regular and explicit references to the natural and the animal, the black female body and black sexuality continue to be figured as primal, wild, and uncontrollable" (Railton and Watson 2005: 58). Black Panther and Vixen are clearly associated with animals but not in a manner that links their sexuality to being "primal, wild, and uncontrollable." The stories move the characters beyond such simple classifications. It is unfortunate that the covers still rely on this type of stereotype to promote the books because they do not do justice to the progressive representations of Black superheroines that the books offer.

This overreliance and easy association of Black women with animalistic hypersexuality as a way to market Black female characters is the persistent problem. Individual stories such as *Deadliest of the Species* and *Return of the Lion* can represent a progressive step away from rudimentary stereotypes, but the stories and the characters still exist within a larger stereotypical context. In other comics Shuri's version of the Black Panther is lusted after and illustrated to show off her ideal figure to maximum effect. Likewise, Vixen—her very name implies a seductress—is often portrayed as sexually active, physically attractive (she is a supermodel after all) and even a bit of a superhero homewrecker. But in these two books the heroines' sexuality is downplayed in favor of their heroism. The most sexually evocative moment in either story involves the supporting character of Storm who has to strip naked in order to travel to the underworld to rescue her husband T'Challa in *Deadliest of the Species*. Thus, a Black superheroine is displayed as a sexual spectacle, but it is not one of the title characters. And even this minor instance of Storm's disrobing is a far cry from the blatantly erotic way she is normally depicted. It is also very different from the way other Black superheroines are routinely hypersexualized, such as Ant (aka Hannah Washington) from Big City Comics who is always illustrated with her butt thrust out evocatively, or Misty Knight from Marvel who at times seeks out rough and dirty recreational sex with other superheroes just to blow off some steam (for a more detailed discussion see Brown 2011: 178). In contrast to the way most superheroines are depicted, Black or otherwise, these solo adventures of Black Panther and Vixen are remarkably chaste.

Drawing conclusions

As the highest profile books to feature Black Panther and Vixen, *Deadliest of the Species* and *Return of the Lion* demonstrate that comics featuring Black superheroines can be successful without reducing the characters to the most sexist and racist stereotypes associated with Black women. I would not go so far as to suggest that Black superheroines in general are moving beyond the colonial influenced Jezebel stereotype; it is an unfortunate fact that the superhero genre of comic books continues to rely heavily on stereotypes of all kinds. It is not a medium or a genre that lends itself well to mature and nuanced storytelling. But it is a form of mass-mediated popular culture where individual writers and artists can present radically different versions of characters. The fact that both *Deadliest of the Species* and *Return of the Lion* strive to represent Black superheroines as fully three-dimensional characters can be attributed to the fact that the books were written and illustrated by creators who are explicitly concerned with the political ramifications of depicting race and gender.

Reginald Hudlin, the author of *Black Panther: Deadliest of the Species*, is an African American writer with a long history of creating progressive Black characters. Similarly, G. Willow Wilson, the author of *Vixen: Return of the Lion*, is a woman whose work consistently addresses issues not just of gender but of religion and Middle Eastern cultures. In a medium where individual creators can have a direct impact on characterization (more so than in mediums like film and television) the increasing presence of writers and illustrators from a diversity of backgrounds bodes well for the future of diverse superheroes and superheroines.

Even within a genre that is typically derided as juvenile, and which traffics predominantly in stereotypical characterizations and extreme portrayals of gender and sexuality, there can be progressive representations of Black women. The wild, animal-like hypersexual stereotype of Black women that continues to dominate in film, television, music, and even sports, exists in superhero comics as well, but as these specific examples of Black Panther and Vixen indicate there is a very real possibility of challenging the one-dimensional racist and sexist logic. Where Black Panther and Vixen may initially appear to simply reinforce the colonialist stereotype of African women (literally "at first glance" given the deceiving erotic come-on of the covers), what the stories reveal is a message of heroism attributed to these Black superheroines. Rarely are Black women portrayed in any medium as independent, intelligent, and strong both physically and spiritually. Heroic Black women who avoid racist and sexist stereotypes do appear on several police procedural shows on television, but those are generally ensemble casts with White male leads. In headlining their own comic books, Black Panther and Vixen are rare instances of Black heroines taking center stage without resorting to any excessive fetishization of their bodies. These characters may be costumed in the standard superheroine uniform of revealing skin-tight outfits but their heroic actions far outweigh the spectacle of eroticism. What Black Panther and Vixen represent in these specific cases are heroes, first and foremost. They save their families, their villages, and their fictional African nations. They also save themselves from numerous physical and emotional dangers, and model new possibilities for the representation of Black women in popular culture.

References

Brown, J. A. (2001), *Black Superheroes, Milestone Comics and Their Fans*. Jackson, MS: University of Mississippi Press.

—(2011), *Dangerous Curves: Action Heroines, Gender, Fetishism, and Popular Culture*. Jackson, MS: University of Mississippi Press.

Bukatman, S. (1994), "X-bodies (the torment of the mutant superhero)", in R. Sappington and T. Stallings (eds), *Uncontrollable Bodies: Testimonies of Identity and Culture*. Seattle, WA: Bay Press, 92–129.

Chabon, M. (2008, March), "Designing women". *Details*, 26, (6), 196–201.

Collins, P. H. (2005), *Black Sexual Politics: African Americans, Gender, and the New Racism*. New York: Routledge.

Cunningham, P. L. (2010), "The absence of Black supervillains in mainstream comics". *Journal of Graphic Novels and Comics*, 1, (1), 51–62.

Darnton, R. (1984), *The Great Cat Massacre and Other Episodes in French Cultural History*. New York: Vintage Books.

Easthope, A. (1988), *What a Man's Gotta Do: The Masculine Myth in Popular Culture*. New York, NY: Routledge.

Gilman, S. (1992), "Black bodies, White bodies: Toward an iconography of female sexuality in late 19th century art, medicine and literature", in J. Donald and A. Rattansi (eds), *Race, Culture and Difference*. London: Sage/The Open University, pp. 171–97.

Hooks, B. (1992), *Black Looks: Race and Representation*. Boston, MA: South End Press.

Hudlin, R. and Lashley, K. (2009), *Black Panther: The Deadliest of the Species*. New York: Marvel Comics.

Klein, A. M. (1993), *Little Big Men: Bodybuilding Subculture and Gender Construction*. Albany, NY: SUNY Press.

McClintock, A. (1995), *Imperial Leather: Race, Gender, and Sexuality in the Colonial Contest*. New York: Routledge.

McKay, J. and Johnson, H. (2008), "Pornographic eroticism and sexual grotesquerie in representations of African American sportswomen". *Social Identities*, 14, (4), 491–504.

McWilliams, O. C. (2009), "Not just another racist honkey: A history of racial representation in *Captain America* and related publications", in R. G. Weiner (ed.) *Captain America and the Struggle of the Superhero: Critical Essays*. Jefferson, NC: McFarland, pp. 66–78.

Miller-Young, M. (2010), "Putting hypersexuality to work: Black women and illicit eroticism in pornography", *Sexualities*, 13, (2), 219–35.

Mulvey, L. (1975), "Visual pleasure and the narrative cinema". *Screen*, 16, (3), 6–18.

Negra, D. (2001), *Off-White Hollywood: American Culture and Ethnic Female Stardom*. New York: Routledge.

Railton, D. and Watson, P. (2005), "Naughty girls and red blooded women: Representations of female heterosexuality in music videos". *Feminist Media Studies*, 5, (1), 51–63.

Said, E. (1979), *Orientalism*. New York: Random House.

Singer, M. (2002), "'Black skins' and White masks: Comic books and the secrets of race". *African American Review*, 36, (1), 107–19.

Wilson, G. W. and Cafu, G. (2009), *Vixen: Return of the Lion*. New York: DC Comics.

9

Gender, race, and
The Boondocks

Sheena C. Howard

Introduction

The conceptual framework of cool pose (Majors and Billson, 1992) has yet to be examined against the backdrop of a Black comic strip. Thus, this study seeks to expound upon two key aspects of cool pose—playing the dozens and the search for pride and manhood.

Through an analysis of a contemporary Black comic strip—Aaron McGruder's *The Boondocks*—we may become aware of the continuity and extension of Majors and Billson's conceptual framework of cool pose, which raises complex questions about assimilation, accommodation and male–female dynamics within the Black community. Though *The Boondocks* is a comic strip, the relationship between language and society is a bidirectional one; social issues manifest within language and language produces and reproduces social dynamics.

Cool pose—introduced

Research on the concept of *cool* within the African American male community has been studied and explored since the late 1980s (See Boykins 1983; Majors 1989). Cool pose as a conceptual framework was introduced by Majors and Billson in 1992. Kimberly Moffitt (2012) suggests that cool pose "revolutionized our perception of Black masculinity" (p. 178). In *Cool Pose: The Dilemmas of Black Manhood in America* (1992), the authors embark on a comprehensive examination of "how Black males, especially those who are young and live in the inner cities of our nation, have adopted and used cool masculinity—or as we prefer to call it, 'cool pose'—as a way of surviving in a restrictive society" (Majors and Billson 1992: 2).

The authors deconstructed Black masculinity by exploring facets of Black men as it relates to expressivity, Black masking, Black humor and expressive life style—all aspects in which cool is expressed:

> Cool pose is a distinctive coping mechanism that serves to counter, at least in part, the dangers that black males encounter on a daily basis. As a performance, cool pose is designed to render the black male visible and to empower him; it eases the worry and pain of blocked opportunities. Being cool is an ego booster for black males ... by acting calm, emotionless, fearless, aloof, and tough, the African American male strives to offset an externally imposed "zero" image. Being cool shows both the dominant culture and the black male himself that he is strong and proud (Majors and Billson 1992: 5).

Scholars have explored the connection between Black masculinity and slavery, the expressivity of Black males in sports and the historical underpinnings of hyper masculinity (Jackson 2006; Brown 1999; Hill 2005; Neal 2005). Majors and Billson (1992, p. 8) focus on cool pose as a tool to coping with oppression and marginality:

> Presenting to the world an emotionless, fearless, and aloof front counters the low sense of inner control, lack of inner strength, absence of stability, damaged pride, shattered confidence and fragile social competence that come from living on the edge of society.

In short, cool behaviors are coping mechanisms designed to deal with the social systems that limit the opportunities of Black men. The adoption of these "cool poses or postures" arise from the mistrust that the Black male feels toward the dominant society and it is designed to offset an externally imposed "zero image" (Majors 1986).

Aspects of cool pose

Cool pose is an ever expanding and innovative form of expressivity in the Black community. Majors and Billson (1992) dedicated an entire manuscript to the repetitive acts Black males incorporate into their daily lives in order to cope with an oppressive society; however, key areas illustrate cool pose in action; exploring every aspect of cool behavior is beyond the breadth of this study. Therefore, per the literature on cool pose, two overarching aspects will be expounded upon in this chapter: (1) playing the dozens and (2) the search for pride and manhood.

Playing the dozens

A reading of cool pose (see Majors and Billson, 1992) yields three main characteristics of the dozens: verbal war, ambivalence towards women and keeping cool. The dozens is a verbal contest or "war" played largely by Black males. It entails rhyming, slang usage, lyrical style and insults towards another party. The origin of the dozens dates back to the slavery period when slaves were sold by the dozen. The whole system of slavery was demeaning and dehumanizing; and the horror was further marked by those who would purchase slaves by the dozen if they were bruised, old, or had a broken limb. The healthy, strong slaves were sold at a higher premium. So, "playing the dozens" has a double entendre. On the one hand it signifies on those who are lesser in intelligence, wealth, strength, or other resources. Also, it is a game that points out from the very beginning the weaknesses of the weak, while being played primarily by those who are marginalized. Majors and Billson (1992: 92) state, "Mothers are subject to vicious slander; fathers are 'queer, syphilitic'; 'sisters are whores, brothers are defective' ... Accusations of cowardice, homosexuality, or stupidity are common."

The dozens is an element of African American oral tradition in which two people, usually males, go head to head in a verbal war. It is a form of expressivity as well as entertainment. One insult towards a mother is enough to start the game. "Yo momma" usually starts the verbal war and is a common recognized rejoinder in the oral tradition of playing the dozens. An example would be, "Yo mama is so fat, when she jumps in the air, she gets stuck!" Another example is as follows: "You so ugly, when you go to the zoo you've gotta pay to get out." The subject of the insult would respond with something equally or more humiliating than the insult projected by his/her competitor.

Violence resulting from the game may occur but is not the preferred result. Majors and Billson (1992) suggest that if one can handle the insults another aims at his mother, then one can withstand the "insults society might hurl at him" (p. 96). There is a love–hate feeling towards the game; the positive aspect of playing the dozens is the verbal training and development of a Black male who may need these skills when dealing with the dominant society; while the negative aspect of the game is the degradation and humiliation of women in the Black community. The final analysis is that one should be able to "keep cool" and establish a reputation of his own by responding with an equally vicious insult. According to Majors and Billson (1992: 91):

> Playing the dozens exemplifies the expressive life-style, especially for young African American males. It represents a way to act and be cool with astonishingly intricate verbal play. Playing the dozens helps adolescent black males maintain control and keep control under adverse conditions. It prepares them for the socioeconomic problems they may later face and facilitates their search for masculinity, pride, status, social competence and expressive sexuality.

The dozens is a contest of personal power, wit, self-control, verbal ability, mental agility and mental toughness. Playing the dozens allows Black males to remain in control when introduced with humiliations and acts as a training mechanism for Black males to channel their aggression linguistically.

The search for pride and manhood

A reading of cool pose (See Majors and Billson 1992) yields three main characteristics of the search for pride and manhood: cool as protection, being tough and search for adolescent identity. Pride is the driving force behind the masking of cool pose (Majors and Billson 1992). The need for pride develops early in the life of a young Black male.

Majors and Billson (1992) suggest that playing it cool protects the self-esteem and enhances the chances of survival. By keeping it cool, authority figures can be deceived by the cool performance of the Black male. Keeping it cool serves as a behavioral performance used when under pressure. For example, when a Black male is confronted by a White authority figure, such as a policeman, he aims to remain calm and shield any feelings of anger or hostility. This has its negative effects. Majors and Billson (1992: 40) state:

> The masking central to cool pose also trains the black male in the art of self-deception. He may lose the ability to know his own feelings, to feel then keenly, or to express them to others when it is safe to do so.

This may have adverse effects on the Black male as cool behaviors become a constant pattern in the Black male's existence. For example, losing touch with his feelings in various interpersonal relationships, such as romantic and/ or familial relationships. This warrants a negative effect because the original function of cool pose was not deception within intimate relationships but more so a tool to deceive authority figures. Majors and Billson (1992: 41) note:

The masking of true feelings interferes with establishing strong bonds with families and friends. Unfortunately for the black male who constantly puts himself under pressure to prove his manhood and is simultaneously unable to show or discuss his feelings and fears, the risk is very high for black on black crime, especially assault and homicide.

The "tough guy" style includes aggression, risk-taking, violence and threats to use violence (Mancini 1981). Gangs and delinquency also epitomize the pursuit of masculinity through toughness and cool. The gang can become a family who offers belonging, pride, respect and empowerment that may be absent in the home and denied by society (Majors and Billson 1992). The rituals of the gang signify solidarity, acceptance and power for the Black male. These rituals include distinctive hairstyles, handshakes, nicknames, territorial wars and battles. These self-destructive behaviors can be more easily comprehended, not simply as deviant activities of antisocial minority males, but more complexly as symptomatic indicators of the historically devalued status of Blacks in American society (Gibbs, 1994). These indicators are often noticed in the early stages of the young Black male's mental and social development.

Adolescents place value on being cool or being perceived as cool. Being cool enhances the adolescents self-esteem and value; this can be a lot of pressure for a young Black male. Majors and Billson (1992: 46) assert:

This pressure is amplified by the fact that adolescence is typically a period of confusion, ambivalence, emotional instability, identity confusion and doubtful self esteem. Being cool, rather than square may help to enhance the adolescents confidence and popularity.

For an adolescent, activities that may appear un-cool are doing well at school, going on field trips or going to museums. If young Black males conform to the White-dominated standards in educational institutions, they may be accused by their peers of "acting White" or "being a nerd." A young Black male who excels in the educational institution may even be physically assaulted. All of these variables could result in an identity crisis. The young Black male may feel as though he is rejecting or losing his culture by conforming and exceling in the White-dominated educational structure. At the same time resisting the White-dominated educational structure relegates the young Black male to the streets.

Rationale

Cool pose has yet to be examined against the backdrop of a Black comic strip. Thus, this study seeks to expound upon two key aspect of cool pose—playing the dozens and the search for pride and manhood.

Through an analysis of a contemporary Black comic strip we may become aware of the continuity and extension of Majors and Billson's conceptual framework of cool pose. Though *The Boondocks* is a comic strip, the relationship between language and society is a bidirectional one; social issues manifest within language and language produces and reproduces social dynamics.

Major and Billson suggest that as long as discrimination continues to be prevalent, the Black male will enact cool behaviors; thus, an analysis of a contemporary comic strip will illuminate the manifestation or lack of cool behaviors. No notable studies have applied this concept of Black masculinity to the medium of comics.

The Boondocks comic strip is fitting for an examination of masculinity that can be interpreted as cool because it is the site of cultural collision as young African American inner-city boys adapt to life in a predominantly White suburb of Chicago. The content of the strip raises complex questions about assimilation, male–female dynamics, accommodation and race relations in American society, which consequently makes cool pose fitting as a concept of application.

Artifact selection

This research includes comic strips from Aaron McGruder's book *Public Enemy* #2, which is a collection of previously published strips syndicated in over 200 newspaper outlets nationwide between March 2003 and November 2004. This study includes an examination of strips published between January 2003 and November 2004. The researcher's examination occurred from September through December 2009. This research does not attempt to generalize beyond the selected artifact; however, the researcher chose the selected artifact because of the diversity and contemporary nature of the content. In addition, the artifact addresses many social and political issues within not only the African American community, but also American society at large. All the comic strips found in *Public Enemy* #2 previously appeared in syndication (McGruder 2005). The beginning and end of each strip is dated with the month and year it appeared in syndication throughout the book. The syndicated strips in *Public Enemy* #2 begin on March 12, 2003 and end on November 13, 2004. *Public Enemy* #2 was published in 2005.

Cool pose—manifested

This section will expound upon the manifestation of playing the dozens and the search for pride and manhood within *The Boondocks* comic strip.

Playing the dozens

There are numerous instances of the dozens in the content of *The Boondocks* comic strip. One of the first instances of playing the dozens occurs in a May 2, 2003 strip. Huey is concerned about the latest news on the Iraq war. Caesar is concerned about world events; however, Caesar provides the reader with comic relief as he often urges Huey to think about issues outside of politics.

> *"You heard the latest from Iraq?"* (Huey)
> *"Politics, politics, politics. Don't you ever worry about anything else?"* (Caesar)
> *"And just what else should I be worried about?"* (Huey)
> *"Well, for starters your moms is so stupid she sits on the television and watches the couch."* (Caesar)

This segment indirectly calls into question the intellectual capacity of Huey's mother by commenting on her inability to watch television properly. The use of wit is evidenced here by Caesar's use of indirection and humor. Another example of the dozens is manifested in a July 27, 2003 strip.

> *"Hey man, you wanna go see 'The Hulk'?"* (Caesar)
> *"Naw ... I heard it wasn't very good."* (Huey)
> *"Yeah, but I wanna go see your moms ... I heard she was **great** as the hulk's stunt double."* (Caesar)
> *How droll ...* (Huey)
> *"I heard she had to sit in the makeup chair for, like ... **two, three minutes** to look the part!!"* (Caesar)
> [Huey slams door]

There is a pattern of Huey's lack of engagement in the dozens game. Caesar hurls insults at Huey's mom; however, Huey never indulges—this is characteristic of Huey throughout the strip. Manifestations of playing the dozens can be seen in an August 10, 2003 strip.

> *"Don't you hate having lots of hair in the summer ? It feels all hot and itchy ..."* (Caesar)

"Yeah ... (Huey)
"I wonder if your moms has this problem with her full beard and hairy
   back?" (Caesar)

In a September 5–6, 2003 strip, Huey does not participate in the insult war; however, we see Huey become somewhat annoyed with Caesar and his constant "yo momma" jokes. We see Huey yell back at Caesar and get intimately close to Caesar while stating, "I *got* it she's ugly." This is an undesirable result as Huey always remains in control of his aggression, an example of being cool by remaining unaffected and emotionless.

"Your mother is so hairy, her eyebrows connect with her beard." (Caesar)
"Just thought you should know." (Huey)
"Your mother's so ugly she looks like she just got hit with a bag of hot
   nickels ... dropped from the Empire State building ... right after her
   face got run over by ..." (Caesar)
"I got it she's ugly !" (Huey)

In a November 12, 2003 strip, Huey is critiquing Black entertainment television and discussing the lack of respectable television stations aimed at the Black community. Caesar ceases the opportunity to provide comic relief by hurling a "yo momma" joke at Huey. Huey rarely finds Caesar's insult to be humorous and in a later segment actually addresses the lack of humor found in Caesar's insults.

"What bothers me is that there are so few places Black people can
   go for entertainment that respects our intellect and sophistication!"
   (Huey)
"I agree ... by the way your moms is so fat, she sweats grease." (Caesar)
"I'm outta here ..." (Huey)
(sigh) "... so few places indeed ..." (Caesar)

February 4, 2004 provides another example of the dozens.

"Your mothers so fat her clothes have stretch marks" (Caesar)
[Huey walks away]
"I've found my comedic voice but I have yet to find my comedic
   audience." (Caesar)

In this strip, January 25, 2004, Huey inverts the function of the dozens game, by making a case that "yo momma" jokes should challenge the status quo and critique the "folly of the world we live in."

"I've decided that the music industry doesn't offer much security, so I'm working on comedy as a backup" (Caesar)

"Check this out ... your momma is so dumb she set the house on fire using a CD burner." (Caesar)

"... Its okay ..." (Huey)

*"**Okay !?** That was my best joke!"* (Caesar)

"It didn't challenge me. I like my comedy to expose the folly of the world we live in." (Huey)

"We need more comedians using humor to question the status quo. Guys who aren't afraid to get political. Richard Pryor, Dick Gregory, George Carlin, Chris Rock ... that kind of thing." (Huey)

"John Ashcroft's momma is so stupid she set the house on fire using a CD burner." (Caesar)

"Now that's funny." (Huey)

Huey makes an interesting assertion in regard to how the dozens could be redirected to challenge the status quo; this is reminiscent of the signifying monkey, an African American cultural trope. The use of signifying and indirection are characteristic of the dozens as all insults are not a direct insult on Huey's mother as they are insults aimed personally at Huey. Huey seeks to add an element of social relevance laced with wit in the dozens game by challenging Caesar to direct his insult towards John Ashcroft, a United States politician who served under George Bush from 2001 to 2005.

In *The Boondocks* it is evident that the majority of insults situate the Black female as the site of humor in the dozens game. Women become the brunt of the joke, rendering them victim to condemnation within the content of *The Boondocks* comic strips, a popular form of mediated communication. The father figure is never the subject of the dozens game in *The Boondocks*, which is not surprising because historically the patriarchal figure has seldom been the source of humiliation in the dozens game. *The Boondocks* reinforces the degradation of the Black female through the performance of the dozens. This is troublesome due to the mass media's role in shaping and influencing the consumer. In the content of *The Boondocks* comic strips, women find themselves absent, as there is a lack of Black female characters and a Black female voice, while simultaneously casting them as the target of humor through the performance of Black masculinity.

The situating of women as subjects of symbolic annihilation is twofold in *The Boondocks,* as the strips manifest ambivalence towards women, while rendering them virtually nonexistent. This ambivalence can be seen by Caesar's relentless attacks on Huey's mother and Huey's resistance to strike back with an insult equally degrading to the Black female community. Specific to *The Boondocks,* insults directed toward Huey with Huey's mother as the target deal with the Black female body and the intellectual capacity of the Black female. For example, Caesar attacks the physical appearance of Huey's mother when he states, "Your mothers so fat her clothes have stretch marks." He further attacks the intellectual capacity of Huey's mother when he states, "your moms is so stupid she sits on the television and watches the couch."

Huey exhibits self-control and mental toughness as he keeps his cool despite Caesar's insults—all the desired results of playing the dozens per the review of literature. Huey's lack of retaliation and participation in the dozens shows a sense of respect for Black females and exemplifies his character as the one personality in the strip who seeks, in every aspect, to uplift the Black community.

In over 200 strips the presence of the Black female voice is non-existent, yet humor is directed towards Black women on several occasions. The strip renders Huey's mother non-existent and subsequently fails to acknowledge or address the whereabouts of Huey and Riley's mother or grandmother. Thus, by explicating this aspect of cool pose (playing the dozens), we learn that playing the dozens can act as a form of hegemonic Black masculinity, which has significant implications and perhaps consequences for the Black female.

Search for pride and manhood

Riley, in particular, will be the focus of this analysis because he embodies many examples of the search for pride and manhood through exemplifying components of toughness, search for adolescent identity, gang activity and delinquency. Riley rebels against anything he thinks is outside of hip-hop culture or being "cool." Riley is about making money and rap music.

> *"I been thinkin' about the future. I need to make **a lot** of money ... I was thinking about the rap game, but then I realized – I'll never have the discipline and the work ethic of a Master P or Nelly ..."* (Riley)

Like many young Black males, Riley views the hip-hop industry as a symbol of being cool while resisting the status quo, which includes the attainment of education and conformity. In a January 2003 strip, Huey asks Riley what his new year's resolution is.

> *"I'm going to take a more aggressive stance toward everything, break laws when it suits my agenda, and intimidate those weaker than me with brute force and threats of unimaginable pain, suffering and retribution. Plus, I think I'll buy a gun or two."* (Riley)'

*"I can't tell if my brother is becoming more of a thug or more of a
    republican. (Huey)
    ... oh, and I hate Black people."* (Riley)

Riley embodies the "thug" and "gangster" stereotype found too often in
mass media representations of Black males, especially hip-hop culture. Riley
takes the position that embodying a thuggish adversarial stance is the proper
and "authentic" response to the status quo. One of the adverse effects of
the "gangster" lifestyle is Black on Black crime. This effect is evident when
Riley states, "oh and I hate Black people." This is also evident through Riley's
aggression towards Huey. Majors and Billson (1992) suggest that Black males
do not respect other Black males who fail to embody or display a tough
image. This sentiment is echoed in the above mentioned segments of *The
Boondocks*, in which Riley seeks to identify with rappers but denounces the
Black community. Riley views hip-hop artists as cool, but shows a lack of
respect for the Black community in general, including his brother Huey.

Riley frequently refers to Huey and Caesar as "nerds" or "stupid" because
of their complex vocabulary, interest in reading, politics and lack of identification with gangster rappers. Terms such as "nerd," "stupid" or "loser" are
the antithesis of being cool and are considered un-cool. Being called lame
or un-cool are the ultimate insults in Black teenage vernacular (Majors and
Billson, 1992). Take this excerpt for example:

*"If I told you I had a simple and easy way to save the world would you
    doubt me?"* (Caesar)
"It would take more than a wild boast to earn such an accolade." (Huey)
"Say I am the man !!" (Caesar)
"What's the plan?!" (Huey)
"You guys are some %^&$#@ nerds ..."* (Riley)

In several strips Riley physically attacks Huey or expresses the threat of
violence towards Huey, representative of cool behavior. In a November 23,
2003 strip, Huey wakes Riley up because Granddad is calling Riley to do some
chores. Riley, disturbed that Huey has woken him out of his sleep, immediately smacks Huey in the face and goes back to sleep. Another instance of
Riley's aggressive behavior is in a December 21, 2003 strip, in which he waits
in the snow by the chimney with a baseball bat in hopes of beating up Santa
Claus and his reindeers.

Riley is a product of hip-hop commercialization and subscribes to many
of the products young Black boys would consider cool. Riley signifies the
influence the media and popular culture may have on adolescents. Being cool
is a valued trait for Riley and he incessantly seeks to adhere to cool behaviors

through hip-hop culture. This is not surprising as hyper-masculinity juxtaposed with hip-hop culture is a thoroughly explored area of study (See Campbell 2005; Hopkinson and Moore 2006; Jackson 2006).

Cool behaviors are also expressed through male-female dynamics in the strip. Similar to hip-hop culture, masculinity is expressed through the embodiment of misogyny and ambivalence towards women as previously discussed. Cool behaviors may prevent Black males from developing authentic relationships with women (Majors and Billson 1992).

In *Deconstructing Tyrone: A New Look at Black Masculinity in the Hip-Hop Generation* (2006), chapter 11 opens with, "Boys play too much and try way too hard to be cool. Girls have to be strong to demand respect" (Hopkinson and Moore: 132). This was the sentiment outlined by nine Black girls in focus group interviews. Hopkinson and Moore (2006) note that, "Many of them have a strong sense of self that grown women would admire. But some of them still struggle with their self esteem and with abuse from boys, even at their tender age" (p. 134). Women, even as adolescents, struggle to negotiate their own space. Boys and girls need to be armed with tools to be able to cope with a variety of messages carried over the nonstop communications and mass media that rule the world.

Within *The Boondocks* a strong Black female voice is omitted even as the strip deals with significant and relevant issues on politics and race. This in itself symbolizes hegemonic Black masculinity, which subsequently trivializes the Black female. *The Boondocks* creates a world in which the Black female is not needed or represented. In one strip the male–female dynamic is touched upon.

Riley meets Don "Magic" Juan, a hip-hop artist and pimp from Chicago. Riley assesses the legitimacy of Don Juan in the following segment:

Okay then, there's a girl at school I'm in love with. What do I say to make
   her like me? (Riley)
That's a trick question, son. (Don Juan)
You aint supposed to be lovin' 'em in the first place. (Don Juan)
It's him. (Riley)

Cool behaviors prevent Black males from developing authentic relationships with women (Majors and Billson 1992). Inability to put one's feelings on the line prevents the development of sincere relationships between Black males and females as Black men repress their feelings and emotions when it comes to females. This sentiment is evidenced in the aforementioned strip and is representative of cool behavior. Black masculinity is performed while representing women as objects that should not be loved but instead "pimped."

Riley embodies many facets of cool behaviors; however, his character is actually the minority. Riley is ostracized and often ignored because of his lack of political and social awareness. Huey and Caesar often dismiss Riley because of his lack of intellectual thought and excessive identification with popular culture.

> *"Y'know I was thinkin'"* (Riley)
> *"Ok. Stop right there ... I'm gonna reach back here like so ... and if you say something ignorant, I'm gonna smack you real, **real** hard."* (Huey)
> *"Never mind. Wasn't that important."* (Riley)
> *"Thought so."* (Huey)

Riley exemplifies the influence the media and popular culture may have on young, impressionable Black males. *The Boondocks* provides the reader with the realities of the media's influence on young Black males. Riley is not a character that one would look up to or idolize as everything about his character exemplifies the ills within and across the Black community. This is the irony of *The Boondocks*, one may assume the strip glorifies and stereotypes the Black community; however, in many ways it challenges stereotypes and raises complex questions about the messages and effects of hip-hop and popular culture on young Black males.

    The Boondocks paints a clear picture that Black-centered entertainment, the Black community as a whole, reality television shows and Black celebrities all contribute to the state of the Black community and the messages young Blacks interpret and construct. This is particularly evident in a running September 2004 segment in which a new reality television show airs called "Can a N**GA get a job?" produced by Russell Simmons.

> *"You don't think a show called 'Can a n**ga get a job?! Makes Black people look lazy and stupid ?!"* (Huey)
> *"No it makes n*ggas look lazy and stupid."* (Riley)
> *"And as a n**ga this is okay with you ?"* (Huey)
> *"We n**gas appreciate the lowered expectations."* (Riley)

Huey is disgusted because the show further perpetuates, commoditizes and stereotypes the Black community through reality television fueled by the sentiment of capitalism in American society. Riley, as a victim of hip-hop commercialization, accepts the degradation of the Black community and enjoys the entertainment offered by the show. Moreover, Granddad asserts that the show is demeaning, but enjoys the show for its entertainment value despite its discriminatory and over-exaggerated representation of Black culture. This is reminiscent of the state of reality television shows in today's mainstream media, shows such as VH1's *Flavor of Love* and BET's *College Hill*, to name a few, offer a stark parallel to the fictitious show McGruder represents in his strip.

Conclusion

In *The Boondocks* Riley is an exemplar of many examples of cool pose and his character does reinforce the stereotypes that have long hindered Blacks, thus adding to the heurism of Major and Billson's cool pose. Riley is militant, defiant, delinquent and violent, all aspects of being cool. Aaron McGruder uses the character of Riley to comment on materialism, the media and popular culture. McGruder states in an interview with the *Baltimore City Paper* (Scocca and Williams 2000):

> The problem is that a lot of us don't have much experience with satire and irony because we've been inundated with simplistic entertainment from every angle. I created Riley *specifically* to comment on the whole wannabe-gangsta, materialistic culture. A lot of people, period, don't understand. Critical thinkers understand what I'm trying to do with the Riley character. I can't do anything about it if people don't get it.

Riley is portrayed as a problem in society, rather than a functional, contributing citizen and family member. *The Boondocks* does, however, maintain a counter narrative through Huey.

Huey possesses a vocabulary well beyond that of a typical 11year old and positions the well-being of the Black community as an integral part of his mission to uplift the Black community and challenge the status quo. As long as Black men experience discrimination (or there is a perception of discrimination), there will be the need for cool (Majors and Billson 1992). Thus, Huey and Riley's manifestation of cool behaviors makes evident the continued perceived or actual discrimination prevalent within society as comic strips often mirror reality. According to Fairclough (2004), language may have a more significant role in contemporary socioeconomic changes than it has had in the past. The relationship between language and society is a bidirectional one; social issues manifest within language and language produces and reproduces social dynamics. Therefore, comic strips are a site in which real social issues manifest within the language of the strip.

Even though, *The Boondocks* depicts varied personalities, perspectives and social locations among the Black male characters, it is still evident that the main characters feel the need to enact cool behaviors, signifying the continued necessicity of coping within a restrictive, oppressive system.

The Boondocks also depicts Caesar, Huey's friend as a young, sophisticated, articulate Black boy concerned about politics and the larger community. However, oftentimes Caesar provides the reader with comic relief by creating a narrative that trivializes and degrades Black women. Thus, as

Black masculinity is performed through the dozens, women are cast as undervalued.

One notable yet unexpected finding which the researcher deems significant is the symbolic annihilation of the Black female in *The Boondocks*. This term, "symbolic annihilation" was first referenced by Gaye Tuchman, Arlene Daniels and James Benet (1978) in a book titled *Hearth and Home: Images of Women in the Mass Media*. Symbolic annihilation is a phenomenon by which the mass media omit, trivialize, or condemn certain groups that are not socially valued (Klein and Shiffman 2009). Therefore, by omitting or marginalizing certain minority groups, a medium symbolically sends a message to consumers about the societal value of that group.

In *The Boondocks* it is evident that the majority of insults situate the Black female as the site of humor through playing the dozens. The dozens is an African American tradition with roots in slavery in which Black males exchange insults in an effort to verbally embarrass one's opponent. The aforementioned is a form of training for Black males as they prepare to face the real world.

In *The Boondocks* women become the brunt of many jokes, rendering them victim to denunciation. *The Boondocks* reinforces the degradation of the Black female through the performance of the dozens, an aspect of Black masculinity. This is troublesome due to the mass media's role in shaping and influencing the consumer. The situating of women as subjects of symbolic annihilation is twofold in *The Boondocks*. The strip manifests hegemonic Black masculinity when women are mentioned, while rendering them nonexistent in appearance. Specific to *The Boondocks,* insults directed towards Huey with Huey's mother as the target deal with the Black female body and the intellectual capacity of the Black female.

The lack of women in a strip that is political and racial in nature symbolically sends a message to women that they do not matter much in society. The lack of a Black female voice in such a politically-driven strip symbolically denigrates and devalues the opinion of the Black female community. The strip also symbolically makes a statement that to be a woman means to have a limited role in society. These messages are reinforced in *The Boondocks* by the treatment of women when they do appear and the insults directed towards women throughout the strip. In addition, Huey is an Afrocentric revolutionary trying to uplift the Black community; however, there is no strong female voice with the same agenda in the strip. This symbolically states that Black men are the only ones who can lead the way to racial equality and social consciousness in the Black community—no female voice is needed.

To date the symbolic annihilation of women has not been studied within Black popular media representations; however, this study shows that the trivialization and marginalization of women is present within modern African

American literature. The comic strip is a site of creating, reflecting and producing ideologies; therefore, future research should further probe the representation of Black women in Black comics.

References

Boykin, W. (1983), "The academic performance of Afro-American children", in J. T. Spence (ed.), *Achievement and Achievement Motives: Psychological and Sociological Approaches*. San Francisco, CA: Freeman, pp. 322–71.

Brown, J. A. (1999), "Comic book masculinity and the new Black superhero". *African American Review*, 33, (1), 25–42.

Fairclough, N. (2001), *Language and Power*. New York: Longman.

Gibbs, J. (1994), "Anger in young Black males: Victims or victimizers?", in R. Majors and J. Gordon (eds), *American Black Male: His Present Status and His Future*. Chicago, IL: Nelson-Hall, pp. 127–44.

Hill, M. L. (2005, June 22), "Breaking the rules: Subverting traditional masculinity on the court and beyond". Retrieved from: http://www.seeingblack.com/2005/x110405/bball.shtml.

Hopkinson, N. and Moore, N. (2006), *Deconstructing Tyrone: A New Look at Black Masculinity in the Hip-Hop Generation*. San Francisco, CA: Cleis Press.

Jackson, R. L. (2006), *Scripting the Black Masculine Body: Identity, Discourse, and Racial Politics in Popular Media*. Albany, NY: State University of New York Press.

Klein, H. and Shiffman, K. (2009), "Underrepresentation and symbolic annihilation of socially disenfranchised groups ('Out Groups') in animated cartoons". *Howard Journal of Communications*, 20, (1), 55–72.

Langley, M. R. (1990), *The Effects of Culture, Gender and Race on the Potential Psychological Treatment of Men: A Critical Review*. Tallahassee, FL: Florida State University.

—(1994), "Effects of cultural/racial identity, cultural commitment and counseling approach on African-American males perceptions of therapists' credibility and utility: Summary". *The Psych Discourse*, 25, 7–9.

Majors, R. (1986), "Cool pose: The proud signature of Black survival". *Changing Men: Issues in Gender, Sex and Politics*, 17, 5–6.

—(1989), "Cool pose: The proud signature of Black survival", in M. S. Kimmel and M. A. Messner (eds), *Men's Lives: Readings in the Sociology of Men and Masculinity*. New York, NY: Macmillan, pp. 83–7.

—(1990), "Cool pose: Black masculinity and sport", in M. A. Messner and D. Sabo (eds), *Critical Perspectives on Sport, Men and Masculinity*. Champaign, IL: Human Kinetics.

Majors, R. and Billson, J. M. (1992), *Cool Pose: The Dilemmas of Black Manhood in America*. New York: Lexington Books.

Majors, R., Tyler, T., Peden, B., and Hall, R. (1994), "Cool pose: A symbolic mechanism for masculine role enactment and coping by Black males", in R. Majors and J. Gordon (eds), *The American Black Male: His Present Status and His Future*. Chicago, IL: Nelson-Hall, pp. 245–59.

Mancini, J. K. (1981), *Strategic Styles: Coping in the Inner City*. Hanover, MA: University Press of New England.

McGruder, A. (2005), *Public Enemy #2*. New York: Three Rivers Press.

Moffit, K. (2010), "Cool pose on wheels: An exploration of the disabled Black male in film", in R. Spellers and K. Moffitt (eds), *Blackberries and Redbones: Critical Articulations of Black Hair/Body Politics in Africana Communities*. Cresskill, NJ: Hampton Press.

Myers, L. J. (1988), *Understanding an Afrocentric Worldview: Introduction to an Optimal Psychology*. Dubuque, IA: Kendall/Hunt.

Neal, M. A. (2005), *New Black Man: Rethinking Black Masculinity*. New York: Routledge.

Scocca, T. and Williams, V. (2000, February 9), "Strip mining: *The Boondocks'* Aaron McGruder and *Liberty Meadows'* Frank Cho take the funny pages in new directions". *Baltimore City Paper*. Retrieved from: http://www.citypaper.com/news/story.asp?id=3624.

Tuchman, G., Daniels, A., and Benet, J. (1978), *Hearth and Home: Images of Women in the Mass Media*. New York: Oxford University Press.

10

From sexual siren to race traitor: Condoleezza Rice in political cartoons

Clariza Ruiz De Castilla and
Zazil Elena Reyes García

In 2004 comedian Dave Chapelle organized the "first and maybe only racial draft" ("The racial draft" 2004). In a sketch that emulated the NFL (National Football League) draft, interracial personalities representing sports, entertainment and politics were to be picked by racial groups that could then claim them as their own. Following this logic Blacks drafted Tiger Woods while Jews chose Lenny Kravitz. Surprise and confusion arose when Whites selected Colin Powell, someone who is "a hundred percent Black" ("The racial draft" 2004). Blacks were not happy with this decision but accepted it under two conditions: they would give up Powell if Whites took Condoleezza Rice and returned OJ Simpson. The deal was then closed with an image of Rice accompanied by a caption that announced: "Given away by Blacks" ("The racial draft" 2004). Condoleezza Rice was now officially White.

Forbes magazine considered Condoleezza Rice, the first African American female Secretary of State, to be "the most powerful woman in the world" for two years in a row (Serafin 2005: para. 1). Her position as Secretary of State, held from 2005 to 2009, was preceded by an impressive career that included a list of "firsts," such as being not only the youngest Provost in the history of Stanford University but also "the first female and first minority to hold the position" (Williams 2007: para. 6). She also became the first woman to serve as National Security Advisor when President George W. Bush appointed her to the job in the year 2000 (Williams 2007: para. 10).

Described by *Ebony* magazine as possibly "the most intriguing of the 66 people who have held the nation's highest diplomatic post" ("Ebony interview", 2005, p. 194), depictions of Rice go from "an inspiration to all people—American or otherwise" (Williams 2007: 17) to "the devil's handmaiden" ("The devil's handmaiden," 2003) and "the purest expression of the race traitor" ("The devil's handmaiden" 2003 para: 2). When it comes to Condoleezza Rice there is an evident tension between those who attempt to look past race and talk about her in terms of her individual achievements, and those who question her allegiance to her race.

For the purposes of this chapter, we will look at political cartoons of Condoleezza Rice, the so-called "Warrior Princess" (Serafin 2005: para. 3) in order to answer the following questions: How do political cartoons frame race in relation to Condoleezza Rice? Do they explicitly address race or do they attempt to avoid it? To answer these questions, we will explore critical race theory, as well as concepts of representation, colorblindness and enlightened racism. We will begin by noting the relevance of cartoons as a site to analyze representations of race; consequently, we will explore the different theories that frame our analysis and finally we will use them to conduct a close textual analysis of eleven political cartoons on Condoleezza Rice.

Cartoons as a site for the analysis of representations of race

According to Gilman (1992), it is through "visual conventions" that we "perceive and transmit our understanding of the world about us" (p. 223). Visual conventions can be found in art and in the media where the world is not "presented" but "represented" (p. 223). Thus, these representations shape the way that we look at ourselves and others. Gilman explains the particularities of representing individuals and states that this practice:

> implies the creation of some greater class or classes to which the individual is seen to belong. These classes in turn are characterized by the use of a model which synthetizes our perception of the uniformity of the groups into a convincingly homogeneous image (p. 223).

As a result, representation can produce stereotypes which Gilman says can be "covert, as in eighteenth century portraiture" or "overt, as in the case of caricatures" (p. 223). Whether covert or overt, these stereotypes "serve to focus the viewer's attention on the relationship between the portrayed individual and the general qualities ascribed to the class" (p. 223). In other words, images found in the media, or in this case cartoons, are entrancing because they carry an "ideological force" that "reduces the interpretations an audience can make, filling their eyes with a single, dominating meaning" (Hart and Daughton 2005: 191).

This ideological force of the image can be related to Hall's (1997a) explanation of the representation of the "Other." Hall speaks of representational practices which attempt to fix "difference" and determine "preferred meanings" (p. 228) which create a division between "us," the "'normal' imagined community" and "them" (p. 258). The preferred meaning that is privileged depends on the dynamics of power that attempt to fix "difference" in representational practices (Hall 1997a: 228). It depends on who has the power to name the experiences that a society goes through and how these particular ways of talking about our experiences shape them as well. Hall (1997b) reminds us to think about the subject and to keep our eyes open when analyzing representations because what we see in them is almost as important as what is left out (p. 59).

According to Hall (1997a), those "who are in any way significantly different from the majority—'them' rather than 'us'—are frequently exposed to [a] binary form of representation" (p. 229). Thus, they are "repelling" because they are "different," while at the same time "compelling" because they are "strange and exotic" (p. 229). These "sharply opposed, polarized, binary extremes… are often required to be both things at the same time" (p. 229). Furthermore, Hall posits that "Difference signifies. It 'speaks'" (p. 230). And it does so in ambivalent ways. On one hand, difference "can be positive" since it is necessary for "the production of meaning," "the formation of language and culture," for the creation of "social identities and a subjective sense of self as a sexed subject" (p. 238). At the same time difference can be "negative" and become "threatening," "a site of negative feelings," and "aggression towards the Other" (p. 238).

These binaries that Hall (1997a) addresses are also present in a "racialized discourse" which has historically opposed "civilization" in relation to Whiteness versus "savagery" in relation to Blackness (p. 243). Such discourses are then transcribed into the "racialized body," where "[t]he body itself and its differences were visible for all to see, and thus provided 'the incontrovertible evidence' for a naturalization of racial difference" (p. 244).

These tensions and binary representations can be found in political cartoons. The fact that stereotypes, which attempt to reduce and fix meaning, tend to be overt in caricatures is what makes political cartoons such an attractive site for the study of representations. While cartoons work as an editorial commentary which can work to criticize those in power, they rely in their capacity to tap into "the collective consciousness of readers," (DeSousa and Medhurst as cited in Edwards and Chen 2006: 369) so that instead of working as agents of change they become "a statement of consensus, an invitation to remember cultural values and beliefs and, by implication, to participate in their maintenance" (DeSousa and Medhurst as cited in Edwards and Chen 2006: 369).

Thus, when looking at political cartoons we find not only a political commentary that criticizes those in power, but the ways that a society feels about issues like gender, race and class. As Edwards (2001) reminds us, cartoonists have a "role as journalists and commentators" (p. 2141) something we should always keep in mind as "the amusement potential of editorial cartoons, as political satire, sometimes eclipses their discursive function in creating social reality" (p. 2141). We agree with Edwards' following argument: "Cartoons remain a potent vehicle for political information and analysis. Their typical position on the editorial pages of newspapers 'emphasizes their importance as cultural artifacts that speak with a civic voice and institutional legitimacy'" (Edwards 2009: 193). In addition, the shared group consciousness that cartoonists tap into, "frequently reveals thematic clustering of character representations and references on a given subject which can be appropriately examined as one collective 'text'" (Edwards and Chen 2006: 369).

It is with this framework of understanding cartoons and through the lens of Hall's theories that we seek to analyze the way cartoonists frame race when representing Condoleezza Rice. While some of them do in fact include exaggerations of racial features to represent her body, others seem to erase Blackness and represent Rice as if she was White perhaps in an attempt to appear "colorblind." In addition to looking at Rice's caricatured body, we will also expand the analysis to the stories being told in the cartoons. While most cartoons depicting Condoleezza Rice focus on her politics, there are some other narratives that refer to race as well. These narratives are better understood if we look at critical race theory, as well as concepts of colorblindness and enlightened racism, which are discussed in the next section.

Critical race theory

Critical race theory is a scholarly movement formed in the 1990s by progressive law scholars. It was born as a result of the limitations that they faced in the 1980s, when critical theory was usually separated from discussions on race (Crenshaw 2002). Legal scholars were "looking for both a critical space in which race was foregrounded and a race space where critical themes were central" (p. 19). These students of law were all academic figures of color, and contended that the law upheld certain privileges when it came to race, gender, and sexual orientation.

Critical race theory argues that the nature of race is socially constructed (Crenshaw, 1995; Delgado, 1995; Delgado and Stefancic 1993; Crenshaw 1991) and it calls for an intersectional approach in order to address race, gender, class, and sexuality According to Matsuda (1991) the space of critical race theory can be defined as:

the work of progressive legal scholars of color who are attempting to develop a jurisprudence that accounts for the role of racism in American law and that work toward the elimination of racism as part of a larger goal of eliminating all forms of subordination (p. 1331).

In this viewpoint, American institutions are equated with oppressive social structures. This group of scholars recognized the tyrannical nature of these structures and sought to terminate that which results in subordination. Moreover, they noted that racism does not stand alone and it intersects with other forms of oppression based on issues such as gender and class. These forms of oppression are illustrated through mediums of communication. Thus, the images that are produced through the various channels of the media, whether through television, radio, internet, and/or print, have implications and consequences in this society.

One of the topics addressed in this paper is the manner in which the media indirectly and directly assert Whiteness on Rice. Crenshaw's (1991) thoughts on critical race theory prove useful to analyze these assertions as she discusses the signifiers of Whiteness in legal terms.

White identity conferred tangible and economically valuable benefits, and it was jealously guarded as a valued possession, allowed only to those who met a strict standard of proof. Whiteness—the right to white identity as embraced by the law—is property if by "property" one means all of a person's legal rights (p. 280).

Such laws from the past advance an ideological proposition through subordination. These positions of subordination are examined in our study.

To engage in a serious discussion about race in the United States, we must also consider the "positive testimonials for a colorblind future" alongside "a still-lingering white supremacist past [...] Such a perspective will remind us that insistent proclamations of a new racial day sit uneasily next to patterns of inequality in the present, and not only in the past" (Roediger 2008: x). Racial inequality hardly belongs in the past when today a part of the population in the US still "desires to claim white identity and to defend the relative advantages attached to it" (Roediger 2008: 212). This is not so difficult to understand if we consider that Whites have "on average more than nine times the household wealth of African Americans and Latinos," or that for White men "incarceration rates [are] at less than one-seventh those of African American males" (Roediger 2008: 212).

In spite of this, discourses of colorblindness inundate the media, as it was evident during Barack Obama's campaign which, according to Roediger (2008) "forcefully" and "contradictorily" supported the idea that race is over in the US, as it has been "eliminated by symbolic advances, demographic change, and private choice, if not by structural transformations or political struggles" (p. 213). If uncontested, this idea can work in favor of practices which perpetuate racism. In the words of Gray (2004: xviii): "With the discourse of diversity, the marketing of blackness as an urban lifestyle, and the continued visibility of black images of middle-class success, one begins to sense the terms of a conservative bid for a post-civil rights color-blind America" (p. xviii).

In this vein Quist-Adade (2006) reminds us that "Racism in Euro-America today has ceased to be the overt, crude, 'in-your-face' form of racism of the past. The general consensus is that racism today is generally more subtle, sophisticated and covert" (p. 46). This practice, which he describes as "the benign, smiling face of racism" (pp. 46–7), is problematic because it "has made too many people of all complexions complacent" (p. 47). It seems that people are blind to racism today because they are content with what has been accomplished. Quist-Adade (2006) criticizes the fact that people confuse "improved race relations" (p. 47) with what he calls "tokenism," characterized by "the hiring of a handful of blacks for window-dressing by white employers" (p. 47) and explains:

> They take a few black men and women cracking through the glass ceiling or the appointment of such figures as Colin Powell and Condoleezza Rice to powerful government positions in the US, and the success and fabulous wealth of African-American entertainers and athletes... as clear indications of race relations having "improved vastly." The fact that racism has changed its appearance and form does not make it any better. Indeed, racism in its new garbs is even more insidious and treacherous. (p. 47).

Curiously, Quist-Adade's criticism resonates with Condoleezza Rice's discourse on race. When she was asked, in a 2005 interview by *Ebony* magazine about her "unique" contributions "as the first African-American female Secretary of State" ("Ebony interview" 2005: 196) she answered that her story was not unique, "it's an American story" (p. 196). Then, she referred to the fact that her generation grew up in segregation, "And you look at where people in my generation are. We've broken ceilings as CEOs and as presidents of universities and as Secretaries of State. It shows how change can happen, and how fast it can happen" (p. 196).

While Condoleezza Rice does not shy away from discussions of race, it seems like she is constantly attempting to "transcend" race in some way. Thus, she insists on the rewards of individual merit and on the fact that as a minority "You have to be twice as good" (Jackson 2002: para. 10). This discourse aligns with discussions on the new faces of racism, which can be linked to Jhally and Lewis's (1992) concept of "enlightened racism" (p. 93). These authors explain the following: "Racial discrimination... has usually been predicated on a series of perceived symbolic links between skin color and culture" (p. 95). However, the visibility of some successful Black individuals "against the odds, in a predominantly white environment," has made ideas of "biological determinism... decidedly less fashionable" (p. 96). Thus, as Quist-Adade (2006) also stated, racism, "as an instrument of repression... now takes more subtle forms" (Jhally and Lewis 1992: 96).

According to Jhally and Lewis (1992), "the principle of social mobility" (p. 96) has created the illusion that "we are only what we become" (p. 97) and thus reinforces racism, since it fails to understand the structural disadvantages of minorities. If Whites are more successful, the logic behind it is that they must be culturally superior (p. 97). The authors conclude:

> These beliefs lead to an attitude that separates blackness from the color that defines it. Blackness becomes a cultural notion associated with African Americans, but from a white perspective, not irredeemably so. It is the same perspective adopted by nineteenth century missionaries: blackness is seen as a condition from which black people can be liberated. (p. 97).

Williams (2008) proves helpful for understanding this idea of liberation or transcendence of race in Condoleezza Rice's case. According to Williams, Rice was:

> raised to "style" racial redemption by studying so hard in so many disciplines that no one could ever, ever challenge whether she was "intelligent enough" or "well-qualified." See her do a double axel in ice skates! Hear her play extremely difficult passages of Brahms! Good Lord, she speaks Russian! She's safely asexual! She's miraculous! (p. 2).

Williams explains that Rice's "credibility has always been dependent on modeling the most amazing departure from a welfare queen that anyone has ever met" (p. 2). It is within this framework that we can analyze the way that cartoonists talk about race in their representations of Condoleezza Rice, which is the following section of this paper. But first we will explain our method.

Method

In this chapter, we will utilize close textual analysis to identify and analyze the key themes in the selected political cartoons. Close textual analysis investigates the relationship between the internal workings of discourse and its context in order to discover what makes a particular text function persuasively. To a degree, close textual analysis, or "close reading," is a response to theoretical approaches to rhetorical criticism in the 1970s (Ehrenhaus 2001; Lucas 1990; Leff 1986; Leff and Mohrmann 1974). In other words, close textual analysis attempts to reveal the detailed, often concealed, tools that give a particular text, in this case political cartoons, artistic consistency and rhetorical effect. In this chapter, we use close textual analysis to examine how the powerful figure of Rice is addressed in relation to race; and secondly, to determine how these cartoons construct certain social realities about her.

Our research for the cartoons included in this chapter began on the web, mainly on sites that group the work of several caricaturists such as Daryl Cagle's Professional Cartoonist Index (http://www.cagle.com), About.com (http://political-humor.about.com/od/politicalcartoon) which has a cartoon section, and The Cartoonist Group (http://www.cartoonistgroup. com/). During this search we came across an internet magazine called *The Black Commentator*. We decided to include a selection of their political cartoons on Condoleezza Rice because they represent a particular point of view of the African American community. *The Black Commentator* describes itself as "an independent" online publication "dedicated to the movement for economic justice, social justice and peace" (The Black Commentator 2010) and claims to provide "commentary, analysis and investigations on issues affecting African Americans and the African world" (The Black Commentator 2010). Furthermore the four cartoons we decided to include from this site belong to the same caricaturist: Khalil Bendib, an Algerian American artist. His work brings in a different point of view from the vast majority of the cartoons that can be found online since most of the editorial cartoonists are White and male. Based on Bendib's background and the place where he published the cartoons included in this sample, we argue that he brings a different perspective on the way that Rice, a Black female politician, is represented. In addition to that, most of his cartoons revolve around race, and this makes them valuable artifacts for this study.

We also considered a group of blatantly racist caricatures by major editorial cartoonists that were not found on the online sites mentioned above, but which received attention in several blogs because of the way they depicted race. In total, we considered more than 100 cartoons on Condoleezza Rice; however, our close textual analysis concentrates on 11 of them which represent three large thematic clusters that we found after going through the material: the sexual fantasy, the Whiteness in Condoleezza Rice and finally the racist depictions of Blackness. It is important to note that a significant number of cartoons focused on criticizing Condoleezza Rice as they would any other political figure. Her facial features are exaggerated in a "safe" way, one that does not evidently emphasize any racial characteristics. We decided to leave those cartoons out of this analysis and focus on the ones that address race, gender or sexuality in any way, either by the way Rice's body is depicted—including the clothes that she is wearing, or the lack of clothes for that matter—or by the written text that contextualizes these images.

Once we focused on these cartoons, the classification or thematic clustering was given by the images themselves. Although the cartoons we include here on are not exhaustively representative of the universe of cartoons around Rice, we argue that they are emblematic and useful for understanding cultural assumptions around powerful Black women in the United States. We begin our analysis with representations that clearly emphasize Rice's sexuality.

Sexual fantasies of Condoleezza Rice

While Williams states that Condoleezza Rice has styled herself as asexual (2008), perhaps in an effort to minimize the "threat" perceived in Black sexuality, cartoonists cannot escape this commonplace and produce sexualized representations of her. This practice is not exclusive of representations of women of color; we would argue that it is a resource that is commonly used to minimize women in power, but in the case of a Black woman it acquires a different dimension. Here the work of Gilman (1992), who traces representations of Black sexuality in works of art that date back to the nineteenth century, must be noted. He argues that aesthetic images merged with a scientific discourse of White superiority, which had as a result the construction of Black sexuality in opposition to a White one where "the sexuality of the black, both male and female, becomes an icon for deviant sexuality in general" (p. 228). Black women were labeled "as more primitive, and therefore more sexually intensive" (p. 231).

These ideas of deviant sexuality and the threat that comes with them can be seen in the first cartoon (Jones 2008), where Condoleezza Rice resembles a dominatrix, as she sits on top of the world, legs crossed, wearing a black leather jacket, fishnet tights and high-heeled black boots. In her hand she holds a pair of handcuffs as she looks a little exasperated, perhaps waiting for her next victim. Her facial features are exaggerated in a way that makes her look masculine, reinforcing the idea of how rough she is. In addition, she is sitting on top of the world, perhaps ready to use her position as Secretary of State, to use the military and financial resources of the US to take over.

In the second cartoon (Matson 2005a) we are presented with a similar image. We can only see Rice from the waist up as she is wearing a revealing black corset. In this image Rice is more like a warrior, but a very sexy one; she is "Reelektra." And she looks ready to fight. But the cartoon suggests that she is not fighting for herself, as it tells us: "Between loyalty and the truth stands a warrior." Who is she loyal to? Not hard to infer that the man behind this sexy and exotic warrior, the man that she is fighting for, is her boss, president George W. Bush.[1]

The third cartoon (Matson, 2005b) shows a topless Condoleezza Rice in an "Official portrait of the Secretary of State's triumphant return to France." It is hard to imagine that even a cartoonist could get away with an image that reveals the breasts of the Secretary of State; however, Matson can do it because he is using Delacroix's iconic portrait of the French Revolution: *Liberty Guiding the People.* The cartoonist is using irony to criticize the policies of Secretary Rice, who was not precisely guiding the French to freedom. But political comment aside, he is also tapping into a sexual fantasy that involves a semi-naked Condoleezza Rice standing next to a small cowboy-dressed George W. Bush.[2]

OFFICIAL PORTRAIT OF THE SECRETARY OF STATE'S TRIUMPHANT RETURN TO FRANCE

Finally in the fourth cartoon, "Condoleezza the Gatekeeper" (Bendib 2003b), we see Secretaries Colin Powell, Donald Rumsfeld and Vice President Dick Cheney standing in line outside of the oval office, looking quite angry as they wait for the President to receive them. While they hold folders labeled as "urgent," "ASAP," and "most urgent," the door, which has a "do not disturb" sign hanging from it, opens up just a crack, so that Condoleezza Rice can poke her head out and announce: "Er, not now guys; the president is in the middle of a ... private conference!" The sexual hint is not just in Condoleezza's "er" or in the urgency that she has to get back to that "private conference," an urgency accentuated by the exclamation sign. She is also wearing "red" lipstick, her eyes are closed so that we can see her thick eyelashes and just in case there was a shadow of a doubt on her intentions, she is wearing heart-shaped earrings. In other words, she is dressed to seduce.

All of these cartoons show an anxiety about Condoleezza Rice's sexuality, an anxiety probably heightened by the fact that she is not married. Furthermore, Rice does not discuss her private life in public and because she is not an elected representative, the topic was never a campaign issue. Thus, her sexuality remains a mystery to us all. These cartoons highlight her sexual power, as well as speculate about the sexual ties that she may have to the former President Bush. Again we could think about these anxieties just in terms of the individual; however, there is a history of representations of Black sexuality that inevitably frames any reading of these images.

Condoleezza White?

The first three cartoons analyzed in this section were published in *The Black Commentator*, an online magazine dedicated to the discussion of issues related to African Americans. It is not surprising then to find that this group of cartoons criticizes Condoleezza Rice for being a traitor to her race,[3] an argument that could not be clearer than it is in the fifth cartoon, "The devil's handmaiden" (Bendib 2003a). This cartoon starts with an image that shows Condoleezza Rice climbing the ladder of "Affirmative Action" as she says "Being a Black person in this country is no picnic ..." A sign lets us know that this ladder climbing took place from the 1970s to the 1990s. The cartoon continues, and now Condoleezza is done climbing, she is at the top while she says "Believe me ... I used to be one!" And as she tells us how she *used* to be Black, she kicks the ladder of Affirmative Action so that no one else can climb it. The cartoon reinforces this transformation from Black to White through Condoleezza's clothes, which change throughout the three moments in her life. She is wearing informal jeans and a T-shirt as she is climbing the ladder, then a black dress when she is at the top, and an identical white one that marks her final transformation as she gets rid of affirmative action. This cartoon portrays several changes, from the style of her clothes, to the shift of her race. At the end, she embodies Whiteness and has *climbed* her way to the top. This may signify a dangerous precedent: to be successful in the United States, you need to transcend your body—if you're not White—and embody the White stereotype.

In the sixth cartoon (Bendib 2002) we see Black politicians being manufactured in a factory called "Neo-Black Politicos R-US." In the same manner that one would imagine mass produced toy soldiers that end up in a "Toys R-US" store, Bendib presents us with Clarence Thomas, Condoleezza Rice, Colin Powell and Cory Booker, all lined up, ready to hit numerous stores. This occurs in the background while two very excited White men in suits, representing "right wing foundations" have a happy conversation. One says: "They're so popular we can't produce them fast enough," and the other one exclaims "I hear they always sell out!" This cartoon accuses all of these "neo-Black" politicians of being traitors to their race, as it portrays them as toys that can be manufactured by White conservatives in order to be sold back to the population.

The seventh cartoon (Bendib 2003c) shows George W. Bush and his gang inside a bubble floating above an angry mob. We should note that Donald Rumsfeld and Dick Cheney are identified with signs which label them "Rummy" and "Dick," while Colin Powell and George W. Bush only require a "C" and a "W" printed in their arms. But Condoleezza Rice needs no labeling. Up there, inside the bubble, it seems like humans have gone back in the evolution chain, they have become Neanderthals who happen to be standing on the bones of what is left of Iraq and Afghanistan. George Bush notes that the mob below them looks like they are about to lynch them and says "I don't understand foreign that good, but I think they're all saying how great we are."

The main reason for choosing this cartoon is because it illustrated an article titled "Blind, deaf, dumb and deluded: White America unfit for global role" (2003), which discussed how "the majority of the white people of America" have become "so alienated from the rest of humanity that they represent a collective threat to the survival of the species" (para. 1). It is interesting that two African Americans, Rice and Powell, are among those who represent "the white people of America." Once again, we note that the race of these two African American figures is reversed; their ethnicity is not only erased, but they become White in the eyes of this cartoonist, just like they did for comedian Dave Chapelle in his racial draft.

These three cartoons point out to the topics exposed by theories of new racism. They could be used to illustrate Quist-Adade's (2008) discussion of tokenism, for example. The cartoons reveal the politics behind the success of a particular kind of Black politician. Such advancements by Rice, these cartoons argue, serve the interests of the White right wing. Jhally and Lewis's (1992) discussion of enlightened racism is also present in these cartoons, specifically in "The Devil's Handmaiden," where Bendib illustrates how Rice transcended Blackness and found success by embracing and embodying Whiteness.

The last two cartoons of this section (Marguiles 2004; Telnaes 2006) question Rice's politics. They are not related to race in their criticism but we include them here because in both images Condoleezza Rice looks almost White. If we were not previously aware that these were representations of the former Secretary of State, we might not even recognize her, and perhaps not even identify the woman in the cartoons as Black. We cannot determine if the Whiteness of Rice in these cartoons is intentional or not. Are the cartoonists perceiving Rice as White in a similar way as the previous cartoonist did? Or are they just avoiding racial representations? Even when it is not clear if these cartoons are a subtle critique of colorblindness or a product of it, we believe that they are worth noting as a part of the larger "collective text."

Blunt racism in cartoons of Condoleezza Rice

Finally, we want to include here cartoons that are blatantly racist. Most of the political caricatures produced in the United States do not fit in this category, at least not in "serious" publications or in the so-called "liberal media." Racism, as some of the authors that we reviewed previously point out, has become more subtle. But even in an era of political correctness, racist images pop up and remind us that we are not living in that post-racial moment that some claim. We should also state that the publication of these cartoons did not go unnoticed, and that they were criticized in several websites and blogs on the internet.

In "Condoleezza Rice in the role of a lifetime," our tenth cartoon (Ramblings' Journal 2004) Dazinger depicts Rice as Prissy, the Black female servant from *Gone With the Wind*. In this cartoon Rice sits barefoot on a rocking chair while feeding a bottle to a "baby" aluminum tube. In the cartoon Rice uses African American vernacular English or ebonics as she says: "I knows all about aluminum tubes (correction) I don't know nuthin' about alumnum tubes." Dazinger claimed that his cartoon was not racist, a claim that is hard to sustain when he is using an old racial stereotype of servitude alongside a language that belongs to African Americans, and that in this cartoon is being used to ridicule a Black woman.

Lastly, the eleventh cartoon (Ampersand, 2004) by Oliphant provides an excellent example of the practices of representation of difference addressed by Hall (1997a). In this cartoon Oliphant depicts Condoleezza Rice as a parrot. However this is not a regular parrot but a racialized one, as the cartoonist chose to use the stereotype of the large Black lips to clearly mark Rice's racial "difference." To hear a parrot talking back to its owner, in this case its chief—"ok chief! Anything you say chief! You bet chief! You're my hero chief!"—could be considered "innocent," but if you add the lips, then the idea of a White master-Black servant relationship also hovers around the interpretation of the cartoon. The power relations are very obvious here: the White male, former US President George W. Bush, owns his female African American slave, Rice. Furthermore, this representation can be linked back to Crenshaw's (1991) understanding of Whiteness within critical race theory, where Whiteness connotes property and individual rights through subordination.

Racializing Rice

This chapter analyzed how race was framed in the representations of Condoleezza Rice in the world of cartoons. This discussion is useful as it shows how race intersects with issues of class, sexuality and gender, as seen in the first cluster of cartoons, which show that women in power today cannot avoid being reduced and represented in terms of their sexuality. In this sense, these cartoons highlight how high-powered women are perceived and the trials that they face as they advance in their careers. Furthermore, through close examination representations of Rice reveal another dimension due to her *raced sexuality*, which is accentuated in some of these cartoons. These images are examples of the exoticizing of the "Other," sometimes through the exaggeration of certain features that carry racial connotations, such as the large lips. These physical traits are what make these particular cartoons part of a larger rhetoric of racism.

Some of the cartoons previously analyzed also suggest sexual ties between Rice and White male politicians, specifically George W. Bush. Under this logic, these sexualized and racialized representations suggest on the one hand that Rice was not qualified for the positions that she occupied in Bush's government. In other words, these cartoons seem to argue that her presumed sexual prowess and favors toward her boss were what qualified her for the job. On the other hand, as accomplished as Rice is, the cartoons undermine her power by showing a woman who has no agency and acts as the slave of the wishes and commands of her boss, the President. Thus, according to these cartoons, Rice has no rightful power of her own and is under the domination of (White and male) others; her power resides in her ability to manipulate them.

In terms of the intersection between race and class some cartoons highlight how Rice is perceived to embody Whiteness due to her career and her politics. The cartoons reveal racial tensions; the dispute over whether Rice is Black enough or not reveals a more complex politics surrounding new forms of racism. Due to her high-ranking position in government, as well as the politics she defended and embodied, she was no longer viewed as African American, but as White. As a result, these cartoons address racial tensions, as well as the questions that non-White political figures may face. In other words, Condoleezza Rice, along with Colin Powell, is viewed as not being Black enough due to their political positions and possibly their political ideologies.

The tensions found in these cartoons are not new and while some would like to see clear alignments between a race and a party, the reality is more complicated than that. Furthermore, the parties have shifted over time and former racially liberal parties have now perhaps become the more racially conservative and vice versa. To illustrate this, we may consider the declarations of nineteenth century African American abolitionist Frederick Douglas, who stated: "I am Republican, a black, dyed in the wool Republican, and I never intend to belong to any other than the party of freedom and progress"

(Platt, 1989, p. 300). He believed that this conservative party would best assist African Americans in their quest for political integration. Rice and Powell seem to carry the same beliefs today, and if we follow *The Washington Post* (O'Keefe 2007: para. 1) that argues that African Americans "hold fairly conservative views," then the association between Black politicians and the Republican Party should come as no surprise. But this position clashes with others such as that of former President Nixon, who once described the Democratic Party as " the party of blacks" (O'Reilly 1995: 351); or that of the infamous rapper Kanye West who accused President George W. Bush of not caring about Blacks during the Hurricane Katrina catastrophe. Additionally, if African Americans are as conservative as *The Washington Post* claims, why do they significantly vote Democrat in most elections? And how could we explain that the first African American President came from the Democratic Party? These cartoons confront underlying themes not only of race—and in Rice's case, of gender as well—but also of political alignment among Blacks.

This study on cartoons demonstrates that racism continues to be part of the repertoire of shared meanings that cartoonists share with the society that they live in. These images provide valuable information about racism, sexism, and also about the racial tensions that take place in US politics. As critics we must dissect such features of cartoons, as well as their discourse, in order to understand race relations in the United States.

References

Ampersand (2004, November 20), "Racist cartoons of Condoleezza Rice?" *Alas, A Blog* [blog]. Retrieved from: http://www.amptoons.com/blog/2004/11/20/racist-cartoons-of-condoleezza-rice/.

Bendib, K. (2002, April 5), "Neo black politicos Я-US" [cartoon]. *The Black Commentator*. Retrieved from: http://www.blackcommentator.com/cartoons_black_politicos_r_us.html.

—(2003a, January 30), "The devil's handmaiden" [cartoon]. *The Black Commentator*. Retrieved from: http://www.blackcommentator.com/27/27_cartoons.html.

—(2003b, April 24), "Condoleezza the gatekeeper" [cartoon]. *The Black Commentator*. Retrieved from: http://www.blackcommentator.com/39/39_cartoons.html.

—(2003c, June 26), "Bubble USA" [cartoon]. *The Black Commentator*. Retrieved from: http://www.blackcommentator.com/48/48_cartoons.html.

"Blind, deaf, dumb and deluded: White America unfit for global role". (2003, June 26), The *Black Commentator*. Retrieved from: http://www.blackcommentator.com/48/48_bubble.html.

"Condoleezza Rice: The devil's handmaiden". (2003, January 23), *The Black Commentator*. Retrieved from: http://www.blackcommentator.com/26/26_commentary.html.

Crenshaw, K. (1991), "Mapping the margins: Intersectionality, identity politics, and violence against women of color". *Stanford Law Review*, 43, 1241–99.

—(2002), "The first decade: Critical reflections, or 'a foot in the closing door'", in F. Valdes, J. McCristal Cup and A. Harris (eds). *Crossroads, Directions and a New Critical Race Theory*. Philadelphia, PA: Temple University Press, pp. 9–31.

Crenshaw, K., Gotanda, N., and Peller, G. (eds) (1995), *Critical Race Theory: The Key Writings That Formed the Movement*. New York: The New Press.

Delgado, R. (1995), *Critical Race Theory: The Cutting Edge*. Philadelphia, PA: Temple University Press.

Delgado, R. and Stefancic, J. (1993), "Critical race theory: An annotated bibliography". *Virginia Law Review*, 79, 461–516.

"Ebony interview with Secretary of State Condoleezza Rice". (2005, November), *Ebony*, 61, (1), 194–200.

Edwards, J. (2001), "Running in the shadows in campaign 2000: Candidate metaphors in editorial cartoons". *American Behavioral Scientist*, 44, 2140–51.

—(2009), "Presidential campaign cartoons and political authenticity: Visual reflections in 2008", in R. E. Denton (ed.), *The 2008 Presidential Campaign: A Communication Perspective*. Lanham, MD: Rowman and Littlefield.

Edwards, J. and Chen, H. (2006), "The first lady/first wife in editorial cartoons: Rhetorical visions through gendered lenses". *Women's Studies in Communication*, 23, (3), 367–91.

Ehrenhaus, P. (2001), "Why we fought: Holocaust memory in Spielberg's *Saving Private Ryan*". *Critical Studies in Media Communication*, 18, (3), 321–37.

Gilman, S. (1992), "Black bodies, White bodies: Toward an iconography of female sexuality in late nineteenth century art, medicine and literature", in H. L. Gates Jr (ed.), "*Race*," *Writing and Difference*. Chicago: University of Chicago Press.

Gray, H. (2004), *Watching Race Television and the Struggle of Blackness*. Minneapolis, MN: University of Minnesota Press.

Hall, S. (1997a), "The spectacle of the 'Other'", in *Representation: Cultural Representations and Signifying Practices*. Thousand Oaks, CA: Sage Publishing, pp. 223–79.

—(1997b), "The work of representation", in *Representation: Cultural Representations and Signifying Practices*. Thousand Oaks, CA: Sage Publishing, pp. 13–64.

Hart, R. and Daughton, S. (2005), *Modern Rhetorical Criticism* (3rd edn). Boston, MA: Pearson Education.

Jackson, D. Z. (2002, November 20), "A lesson from Condoleezza Rice". *Racematters.org*. Retrieved from: http://www.racematters.org/lessononlifecondoleezzarice.htm.

Jhally, S. and Lewis, J. (1992), *Enlightened Racism: The Cosby Show, Audiences and the Myth of the American Dream*. Boulder, CO: Westview Press.

Jones, T. (2008, January 29), "Condoleezza Rice" [cartoon]. *Daryl Cagle's PoliticalCartoons.com Store*. Retrieved from: http://www.politicalcartoons.com/cartoon/53bda5ac-f9c1-4ac6-88f8-a40de6cb5cf7.html.

Leff, M. (1986), "Textual criticism: The legacy of G. P. Mohrmann". *Quarterly Journal of Speech*, 72, 377–89.

Leff, M. and Mohrmann, G. P. (1974), "Lincoln at Cooper Union: A rhetorical analysis of the text". *Quarterly Journal of Speech*, 60, 346–58.

Lucas, S. E. (1990), "The stylistic artistry of the Declaration of Independence". *Prologue: Quarterly of the National Archives*, 22, 25–43.

Marguiles, J. (2004), *Daryl Cagle's Political Cartoonists Index*. Retrieved from: http://list.cagle.com/etoon.aspx?cartoon=/news/Rice-9-11/0406l_margulies-1.gif.

Matson, R. J. (2005a, January 18), "Condoleezza Rice is a loyal warrior for President Bush" [cartoon]. *Daryl Dagle's Political Cartoons.Com Store*. Retrieved from: http://www.politicalcartoons.com/cartoon/5fed7249-397c-43b5-8097-2d53b9708ffb.html.

—(2005b, February 15), "Condoleezza Rice makes a triumphant return to France". *Daryl Dagle's Political Cartoons.com Store*. Retrieved from: http://www.politicalcartoons.com/cartoon/0be7e886-a039-4346-bc60-da01920544e0.html.

Matsuda, M. (1991), "Voices of America: Accent, antidiscrimination law and a jurisprudence for the last reconstruction". *Yale Law Journal*, 100, 1329–1407.

O'Keefe, E (2007, November 28), "Why Don't Black People Vote Republican?". *The Washington Post*. Retrieved from: http://voices.washingtonpost.com/channel-08/2007/11/question_29_why_dont_black_peo.html.

O'Reilly, K. (1995), *Nixon's Piano: Presidents and Racial Politics from Washington to Clinton*. New York: Free Press.

Platt, S. (ed.) (1989), *Respectfully Quoted: A Dictionary of Quotations Requested from the Congressional Research Service*. Washington, DC: Library of Congress.

Quist-Adade, C. (2006), "What is 'race' and what is 'racism'?". *New African*, 450, 46–9.

Ramblings' Journal. (2004, October 12), "You remember the Ted Rall debacle this summer. Now comes yet another one" [Web log post]. Retrieved from http://mhking.mu.nu/archives/049887.php.

Roediger, D. (2008), *How Race Survived U.S. History: From Settlement and Slavery to the Obama Phenomenon*. New York, NY: Verso.

Serafin, T. (2005, July 29), "The 100 most powerful women". *Forbes*. Retrieved from: http://www.forbes.com/lists/2005/11/MTNG.html.

Telnaes, A. (2006), "Energy policy" [cartoon]. *Ann Telnaes' Editorial Cartoons*. Retrieved from: http://www.cartoonistgroup.com/store/add.php?iid=37536.

The Black Commentator (2010), Retrieved from: http://www.blackcommentator.com/

"The racial draft". (2004, January 21), *Dave Chappelle Show*. Retrieved from: http://www.comedycentral.com/video-clips/b224ei/chappelle-s-show-the-racial-draft.

Williams, A. (2007, February 22), "Condoleezza Rice is an inspiration to us all". *Newsmax.com*. Retrieved from: http://archive.newsmax.com/archives/articles/2007/2/22/111813.shtml.

Williams, P. (2008, October 9), "The politics of Michelle Obama's hair". *The Daily Beast*. Retrieved from: http://www.thedailybeast.com/blogs-and-stories/2008-10-09/the-politics-of-michelle-obamas-hair.

Notes

1　© R. J. Matson, *New York Observer*, 2005. Reprinted with permission.

2　© R. J. Matson, *New York Observer*, 2005. Reprinted with permission.

3 All of these cartoons were drawn by the same artist, Algerian American Khalil Bendib. We only discuss three of them in this section, although we have eight in the larger sample. It is interesting to mention that although Bendib's work focuses on politics, he also recurs to the exploitation of the sexual fantasy in his cartoon *Condoleezza The Gatekeeper* (cartoon 4). It seems that when there is no clear political critique, a woman's sexuality can always give cartoonists a pretext to construct one.

PART THREE

Comics as political commentary

11

"There's a Revolutionary Messiah in Our Mist": A pentadic analysis of *Birth of a Nation*: A comic novel

Carlos D. Morrison and Ronald L. Jackson II

Introduction

African American artists have often found a variety of mediums or outlets in which to provide social, historical and political commentary on the issues affecting their communities. Jackie Ormes, the first African American woman cartoonist, introduced the comic strip *Torchy Brown* in 1937 to African American readers, particularly Black women. In the strip, "Torchy was an intelligent, self-reliant Black career woman, whose stories showed her fighting racism, sex discrimination, and environmental hazards (Strömberg 2003: 109). Tom Feelings created a strip for the *New York Age* in 1958 entitled *Tommy Traveller in the World of Negro History* where the main character "traveled" back in time and ended up in Black American history (p. 115).

Moreover, the importance of Black history was further conveyed in a graphic novel entitled *Still I Rise A Cartoon History of African Americans* written by Roland Owen Laird, Jr and illustrated by Elihu "Adofo" Bey in 1997. The novel was an illustrated history of Black people in America that chronicled their trials, tribulations, and struggles. And finally, Aaron McGruder unleashed upon the world his groundbreaking comic strip entitled *The Boondocks*. The strip featured Huey and Riley Freeman, who lived with their granddad out in the "boondocks" of predominated white Woodcrest where they "engage the issues of the day:" racism, racial identity, and media exploitation.

In addition to *The Boondocks*, Aaron McGruder, along with Reginald Hudlin and illustrator Kyle Baker (here after McGruder et al.), created a graphic novel, entitled *Birth of a Nation: A Comic Novel* (here after *Birth of a Nation*) that addressed issues of racism, political disenfranchisement, and Black nationalism. The question we raise about the text is this: What was McGruder et al.'s motive for producing the novel? What situation(s) did their motive "size up" or name? This essay is a pentadic analysis of the *Birth of a Nation* text. There will first be a review of literature followed by a discussion of dramatism as method. The analysis of the novel then follows.

Comic books—the literature

Within the last 25 years, academics have critically examined comic books, comic strips (Turner 1977), cartoons, and recently graphic novels as a serious art form (McCloud 1993). The works by literary, cultural and communication studies scholars has increased our understanding of the influence of comic book and comic book culture. Some students of literary and cultural studies focus their analysis of comic books on the "text as literature" and on the revision of comic book characters (Wandtke 2007; Heer and Worcester 2004; Pearson and Uricchio, 1991). However, other scholars focus their analysis on culture (Inge 1990), power (Duncan and Smith 2009), fandom (Pustz 1999), censorship (Nyberg 1988), ideology, (McAllister et al. 2001; DiPaolo 2011), audience reception (Cornwell and Orbe 2002), African American cartoonists, Black superheroes, and Black images (Jennings and Duffy 2010; Goldstein 2008; Foster 2005; Strömberg 2003; Brown 2001).

Our study of *Birth of a Nation* adds to the literature by addressing two important issues: (1) the need to focus the analysis on an "African American graphic novel" (Chaney 2009) and (2) the need for *a rhetorical analysis of the novel* using Kenneth Burke's dramatistic pentad as a critical method. While most studies of sequential art tend to focus on comic books, comic strips, and comic-related movie images, our study will shift focus to the graphic novel. Tabachnick (2009) defines a graphic novel as "an extended comic book that treats nonfictional as well as fictional plots and themes with the depth and subtlety that we have come to expect of traditional novels and extended nonfictional texts" (p. 2).

Birth of a Nation—the text

Birth of a Nation is a work of literary and political satire that is a recreation, within the context of sequential art, of the 2000 presidential election. The story is about Fred Fredericks and the residents of East St Louis, Illinois or "East Boogie" who, as a result of being "dissed" and disfranchised by federal authorities at the polling place on Election Day, decides to separate from the Union and form their own independent homeland called the "Republic of the Blacklands." The residents soon develop feelings of nationalism as they rally together to develop a "Black bank," a Black liberation flag (with a picture of Jesus in the center), and a song entitled "Blacklands" (sung to the tune of *Goodtimes*, i.e. *"Ain't we lucky we got it! Blacklaaaaaaad"*).

However, their "new nation" does not go unnoticed, particularly by the federal government. The Caldwell administration, which consists of President Caldwell (President George W. Bush), Secretary of State Colin "Jack" Powell, Advisor Condoleezza "Condice" Rice and Vice-President Dick "Richard" Cheney, seeks to force Fredericks and the residents to return to the Union by "any means necessary." Despite the government's use of harassment, assassination, and "divide and conquer" tactics, as well as the internal struggles taking place within the "new nation," Fredericks and his followers "stay the course" which, in the end, leads to the signing of the "US–Blackland Treaty."

As suggested earlier, *Birth of a Nation* is a graphic novel worthy of study and analysis. In addition to the Afrocentric orientation, i.e. Black protest theme, characters, etc. of the novel, the story is driven by a powerful dramatic narrative. It is a narrative equipped with "actors" fit for a play. For that reason, our discussion turns now to our critical method, the dramatistic pentad.

Dramatistic pentad—the method

The method that Burke (1969) develops for analyzing the use of language in human motivation is called a "pentadic analysis". "Burke argues that when people explain the world to themselves and thus formulate motives for acting in the world, they do so by anchoring their explanation in one or a combination (a ratio) of five basic terms, which he called the pentad (Brummett 2011: 193). The five terms that constitute Burke's "grammar of motives" are: agent, act, agency, scene and purpose. Burke (1969) says the following:

> In a rounded statement about motives, you must have some word that names the *act* (names what took place, in thought or deed), and another that names the *scene* (the background of the act, the situation in which it

occurred); also, you must indicate what person or kind of person (*agent*) performed the act, what means or instruments he used (*agency*), and the *purpose*. (p. xv).

To make Burke's "grammar of motives" more "user-friendly" for the rhetoric critic, Foss (1996) provides a more systematic and methodological approach to pentadic criticism. The procedures for conducting a pentadic analysis are a three-step process. According to Foss, the critic, in analyzing the artifact (i.e. graphic novel, *Birth of a Nation*) does the following: (1) label, identify and describes the five dramatistic terms, (2) identify the dominant term or set of terms in the text, and (3) name the rhetor's motive.

We believe that Burke's pentad is an appropriate method for analyzing the graphic novel *Birth of a Nation* for three reasons. First, both the method and the text place an emphasis on drama. There are heroes (Fredericks) and villains (President Caldwell) and a plot that takes a "good versus evil" form that is fertile ground for a pentadic critique. Secondly, the method would be appropriate for analyzing the actual sequential art (pictures) aspect of the text as a language system. And finally, the method has not been applied to an analysis of the text based on our review of the literature. We will now apply such a method in the next section.

The analysis: Labeling the terms

As suggested earlier, the first step in conducting a pentadic analysis is to identify the five elements of the pentad in the rhetorical artifact from the vantage point of the rhetor (Foss 1996). Here, the terms are presented as a sort of "dramatistic roadmap" for further purposes of analysis. In our study, McGruder et al. are the rhetors who use the graphic novel form as the medium through which they establish comedic drama in the text. In the novel *Birth of a Nation*, we have identified the following dramatistic elements:

Agent   (Fred Fredericks, energetic mayor of East St. Louis and later president of The Blacklands)

Act   (Secession, the creation of the Republic of the Blacklands, leaving the Union)

Agency   (The Declaration of Independence)

Scene   (East St Louis, Illinois, a city of decay, destitute, and the downtrodden)

Purpose   (Self determination, freedom and independence)

Description of the terms

In *Birth of a Nation,* McGruder et al.'s (2004) main character or protagonist is Fred Fredericks; while there are several characters who could be potential agents, Fredericks is the main *agent* in the novel. Fredericks, who is mayor of East St Louis, Illinois, can best be described as a young, energetic, and optimistic "agent for change." He is a thoughtful and caring politician who is committed to his predominate Black constituents of East St Louis. On one occasion in the story, Mayor Fredericks, as a result of a city-wide garbage strike, uses his car to pick up the trash and garbage for the elderly in the community.

Nevertheless, while Fredericks engages in a variety of acts ranging from collecting the garbage of the elderly to giving political speeches to motivate the masses to action, the most significant act that McGruder et al.'s character carries out is the *act of secession and the creation of a new Black nation or homeland.* As a result of the disenfranchisement of East St Louis residents at the ballot box and the subsequent Republican victory, Fredericks gives the following statement to the media and the citizens of East St Louis:

> I do hereby dissolve all political bonds between the city of East St. Louis and the government of the United States of America. We will create a new nation and chart our own destiny, as the forefathers of this country did when their freedom was threatened. And history will say America never forgot the true meaning of liberty. Thank you (McGruder et al. 2004: 34).

In addition to the act, the *purpose* is another dramatistic concept. The purpose is the reason for the action or the end goal of the action (Hauser, 1986). For Fredericks and the citizens of East St Louis, the major purpose of the act of separation was the right to engage in self-determination and be independently free from government tyranny in the polling place and beyond.

Clearly, Fredericks' act of separation was grounded in the Declaration of Independence (agency). His appeal to the "forefathers of [America]" and the "true meaning of liberty" are the "ideological nuggets" that form the substance for the need for separation and independence in East St Louis (the *scene*).

From "East Boogie" to "The Blacklands"— the scene

The setting or scene depicted in *Birth of a Nation* is the city *of East St Louis, Illinois*. The city is shown as one of the most impoverished communities in Illinois that has suffered a substantial loss in population. The decline of industrial activity has brought about widespread unemployment for those who remain. The city is de facto segregated with a large African American population. Moreover, "East Boogie" is the name of the predominated Black community in East St Louis. "East Boogie" is also consistently ranked among the most crime-ridden cities in the nation according to the text.

Nevertheless, despite poverty, unemployment, and crime that is affecting the city, residents of East St Louis are gearing up for the upcoming presidential race with the hopes of electing a president who will work to change the hardships faced by the residents of "East Boogie." The mayor of East St Louis, Fred Fredericks is rallying the Black community together to vote for Vice-President Holden. Casting a vote for Holden is casting a vote against Texas Governor Caldwell who is the favorite to win the election. As residents, i.e. shop keepers, ministers, postal workers, and the elderly converge on Martin Luther King, Jr Elementary School to exercise their right to vote, they are confronted with some disturbing news from poll officials—A substantial number of residents, all Black and including Mayor Fredericks, are barred from voting because they are thought to be felons. A melee brakes out between the sheriffs and residents leading to the arrest of the mayor.

In the end, 1,023 Black residents, who had never committed a crime, were purged from the voting rolls. With the presidential election being decided by a single state, i.e. Illinois, this voting faux pas on the part of the Illinois government made it possible for Texas Governor Caldwell to win after three recounts of the votes. The Supreme Court reaffirmed the lower court's decision.

As suggested earlier, the rhetorical critic is charged first with the responsibility of labeling and describing, and interpreting the five basic elements of the pentad. McGruder et al. uses the characters, in the graphic novel, to convey an important dramatic narrative. The narrative is as follows: as a result of being *intentionally* disenfranchised at the polling place in East St Louis (scene), Fred Fredericks (agent) "calls" for the citizens of East St Louis to "secede from the Union" (act) in order to invoke in the Black citizens of East St. Louis the need for self-determination, independence, and freedom from political oppression (purpose) as guaranteed by the Framers in the Declaration of Independence (agency).

Labeling the terms

In addition to the above set of terms, there is also a second set of dramatistic elements in the story. These elements are, to a greater extent, in opposition to the first cluster of terms. And as a result, these terms serve as the "fuel" that moves the overall narrative along. The following "oppositional terms" in the story are:

Agent(s)   (Secretary of State Colin "Jack" Powell, and Vice-President Dick "Richard" Cheney, Advisor Condoleezza "Condice" Rice and President Caldwell (George W. Bush)

Act   (Return East St. Louis to the Union)

Agency   (Government and military authority, strategies and tactics, harassment, suppression of financial means, etc.)

Scene   (The Oval Office at the White House)

Purpose   (To maintain the credibility of the Caldwell Administration, The Republican Party, and to preserve the Union)

Description of the terms

In *Birth of a Nation*, McGruder et al. (2004) introduce a very familiar group of agents or "politicos of power" in the story. One of the characters who immediately stands out (literally) is President Caldwell. Kyle Baker's artistic talent shines through as he draws Caldwell in the striking image of former President George W. Bush. President Caldwell, throughout the novel, spends most of his time relinquishing his ability to think and make decisions to Secretary of State Colin "Jack" Powell, Advisor Condoleezza "Condice" Rice and Vice-President Dick "Richard" Cheney. Moreover, when President Caldwell makes an attempt to "think and speak at the same time," he substitutes the wrong word or phrase while making his statement. For example, in response to Colin "Jack" Powell suggesting that military intervention into East St Louis would cast the administration in a bad light, President Caldwell says to the General, "You're saying we don't want to *screw* [my italics, i.e. shoot] ourselves in the foot" (McGruder et al. 2004: 38). And when the administration was unsuccessful in "freezing" the monetary assets of East St. Louis' major financial backer, John Roberts, President Caldwell said the following to his political high command, "Gentlemen, please! Now is the time for a new plan. Only together will we triumph over *diversity* [my italics, i.e. adversity]" (p. 63).

Clearly, McGruder et al. were using their character's speech behavior as a way to bring attention to President George W. Bush's misuse of the English language during his public speeches. President Bush was known for using malapropisms, spoonerisms, and unconventional words and phrases in his political rhetoric, which is known in the literary circles as *Bushism.* The use of Caldwell's malapropisms are important for at least three reasons: (1) first, the use of the malapropisms by President Caldwell help the reader(s) to further identify Caldwell with President George W. Bush and not his father, H. W. Bush, (2) the use of malapropisms by Caldwell provides *comic relief* in the novel, and (3) President Caldwell's use of the malapropisms serve to under-score his lack of intelligence and credibility. However, in the final analysis, McGruder et al. have created a character who, while lacking intelligence and credibility, has a tremendous amount of influence and power beyond the Oval Office; he has power and influence that will be felt in the "Republic of the Blacklands."

In addition to President Caldwell, there is Vice-President Dick ("Richard") Cheney. Once again, Baker's artistic talents capture Cheney's likeness making him very recognizable to the reader. In the story, Richard is portrayed as a conservative "hard-liner" or even an extremist. In response to hearing that East St Louis has seceded from the Union, Richard, with a clinched fist and an angry grimace on his face, says the following to President Caldwell and his executive staff in the Oval Office, "I say we hang every last one of those treasonous bastards!" (p. 37). Moreover, in response to the administration inability to cut off the flow of financial support to East St Louis, Richard says to President Caldwell, "I also think we need to get the CIA in on this. They have a plan that I think will work" (p. 63).

The plan of the CIA "black ops" is a "divide and conquer" strategy whereby the CIA is able to get President Fredericks' military to turn against him by "planting" "seeds of doubt" in the mind of General Roscoe. The bait that the CIA uses is that President Fredericks is "holding out" on the amount of money the bank is accumulating. And when President Fredericks says "No!" to General Roscoe's monetary demands, the General and his men try to assassinate President Fredericks at City Hall. However, their plan is foiled when the General and his henchmen are killed by a crashing jet towards the end of the story.

It is clear from the story that Dick "Richard" Cheney and President Caldwell, coupled with the CIA, are the "masterminds" behind such a plot. When Secretary of State Jack Powell asks Richard, "What is the CIA plan?" Richard's response is "That's need-to-know information" (p. 87). President Caldwell chimes in with the following statement, "A plan that's worked in more than one African nation" (p. 63). Given that the "real" Dick "Richard" Cheney, as Secretary of Defense under "Daddy" H. W. Bush, was one of the "masterminds" behind the use of economic sanctions and political pressure to oust Panama General Manuel Noriega, his actions in the novel are not too surprising. At least that is what McGruder et al. would have us think about the story.

While Dick "Richard" Cheney's character was an extremist in his approach in dealing with President Fredericks and the residents of the Republic of the Blacklands, both Secretary of State Colin "Jack" Powell and Advisor Condice Rice are characters that are portrayed as taking a more moderate wait and see approach to deal with President Fredericks, particularly Jack Powell After the secession of East St Louis from the Union, it is Jack Powell that convinces President Caldwell not to send in the National Guard to take control of the city. Jack believed that if any of the residents were to be harmed or killed as the result of an "invasion," the administration could possibly suffer repercussions. Jack says the following to the President, "Understand what's at stake, gentlemen. Maybe the country, but definitely this administration … And remember, this isn't a bunch of Branch Davidians in Waco. It's old black grandmothers who just wanted to vote. If people, anyone, started dying …" (p. 38). Again, Jack is a voice of reason that, in the end, influences President Caldwell to "hold off" on sending in the Guard, but only for a while.

Condice's character, on the other hand, is President Caldwell's advisor. In the story, she not only provides the President with Intel about East St Louis, Illinois, but she also "instructs" the President on his word usage by explaining to him the difference between the word "succeed" and "secede." Upon hearing that East St Louis has *seceded* from the Union, President Caldwell proclaims, "So, they succeeded?" (p. 36). Condice then points out to the President the following, "You're saying suc-ceed, with a hard 'C'—as in 'to achieve.' To leave the union is to se-CEDE. While they have apparently seceded, they have not necessarily succeeded in whatever … they hope to accomplish" (p. 37).

Both Condoleezza "Condice" Rice and Colin "Jack" Powell are clearly identified by Kyle Baker's artwork in the novel. Their names and likeness help to identify them to the novel's readers. More importantly however, Condice and Jack's characters are smart, yet cautious advisors who are trying to help the Caldwell administration to navigate a potential explosive situation with the "Republic of the Blacklands"-the force return of the residents of East St Louis to the Union.

McGruder et al.'s cast of "oppositional characters" have one major objective or act to perform in the graphic novel. That act is to *return East St Louis, Illinois to the Union*. The Caldwell administration has two perceptions concerning East St Louis' act of secession. The perception presented to the media by the administration is that the act of secession amounts to a "family disagreement" that will be worked "out as a family" (p. 40). This view is little more than an attempt by the administration to put a good "public relations spin" on the secession crisis so that the President and his administration will look good in the media and in the "eyes" of the American public. However, within the confines of the Oval Office (the scene), East St Louis' act of secession is viewed strongly, particularly by Dick "Richard" Cheney, President Caldwell, CIA, etc., as an act of treason that: (1) threatens the Union, (2) threatens the American mythology of "one nation under God, indivisible, with liberty and justice for all" and (3) threatens the credibility of the administration. As a result, East St Louis must be returned to the Union at all cost.

At this point, it is important for us to discuss scene, act, agency and purpose together. As suggested above, the Oval Office is the scene where the "politicos of power" exert their power, control and influence over both foreign and US domestic policy. It is the context where agents, i.e. President Caldwell, Dick "Richard" Cheney, Condoleezza "Condice" Rice and Colin "Jack" Powell make the "domestic decision" that the act of returning East St Louis to the Union is paramount to preserving the Union and national security (purpose). The Caldwell administration uses its government authority and military strategies as instrument (agency) to force Fredericks and the residents into compliance.

As suggested at the beginning of our discussion, the above dramatistic elements represent an "oppositional cluster" of terms in the story. Here, McGruder et al. provide an oppositional narrative that captures the perspective of the status quo in the novel. The opposing dramatistic narrative is as follows: the agents or "politicos of governmental power," i.e. President Caldwell, Dick "Richard" Cheney, Secretary of State Colin "Jack" Powell, and Advisor Condoleezza "Condice" Rice make the decision in the Oval Office (scene) to force East St Louis to return to the Union (act) through the use of governmental and military authority (agency) in an effort to maintain the credibility of the Republican Party and the Caldwell administration while preserving the Union (purpose).

Identification of dominant term(s)

After the terms have been labeled, described and analyzed, the critic, as suggested in the methods section, identifies the dominant term(s) in the rhetoric. Foss (1996) posits that the next step in a pentadic analysis "is to discover which of the five elements identified dominates the rhetoric or is featured by the rhetor. Discovery of the dominant term provides insight into what dimension of the situation the rhetor privileges or sees as most important" (pp. 459–60). After a critical examination of the various ratios, we have identified two dominant pentadic terms or ratios in the graphic novel: act-agent (protesters) and agency-purpose (establishment).

Secession as motivation: Fred Fredericks as "Messiah" (act-agent ratio)

In *Birth of a Nation*, McGruder et al. (2004) call our attention to the importance of Fred Fredericks and his political antics in the narrative. More specifically, McGruder et al. clearly identify the "perils of secession and the estab-lishment of the Republic of the Blacklands" as the dominating act in the graphic novel that transforms Fredericks' agent political life in a radical way. Throughout the story, Fredericks is an important symbol of the "messianic idiom" Asante (1987) or style in African American protest rhetoric. Moreover, *Fredericks as symbol of the messianic idiom is the strongest justification for the predominance of the act-agent ratio in the discourse amongst the protesters*; moreover, we are suggesting here that the *act (of secession and the creation of the Blacklands) transformed the agent (Fred Fredericks) into a "messiah" thus causing him to embracing a messianic style of leadership.* The messianic style is best describe as an individual who, empowered with a sense of mission and deliverance, moves to liberate a people from "strife" and/or "bondage."

Moreover, Fred Fredericks, John Roberts, the residents of "East Boogie" and others comprise what we call the "protest cluster" in the novel. In this "protest cluster," the main dramatistic ratio is act-agent. The act (of secession and the formation of the Republic of the Blacklands) is central to the *revolu-tionary situation* that defines the nature of the text. In the story, Fredericks (agent) is transformed from mild-mannered and politically astute Mayor Fredericks into a "revolutionary messiah" as a result of being transformed by his act of secession. In addition to Fredericks, the act also transforms the scene (*East St Louis*). Poverty-stricken "East Boogie" is transformed into the "Republic of the Blacklands" which suggests that the "act of secession" brings about both *transformation* and *liberation* in a people and in their environment.

Suppression as motivation: The government's assault on "East Boogie" (agency-purpose)

In addition to the act-agent ratio, there is also the *agency-purpose* ratio located in the text. In this "establishment cluster," the agency (government and military authority of the Caldwell administration, strategies, tactics) *influ-ences t*he purpose (maintain the credibility of the Caldwell administration, the Republican Party and to preserve the Union). Specifically, the "establishment cluster" is agency-centered.

First, it is important to say that Fredericks' act of secession was the *exigency* that caused government officials in the Caldwell administration to respond by developing a rhetoric of control. By rhetoric of control we mean the discursive and nondiscursive use of communication by the establishment (Caldwell administration) to thwart external attacks to its power or ideology (Bowers and Ochs 1971). As we suggested earlier in the essay, the act of secession was viewed by government officials, particularly Dick "Richard" Cheney, as an act of treason that not only threatened the credibility of the Caldwell Presidency, but also was a threat to the American mythology of a *United* States or "*union* of states." As a result, this act and the rebels (Fredericks, etc.) of East St Louis who brought it into existence had to be dealt with severely.

In order to carry out the act of returning East St Louis to the Union, the establishment relied on the *strategy of governmental and military authority.* Power, control and influence are brought to bear on the Black residents of "East Boogie" in order to bring them into compliance with the national government and more specifically, with the edicts of the Caldwell admin- istration. Moreover, the strategy of governmental and military authority is carried out in the novel through at least two tactics: (1) suppression of financial means, and (2) "divide and conquer." We define *suppression of financial means* as the *denial* of monetary gains, i.e. welfare or government checks by a governmental authority or entity. After President Fredericks announced that the residents of East St Louis would secede from the Union, Secretary of State Jack Powell suggests to the President that "the whole damn city is dependent on the government, whether it's a government job or a welfare check. Cut them off and in two weeks they go away for an apology ..." (p. 39).

And finally, the government uses the tactic of "divide and conquer" in an effort to get the "weakest link," i.e. General Roscoe in President Fredericks' "inner circle" to turn against him. The government knew that Roscoe's weakness was the issue of money given his background as a "street hustler" in "East Boogie." Moreover, had Roscoe and his henchmen assassinated Fredericks, the government would: (1) be exonerated of any wrongdoing concerning Fredericks' death, and (2) have ended the rebellion thus restoring the Union and the credibility of the administration.

The act (return East St Louis to the Union) and the *agency* (suppression of financial means, "divide and conquer") were all concocted by the "politicos of power" for one sole *purpose: to maintain the credibility of the Republican Party in general and the Caldwell administration specifically in light of the recent presidential election.* The "secession issue" and the fact that President Caldwel was never *elected* President create a credibility crisis for the Republican Party and the Caldwell administration. In speaking with Jack

Powell, President Caldwell says, "Actually, if you think about it ... [I wasn't] elected President! Get it ... cause I really didn't win the election, Remember, this is how this whole [secession] thing started ..." (pp. 86–7).

Writers Aaron McGruder, Reginald Hudlin, and illustrator Kyle Baker have produced a very funny, yet thought-provoking work in *Birth of Nation*. Following in the tradition of the cartoonists before them, McGruder et al. pointedly use the power of satire coupled with the graphic novel to address the hopes, fears, frustrations, and disappointments faced by African Americans as a result of the 2000 presidential election. While the satire is strong, the identification with realism associated with Baker's illustrations and McGruder and Hudlin's writings is even stronger. The images and the actions of Fred Fredericks, President Bush, Colin Powell, Condoleezza Rice and Dick Cheney in the text "ring true" with the readers, particularly with African American readers, who took part in the 2000 presidential election and watched their own hopes and aspirations for change go down the "political drain" after the election was "stolen" by President Bush as suggested in the text.

The rhetor's motive(s)

While identification, which is also an important concept in Kenneth Burke's theory of dramatism, is concerned with our ability to share substance (hopes, fears, etc.) with the text and as a result be persuaded by the text, it is Burke's pentad that addresses the use of language in determining a rhetor's "grammar of motives." In *Birth of a Nation,* we identified two dominant and important "grammar terms" or ratios in the graphic novel: *act-agent (protesters) and agency-purpose (establishment).* As we suggested in the analysis, the "act of secession and the establishment of the Republic of the Blackland" was the dominant *act* in the novel that transforms Fred Fredericks *(agent)* into a "messiah" and thus, a powerful leader of his people. This act-agent ratio is important for three reasons in the text. First, the act-agent ratio in the text "sizes up," or "names" a *situation of crisis (election fallout), revolution (the secession and the forming of the Blacklands), and tranquility (the forming of the US–Blackland Treaty).* Secondly, the act-agent ratio suggests that only a leader who is *transformed by his own act(ions) into a "messiah"* is capable of leading his people through such a situation or ordeal. And thirdly, the act-agency ratio, in the end, is a "self-discovery" ratio. The crisis situation (election fallout) allows Fredericks to come to the realization that while the establishment took away his right to cast his ballot (act of voting) and treated him like a second-class citizen (harassed and jailed), he could *secede* (act of secession) from that establishment and liberate "his people" by becoming their "messiah."

In addition to the act-agent ratio that defines the "protest cluster" of terms, there is also the agency-purpose ratio that defines the "establishment cluster" of terms in the text. In the "establishment cluster," the Caldwell administration relies on the strategy and tactics of government and military authority, i.e. a rhetoric of control (agency/means) as a *justification* for maintaining the credibility of the administration, the Republican Party and for preserving the Union (purpose/ends). The agency-purpose ratio is also important for three reasons in the text. First, the agency-purpose ratio "sizes up" or "names" a *situation of unbridled power and control* embraced by government officials in the Oval Office. As the rebellion progresses in the story, the administration uses various strategies and tactics with reckless abandon in order to *force* the "Republic of the Blacklands" to return to the Union. Secondly, the agency-purpose ratio suggests that a situation of unbridled power and control "sets the stage" for the development of a *Machiavellian persona* among establishment leaders. In an agency-purpose ratio, "the means justify the ends mantra" is a form of extreme pragmatism embraced and carried out by government officials. And finally, the agency-purpose ratio "names" in the end, the *unethical attitude* of the Caldwell administration. The government's use of control tactics coupled with a "touch of Machiavellianism" in a situation of unbridled power are all examples of unethical behavior "masking" as legitimate government directives.

The "Grand Motive" in *Birth of a Nation*

While the 2000 presidential election may have been the reason why McGruder, Hudlin and Baker created the novel *Birth of a Nation*, the 2000 presidential election was not their motivation for creating the work. McGruder et al.'s motive for producing *Birth of a Nation* was to *expose American hypocrisy*. Smith (1969) posits that one of the major recurring themes in the rhetoric of the Black Revolutionist is the idea that "America is a hypocritical country" (p. 50).

From a historical perspective, European Americans understand the meaning and significance of revolution. Two of the best historical examples are: the American Revolution and the Civil War. During the American Revolution, the 13 original colonies, as a result of being heavily taxed, banded together and revolted against the British Empire in order to gain their *independence.* Interestingly enough, British officials labeled the colonists "traitors." Moreover, during the "War Between the States," the Southern states *seceded* from the

"*Union* North" and formed the *Confederate States of America*. And once again, interestingly enough, North Whites at the time labeled the southern secessionists "traitors" and "rebels."

Our intention here is not a history lesson per se, but we want to show that, as we stated, White America has a point of reference for revolution; however, *the idea of revolution, as far a White America is concerned, does not apply to African Americans*—this is the central theme in *Birth of a Nation*. The three most important examples of this is: (1) the government's response to Fredericks' act of secession, (2) Cheney's "treasonous bastards" comment, and (3) in response to Fredericks' act of secession, a southern senator tells President Caldwell, "the good Christian people of Mississippi don't take too kindly to secession" (McGruder et al. 2004: 53).

Nevertheless, McGruder et al. tell us in the text that the act of secession and more importantly, the subsequent development of the "Republic of the Blacklands" is critically important for the former "residents" of East St Louis and for us, the readers of the text also. The survival of the "Republic of the Blacklands" is a significant motif in the text because it reaffirms for the reader the notion that the ideas expressed in the Declaration of Independence apply to African Americans. And we have a mild-mannered Fred Fredericks turned "revolutionary messiah" to thank.

References

Asante, M. (1987), *The Afrocentric Idea*. Philadelphia, PA: Temple University Press.

Benton, M. (1989), *The Comic Book in America: An Illustrated History*. Dallas, TX: Taylor Publishing Company.

—(1993), *Crime Comics: The Illustrated History*. Dallas, TX: Taylor Publishing Company.

Bowers, J. W. and Ochs, D. J. (1971), *The Rhetoric of Agitation and Control*. New York: Random House.

Brown, J. A. (2001), *Black Superheroes, Milestone Comics and Their Fans*. Jackson, MS: University of Mississippi.

Brummett, B. (2011), *Rhetoric in Popular Culture* (3rd edn). Los Angeles, CA: Sage.

Burke, K. (1969), *A Grammar of Motives*. Berkeley, CA: University of California Press.

Chaney, M. A. (2009), "Is there an African American graphic novel?", in S. E. Tabachnick (ed.), *Teaching the Graphic Novel*. New York: The Modern Language Association of America, pp. 69–75.

Cornwell, C. N. and Orbe, M. P. (2002), "'Keepin' it real' and/or 'sellin' out to the man': African-American responses to Aaron McGruder's *The Boondocks*", in R. M. Coleman (ed.), *Say It Loud!: African American Audiences, Media, and Identity*. New York: Routledge, pp. 28–43.

DiPaolo, M. (2011), *War, Politics and Superheroes: Ethics and Propaganda in Comics and Film*. Jefferson, NC: McFarland.

Duncan, R. and Smith, M. J. (2009), *The Power of Comics: History, Form & Culture*. New York: Continuum.

Foss, S. K. (1996), *Rhetorical Criticism: Exploration & Practice* (second edn). Prospect Heights, IL: Waveland Press.

Foster, W. H. (2005), *Looking for a Face Like Mine*. Waterbury, CT: Fine Tooth Press.

Goldstein, N. (2008), *Jackie Ormes: The first African American Woman Cartoonist*. Ann Harbor, MI: University of Michigan Press.

Hauser, G. A. (1986), *Introduction to Rhetorical Theory*. Prospect Heights, IL: Waveland Press, Inc.

Heer, J. and Worcester, K. (2004), *Arguing Comics: Literary Masters on a Popular Medium*. Jackson, MS: University Press of Mississippi.

Inge, M. T. (1990), *Comics as Culture*. Jackson, MS: University Press of Mississippi.

Jennings, J. and Duffy, D. (2010), *Black Comix: African American Independent Comics, Art, and Culture*. New York: Mark Batty Publishers.

McAllister, M. P., Sewell Jr, E. H., and Gordon, I. (eds) (2001), *Comics & Ideology*. New York: Peter Lang.

McCloud, S. (1993), *Understanding Comics: The Invisible Art*. New York: Peter Lang Publishing.

McGruder, A., Hudlin, R., and Baker, K. (2004), *Birth of a Nation: A comic Novel*. New York: Three Rivers Press.

Nyberg, A. K. (1998), *Seal of Approval: The History of the Comics Code*. Jackson, MS: University of Mississippi.

Pearson, R. E. and Uricchio, W. (eds) (1991), *The Many Lives of the Batman: Critical Approaches to a Superhero and His Media*. New York: Routledge.

Pustz, M. J. (1999), *Comic Book Culture: Fanboys and True Believers*. Jackson, MS: University Press of Mississippi.

Savage, W. W. (1990), *Comic Books and America, 1945–1954*. Norman, OK: University of Oklahoma.

Smith, A. (1969), *Rhetoric of Black Revolution*. Boston: Allyn and Bacon.

Strömberg, F. (2003), *Black Images in the Comics: A Visual History*. Seattle, WA: Fantagraphics.

Tabachnick, S. E. (ed.) (2009), *Teaching the Graphic Novel*. New York, NY: The Modern Language Association of America.

Turner, K. J. (1977), "Comic strips: A rhetorical perspective". *Central States Speech Journal*, 28, 24–35.

Wandtke, T. R. (ed.) (2007), *The Amazing Transforming Superhero!: Essays on the Revision of Characters in Comic Books, Film, and Television*. Jefferson, NC: McFarland.

Wright, B. W. (2001), *Comic Book Nation: The Transformation of Youth Culture in America*. Baltimore, MD: The Johns Hopkins University Press.

12

Inappropriate political content: Serialized comic strips at the intersection of visual rhetoric and the rhetoric of humor

Elizabeth Sills

The following prayer was printed in over 250 newspapers across the United States on November 22, 2001—roughly two months after the September 11 attacks. Its text was written above an image of a small boy bowing over family's Thanksgiving dinner to say grace:

> In this time of war against Osama bin Laden and the oppressive Taliban regime ... We are thankful that OUR leader isn't the spoiled son of a powerful politician from a wealthy oil family who is supported by religious fundamentalists, operates through clandestine organizations, has no respect for the democratic electoral process, bombs innocents, and uses war to deny people their civil liberties.

This prayer was published during a time when it was still popular to display cut-out American flags in windows and yellow ribbons on doors. It was not printed in the editorial pages or in any kind of political advertisement. This remarkably radical statement was printed, instead, in the funny pages, in an installment of Aaron McGruder's comic strip *The Boondocks*.

The potential of the serialized comic strip (one that is published in regular installments over time) to condense and disseminate ideas in the public sphere was recognized by Turner (1977), who noted that strips' significance stems from their prominent place in the public forum. She also observed that comic strips "both reflect and affect society" (p. 28). Their premises are drawn from societal principles, and the inherent fantasy appeal of the strips often gives ideas an influential new fulcrum upon which to pivot. Turner concluded that comics may not themselves account for widespread social change, but "they may contribute as much to the social consciousness and social reality as news reports or political speeches" (p. 29).

Whereas Turner focused primarily on the capacities of comics as fantasy narratives, this chapter analyzes the serialized multi-frame comic strip as a unique intersection of visual and humorous rhetoric. I build upon Turner's conclusions by examining the way that images in *The Boondocks* act enthymematically as much as the ostensible fantasy narrative. Furthermore, I explore ways in which the humorous aspect of the strips enhances their social consciousness and encourages self-reflection within their audience. Bostdorff observed in 1987 that the "potent punch" of political comics lies in their combination of graphics and words (Bates et al. 2008). As such, because the "punch" of the funnies can carry societal weight far beyond the implications of their lighthearted name, this chapter will examine the combined potentials of visual and humorous rhetoric in *The Boondocks* to catalyze a radical, subversive ideology in the immediate aftermath of September 11, 2001.

The Boondocks comic strip

In the aftermath of the September 11, 2001 attacks on the United States, interest in national unity rose to a patriotic frenzy. American flags, yellow ribbons, and other national icons illustrated the pervasive sentiment that the people of the United States were rallying into a collective. The universal message iterated through word and image in the public consciousness was clear: America prevails, God bless it.

Amid all this fervor, however, a contrasting perspective emerged. *The Boondocks* resolutely criticized the post-9/11 media coverage, as well as the federal government and then-President George W. Bush, and it did so in no uncertain terms (McGrath 2004; Ulin 2002). This scathing critique began within a month after the attacks, during a time when public sentiment still revolved around solidarity (Nichols 2002). Its unwillingness to stroke the American government did not go unnoticed; it was soon pulled from the funny pages of at least three newspapers in a swift and decisive show of censorship (Lemons 2001). However, the most remarkable aspect of the situation was not the censorship itself, but rather the fact that it was not more widespread. This example of subversion, stemming from the creative energies of a writer named Aaron McGruder, took the form of a popular serialized comic strip called *The Boondocks*, which appeared daily in newspapers in many major cities. Its message, though uncompromising and often antagonistic, was accepted via comics in a way it might not have been in any other format.

Pilgrims in an unholy land

The strip follows the exploits of the Freeman family: two children, Huey and Riley, and their grandfather, all of whom have moved from the South Side of Chicago to a heavily whitewashed suburb called Woodcrest. Aaron McGruder has noted that the family represents "three different facets of the sort of angry-black-man archetype." Riley embodies the thug spirit of BET-laced culture, while Granddad remains staunchly "old school," steadfast in his views and immovable in the face of change. Huey, the true protagonist of the strip, is marked by "an Afro, a high forehead, perpetually knitted brows, and an unnatural familiarity with the precepts of socialist black nationalism. He has roughly equal contempt for Dick Cheney, Cuba Gooding, Jr, and Santa Claus" (McGrath 2004: 2). Although each Freeman embodies a distinct philosophy, they form a tight-knit family, and their opposition often results in synthesis that demonstrates the potential for solidarity among different facets of the Black community (Santo 2009).

Much of the humor of the strip was initially situational, revolving around the culture clash faced by the family after transplantation. Huey started a "Neighborhood Klanwatch," Riley launched a graffiti-based campaign to change his new street name from "Timid Deer Lane" to "Notorious B.I.G. Avenue," and both boys came to the jarring realization that "real-life white people are not all as funny as the ones on *Seinfeld*" (McGruder 2003). As the strip progressed, McGruder began to turn his humor toward the Black community itself, using vehicles such as Huey's annual "Most Embarrassing Black People Awards" to criticize prominent African Americans who the author felt were allowing themselves to channel unflattering stereotypes (Kaplan 2004).

At the time of its nationwide debut in 1999—one of the largest in the history of serialized newspaper comics—*The Boondocks* joined the ranks of Ray Billingsley's *Curtis* and Robb Armstrong's middle-class conscious *Jump Start* as the only widely distributed strips penned by Black men (McGrath 2004). *The Boondocks* stood out among these offerings, however. *Candorville* cartoonist Darrin Bell observed that:

[*The Boondocks*] shattered the notion that African Americans on the comics page had to be tame and non-threatening in order to appeal to white readers. It demonstrated that the country's come far enough, and newspaper readers are sophisticated enough, to appreciate hearing from minorities with provocative views on the comics page (Astor 2006).

The cartoonist's chutzpah in this regard contrasts with numerous Black artists, athletes, and other entertainers who seem to have their ethnicity thrust upon them as they gain celebrity (Turner 1994). Furthermore, it bridges the gap between racial ideology and humor that has resulted in part "because of a tendency to restrict public discourse on issues of ethnicity and race to polite but ultimately disengaged exchanges that suppress true feelings" (Entman and Rojecki 2000: 160). *The Boondocks* spans this divide because it is not humorless, nor are its observations of racial ideology "tame and non-threatening." McGruder embraces his remarkable role in the Black comic scene, noting that "Somebody has to sort of translate the drums for white folks, and occasionally they call me to try to do it" (McGrath 2004: 3). His appeal succeeded with its determination: by the time McGruder ended the strip in 2006 to pursue other interests—among them an animated cartoon version of *The Boondocks* that premiered in 2005 on Cartoon Network's *Adult Swim* (Santo 2009)—it was carried by over 300 print and online outlets (McGrath 2004).

Illustrating the revolution

The popularity of *The Boondocks* has been attributed to its "edginess" and its appeal to a demographic that newspapers are increasingly trying to attract (Astor 2006). However, the broad base of its appeal also taps into sources beyond hip-hop culture. Aaron McGruder, despite often expressing distaste for the serialized newspaper comic genre—which he views as the stomping ground of "seventy-year-old white men"—has counted *Peanuts*, *Calvin and Hobbes*, *Bloom County*, and *Doonesbury* among his influences (McGrath 2004). Many of these strips are referenced periodically throughout the series. Furthermore, the Freeman family and their neighbors are illustrated in the style of Japanese *manga*; in the words of Huey's friend Caesar, the appeal is "kinda 'anime'—like Pokemon. That's popular" (McGruder 2003: 63). Huey himself has also been compared with Bart Simpson in their common attitudes of youthful angst (Kaplan 2004).

In the manner of *Peanuts* and *Calvin and Hobbes*, *The Boondocks* achieves hilarity in part by featuring unusually analytical children as main characters.

According to McGruder, "The characters couldn't be adults. Huey's politics are so strong and uncompromising that if he gets any older, he becomes Louis Farrakhan" (Ulin 2002). In fact, Huey's agenda is often halted by his juvenile stature: he expresses his radical sentiments to old, White ladies who respond that he is "just a big ole cutie pie," and his revolutionary plans are occasionally derailed by the fact that he cannot drive (McGruder 2003). However, although the strip's main characters appear youthful, the views they express are far from immature. Huey and Riley are both precocious, each in his own distinct manner, and the unapologetically Black nature of their worldview makes them remarkable in the mythos of a pop culture that has consigned its young black characters to "intelligence rooted in a lily-white environment" (Turner 1994: 125).

The strip became increasingly politically conscious and indeed radical throughout its run, but despite its content it remained solidly amid the funnies rather than on the opinion page. Because greater numbers of newspaper readers gravitate toward the comics section than they do to more overtly political fare, this gave McGruder more clout than that enjoyed by editorial cartoonists (Nichols 2002). The singularity of the strip has been observed by its author:

> I cannot be made into the commentator for the unspoken black masses. But I will say that the strip represents a political perspective that people black and white hold that is not being put out in the mass media. I just happen to have incredibly wide distribution in a medium that doesn't draw a lot of attention to itself (Lemons 2001).

The transcendence of cultures mentioned here is key: Entman and Rojecki (2000) observe that in many mass media outlets, Black people and White people are made to seem as if they "occupy different moral universes" (p. 6). That is, the ethical mindsets of the two groups are projected to operate in fundamentally different ways. Thus, McGruder's decision to move toward commentary about a political issue pervading the national mindset allowed the comic to take a step beyond "translating the drums." Rather than iterating critiques of Black racial ideology for a wide audience, the strip's political commentary was able to tap already familiar social issues—for myriad ethnic groups—and build upon broad public discourse in a manner that was at once confrontational and engaging.

This is not to say that *The Boondocks* had moved on to address uncontroversial material—quite the opposite, in fact. However, in light of McGruder's "incredibly wide distribution," it may be that the author's radicalism, much like Huey's, happened to sneak under the radar of the powers that be. In this format, armed with pop culture appeal, the ostensible innocence of youth, and biting political commentary, McGruder turned to face the United States government in the weeks after September 11, 2001.

Staying cynical

"Everything's different now. The whole country has changed, but not me. I'm going to stay cynical," stated Huey Freeman defiantly on October 1, 2001 (McGruder 2003). His attitude reflected a long-deliberated decision by Aaron McGruder. "I really had to be prepared to lose my career," noted the cartoonist. "Because this was such an unprecedented thing going on, nobody could predict how people would react." (Ulin 2002). Because his deadlines fell on Tuesdays at the time, McGruder had one week after the attacks to decide whether or not to use the strip to express sentiments counteracting the overwhelming patriotism pervading the country (Lemons 2001). Then, on September 25, McGruder—and Huey—launched a no-holds-barred criticism of the news media, the investment of multinational corporations in the country's grief ("Nike would like to remind all freedom-loving, brave American soldiers to 'Just do it!'"), and the dramatic nature of the ensuing military initiative to find and punish those responsible for the attacks (McGruder 2003). "I was shocked by what happened," McGruder later noted. "But I was also shocked by the simplistic nature of the commentary—this whole 'good' vs. 'evil' analysis that sounded like something from fifth grade" (Nichols 2002).

Eventually, the scope of *The Boondocks* moved beyond media hype and zeroed in on the actions of the United States federal government. The October 4 installment of the strip, one which has become notorious among many high-profile moments in the series, depicted Huey calling the FBI's Terrorism Tip Line to report the names of some Americans guilty of aiding and abetting Osama bin Laden: "All right, let's see ... the first one is REAGAN, that's R-E-A-G ... Hello? HELLO?" (McGruder 2003). This exchange prompted the New York *Daily News* to drop the strip for the next month and a half, followed shortly by Long Island's *Newsday*, and the Dallas *Morning News* moved *The Boondocks* from the funnies to the editorial page. Representatives of these publications refused to refer to their actions as censorship—rather, they simply thought that McGruder had become "a little too political" (Lemons, 2001; Nichols 2002; Ulin 2002). The strip had been barred from other papers on previous occasions for subject matter ranging from criticism of the National Rifle Association to condemnation of Black Entertainment Television to Huey's quest to expose Santa Claus as a member of the Illuminati. "A few papers have pulled the strip, but most of them haven't. And the publicity has just drawn attention to what I'm doing," noted McGruder (Lemons 2001; Nichols 2002).

In fact, the cartoonist's confidence remained so firm that he began to poke fun at his would-be censors. On October 17, the strip began with a mock Editor's Note explaining that the "inappropriate political content" of *The Boondocks* had been replaced by a new children's series called "The Adventures of Flagee and Ribbon," featuring a larger-than-life American flag with a yellow ribbon as his yes-man sidekick. "Hey, Flagee, there's a lot of evil out there," began Ribbon in the characters' debut cell. "That's right, Ribbon," responded the flag. "Good thing America kicks a lot of *@!" (McGruder 2003).

The series' political commentary continued, reinstating the Freeman clan and Huey's ever-radical political views, and touched on issues such as the growing societal distaste for Arab Americans and the unrealistic terror behind the anthrax scare. The next great tumult created by *The Boondocks* did not occur, however, until the November 22 Thanksgiving holiday installment. This strip, the infamy of which remains notable, shows Huey saying grace over his family's Thanksgiving dinner—the content of this prayer can be found in the introduction to this chapter. "The best thing about that strip is that it never says George W. Bush. The reader has to make the connection," McGruder observed in the wake of public resentment toward Huey's statement, the content of which the cartoonist had paraphrased from an e-mail forward. "So I didn't make it up; you came to the conclusion as well. And if that's true, why are you mad at me?" (Lemons 2001). Perhaps unknowingly, the cartoonist expressed one of Turner's (1977) arguments for the rhetorical potential of comic strips: their enthymemes are based on societal consciousness, giving them great persuasive impact.

Although McGruder continued to express his views through the comics, the Thanksgiving strip marks, for the purposes of this analysis, the end of the controversial reaction to 9/11 voiced in *The Boondocks*. Again, the most remarkable aspect of the flak following these strips is not that it occurred, but rather that it remained as minimal as it did. Even the cartoonist himself noted that "The shit I was able to get away with after September 11 was astounding" (McGrath 2004).

In this light, I move on to examine the comic strip identity of this artifact in an effort to illuminate the ways in which the medium itself may have enabled McGruder's dissent. Again, the rhetorical nature of the humorous serialized comics incorporates, in a unique way, visual rhetoric and the rhetoric of humor. I will briefly overview each approach to analysis in turn and then explain how the tandem effect of the two may have increased the palatability for popular consumption of radical, subversive material via *The Boondocks*.

Visual rhetoric

Aaron McGruder's characters give human faces to cultural and political ideas much in same way Rockwell's paintings gave face to the ideological undertones of the Civil Rights era (Gallagher and Zagacki 2005). Notably, these faces are—for the most part—the faces of children. Recall McGruder's own words: "Huey's politics are so strong and uncompromising that if he gets any older, he becomes Louis Farrakhan" (Ulin 2002). That is, through another mouthpiece—especially that of an angry Black man with more agency to address his grievances—the content of *The Boondocks* could seem threatening or, in the case of the post-9/11 strips, treasonous. Because the main characters represent a cultural embodiment of innocence, though, readers are more disposed to process their socialist or gangsta ideas. This deliberate rhetorical decision on the part of the cartoonist lays the visual premise for his argumentation and gives him positive *pathos*. The dissent of the strip becomes palatable when issued from the mouth of babes. Theoretically, this serves as an echo of Turner's observation of the potential potency of comic strips noted above. Phillips and McQuarrie (2004) theorize that symbols channeled through visual images have as great an impact on audiences as those channeled through their verbal counterparts. In instances where images are intended to represent people, their effect can become even more powerful. Images can put human faces on political concepts and remind viewers that these concepts are only as pervasive as those they affect. In many ways, images of people confer a sense of identity upon abstract ideas (Gallagher and Zagacki 2005).

Furthermore, because visual images are often aesthetically interesting, they may indeed pique more audience attention than words alone (Phillips and McQuarrie 2004). When a verbal argument is coupled with an image, its appeal becomes all the more potent. The aesthetic appeal of images in general certainly plays a part in the appeal of *The Boondocks*. Because—as noted above—images can increase the attractiveness of idea, the fact that McGruder's arguments take the form of a comics rather than an editorial script does them a great service in terms of general appeal. The cartoonist's choice of medium allows him to address individuals who gloss over the opinion pages and head straight for the funnies, which gives him a broader base than he would enjoy with a generic syndicated column, or even a single-cell political cartoon. The post-9/11 strips are also singular in the sense that they expressed views which had been all but completely eliminated from the mainstream media, "more the stuff of rants and mass e-mailings" than of the voices of the media conglomerates (Nichols 2002; Ulin 2002). Whereas a simply verbal expression of McGruder's subversive ideas might have been considered more offensive, the comic strip nature of his expression let him enjoy relatively limited backlash toward his subversive sentiments.

The cognitive processes of recognition prompted by strips such as "The Adventures of Flagee and Ribbon" could be described in terms of enthymeme, making sense and creating arguments based on cultural themes with which the audience is already aware (Scott 1994). Audiences were grabbed by the presentation of images, which they found culturally resonant, and understood the relevance of the commentary based on the visual presentation of the characters. This segment capitalized on the enthymematic capacity of visual images in a highly attractive and easily accessible manner, and while doing so got away with ridiculing two of the nation's most revered cultural symbols, the American flag and the wartime yellow ribbon. The accessibility and attractiveness of the visual image is made quite clear through the inclusion of these two characters. The presentation went a step beyond mere presentation thanks to the obnoxiousness of its protagonists, who encouraged the audience to repackage their usual conceptions of patriotic symbolism and language by pushing forward in an obnoxious way that encouraged the audience to push back. Needless to say, this was a phenomenon not usually associated with the presentation of these images. This sort of ideological repackaging through image presentation is not unprecedented: Gallagher and Zagacki (2005) discuss ways in which Norman Rockwell's Civil Rights-era paintings function as visual arguments, demonstrating "that certain individuals [depicted in the paintings] possessed a virtue or, conversely, that they were vicious racists or somehow implicated in the act of racism as a result of their apathy or acquiescence" (p. 180). They also outline the use of powerful images in other aspects of social movements, from the 1960s struggle for Civil Rights to the Jim Crow culture that necessitated it. In this process, they note the reflexivity of arguments made through visual image: they are rooted in culture, but they also have persuasive power to influence culture. Turner noted this same phenomenon in her general observations of the rhetorical potential of the comic strip.

McGruder's root artistic influences may serve as an argumentative asset as well. As previously noted, the cartoonist counts *Peanuts* and *Calvin and Hobbes* among the strips from which he draws creative inspiration, and his artistic style is influenced heavily by Japanese anime. All these emulations are blatant and easily recognizable to those familiar with them—which given their popularity probably includes much of the target audience. Cells of *The Boondocks* often explicitly visually mimic other strips, with Huey poking his head out of his front door to speak to a friend on the doorstep after the fashion of *Peanuts* characters, or Huey and a friend going sledding, as *Calvin & Hobbes* often did. The similarities among strips become even stauncher when Huey and his friends make explicit references to comic mainstays.

In one strip, for example, Lucy van Pelt joins the ranks of several world dictators—and Santa—in Huey's "Hate Book" because "the whole pulling the football away thing ... still bugs [him]" (McGruder 2003).

Phillips and McQuarrie's (2004) typology of human processing of visual rhetoric proves illuminating for the study of comic strips. They argue that "visual figures, like all rhetorical figures, are fundamentally concerned with the relationship of one thing to another" (p. 117). Their assertion that visual rhetoric prompts audiences to make connections is powerful: the implications are that visual images are conducive to the formation of analogies. Phillips and McQuarrie feel that this cognitive process is an especially likely reaction in the sense that analogic thinking has been identified as one of the primary focuses of human cognition, an ability which develops early in life and remains one of the most common lenses through which humans process information. In a way, this process boils down the enthymematic nature of argumentation into a quick and easy deduction: what looks like X must be like X. The capacity of images to encourage the perception of similarities proves key in the analysis of comic strip text.

The manner in which objects within a visual presentation are arranged reflects a conscious decision on the part of a rhetor, and affects to a great degree the cognitive processes in which the audience engages upon viewing the piece. While the reaction of different individuals to different visual stimuli will vary, the common thread of cultural constants usually enables most of the audience to interpret similar presentations in similar ways (Scott 1994). The implications of this theory become clear in an examination of *The Boondocks*: McGruder's presentation intentionally takes after other popular strips like *Peanuts* and *Calvin and Hobbes* because the cartoonist has made an effort to channel them. Furthermore, he has made a conscious decision to model his characters after those in popular anime shows. These choices enable Phillips and McQuarrie's (2004) notion of analogic thinking within McGruder's audience: the strip looks and quacks like the popular and beloved *Peanuts*; therefore, it seems reasonable at first glance that the content should be something akin to *Peanuts*—or *Calvin and Hobbes* or anime cartoons, etc. The enthymeme behind the analogy is clear. The process is a step beyond simply recognizing that the main characters are children and therefore non-threatening. It enables the viewers to connect McGruder's dissent with cultural mainstays that they already know and like—even with largely white institutions like *Peanuts* and *Calvin and Hobbes*—thus they may be more disposed to read the strips and then process the ideas. The cartoonist's approach can appeal to readers who dislike Malcolm X but enjoy Charlie Brown. Thus, his dissent can affect a much more pervasive segment of American society, and avoid the greater scrutiny it might have had to endure in another format.

The contribution of humor

Rhetorician Kenneth Burke, cautions critics that the purpose of analyzing any medium is to pinpoint the ways in which it enables people to suit their cognitive faculties to their environments (Germeroth and Shultz, 1993). This imperative creates a useful impetus with which to analyze the rhetorical function of the humor in *The Boondocks*. Because Aaron McGruder took such a no-holds-barred approach to humorously address controversial issues in post-9/11 America, his contributions to significant factors of his time are clear. The issue becomes, then, the manner in which his humor constructed that "mental equipment" (Germeroth and Shultz 1993).

The Boondocks fosters identification and clarification—according to Meyer's (2000) classifications of the rhetorical functions of humor—through its use of common societal themes and appealing characters. Huey often breaks the fourth wall[1] and looks directly at the audience as he reacts to the overly dramatic media coverage after the attacks. Because the audience has more than likely been watching similar newscasts, Huey's eye contact encourages a feeling of empathy and thus identification. Then, because the nature of a two-to-four panel comic strip is limiting in terms of plot, situations are boiled down to their very essentials before being given a humorous spin in the strip. Because they are so reduced in this format, their clarity and accessibility become much greater. McGruder cannot skirt around the issue that Osama bin Laden may have benefited from the actions of the Reagan administration—he is forced to make his point quite immediate and clear. Since Meyer noted that identification and clarification create a feeling of unity between the rhetor and the audience, it is logical to assume that at least some of the cartoonist's readership found these aspects of his humor appealing—he has thus created a sense of cultural unity. The interlude of "The Adventures of Flagee and Ribbon" contributes to a sense of differentiation: McGruder prompts his audience to reconsider the practical application of these popular symbols of national unity, as well as the lofty ideals they represent. Because Flagee often expresses abrasively nationalistic sentiments in a Stephen Colbert-like fashion (Baym 2009), he encourages distance from that kind of inflated bravado and focus on more critical analysis of the actions of the federal administration.

All of this lends itself to discussion of the dependence of humor on enthymeme. Media such as comic strips utilize narrative humor—that is, build upon a plot—and must develop their storylines logically. Each event leading up to the punch line, which usually falls in the final frame of a strip, builds upon the event before it; furthermore, each individual strip builds upon the characters and plot developed in previous strips. According to Germeroth and

Shultz (1993), this adds up to a sense of "forensic causality," the idea that the premises upon which a comic is based can be syllogistically deduced and lend themselves to greater apparent *logos* within a strip's conclusions.

The enthymematic function of humor aids greatly in McGruder's dissent. The cartoonist plays upon widely held societal beliefs in an almost hypophoric fashion, exposing questions that had been left open by the media or the government and then confidently answering them. The notorious ironic Thanksgiving strip exemplifies this tendency: as McGruder pointed out, no mention is made of George W. Bush at any point in Huey's monologue. However, the notoriety of the strip makes clear the fact that the attributes in the prayer referred not only to the enemy figurehead, but to the leader of the US as well. Remember, "for ironic discourse to function ironically the audience must join with the author in creating its meaning" (Gring-Pemble 2003).

Finally, because of the ability of humor to address pervasive societal issues in an appealing manner, McGruder was able to issue harsh criticism against no less than the purported leader of the free world—and get away with it. Burke's concept of "maximum consciousness" rings out through the comics: the Thanksgiving strip certainly illuminates the essentials of the contemporary political situation, which at face value were not palatable to the grieving American public, but the sense of humorous irony kept the mood—for the most part—lighthearted, which opened the door for thoughtful consideration of the comparison rather than anger at the expression of a subversive idea. The post-9/11 strips, as a text, enact well the use of humor as a means to critique cultural incongruities in a socially acceptable manner. They channel McGruder's subversive ideas in a palatable manner that encourage the American public to reflect upon itself while evading, in all but three instances, the hurdle of censorship. Again, the strips embody Turner's (1977) notion that comics both reflect and affect culture, but through their use of humor they may be able to do it even more effectively than she could account for through her explanation of the fantasy narratives they embody. Rather than encouraging escapism, humorous comic strips can and do induce self-reflection and critical thinking.

As evidenced by the subversive success of *The Boondocks,* the happy emotions triggered by humor can contribute ease and goodwill to the analysis of a text. Comedy illuminates a situation, but it does so in a manner that encourages good feeling and thus a "charitable" view of things rather than an intensely critical one. With a sense of *reductio ad absurdum,* Burke notes the ability of humor to write a situation in simple terms, such that it may be more easily understood and analyzed (Gring-Pemble and Watson 2003). Because they have been reduced to such an easily observable size, assumptions become more accessible and "one possible outcome is for people to realize how outrageous their initial assumptions are" (Germeroth and Shultz 1993). Germeroth and Shultz also observe that when an argument is made in a humorous fashion—dangerous or subversive though it may be—audiences tend to find it less offensive and more fun. In this spirit of happiness, they are more willing to process the argument than they would be if it were presented combatively. Audiences are attracted to humorous situations because they anticipate a happy "affective payoff" (Young 2008: 122). Indeed, funny presentation may make audiences more open to receiving particular messages, because the presence of humor as a "discounting cue" makes a critical mindset seem undesirable lest the happy mood be dampened (p. 123). Although studies have shown that humor itself does not inherently persuade audiences toward action—and can actually distract them—repeated exposure to funny commentary has been shown to erode audience resistance and make its enthymematic assumptions seem increasingly logical, so that "repeated exposure over time could foster attitude change" (Young 2004; 2008: 134).

The complexities of current events

Turner's (1977) contributions to the theory of the rhetorical functions of comic strips remain sound. Their true scope, however, cannot be appreciated without recognizing the interplay of visual images in humor that lie at the definitive nature of the modern serialized comic strip. Both aspects of rhetorical theory contribute to Turner's notion of comic-as-enthymeme, but each functions on such a deep cognitive level that the combination of the two makes the deductive abilities of the strip even more powerful than a simple recognition of comics' brevity would imply. Turner hinted at the fact that comics both influence and affect culture, but the way in which they can both consciously and unconsciously address preconceptions and consequences makes them much more powerful catalysts of ideas than Turner had in mind. While she observed that "they may contribute as much to the social consciousness and social reality as news reports or political speakers" (p. 29), she failed to take into account the potentially greater power of the easily recognizable visual scripts channeled by the simple graphics as well as the good feeling and self-reflection encouraged by comics' use of humor. If the success of subversive comics like *The Boondocks* is any indication, these two attributes of the genre may give it a much more potent appeal than previous work can explain. Given the rhetorical finesse of the comic strip, the dissent that Aaron McGruder was able to popularize after 9/11 is not so surprising. Three papers censored the strip, but over 250 did not. Those who continued to carry its blatantly political humor could have done so for any number of reasons: its hip-hop "edginess," its biting wit, its resemblance to well-loved strips of the past, or maybe the fact that the combination of all its rhetorical functions made its audience process and consider a dissenting opinion amid overwhelming calls for uncritical American solidarity. Thus, rooted in the realm of Black comics, McGruder has succeeded in "translating the drums" and then some. He has built upon common societal themes and then challenged them, giving his audience a chance to use its common knowledge for valuable self-reflection.

References

Astor, D. (2006, September 27), "Colleagues praise 'Boondocks,' aren't surprised it may have ended". *The Hollywood Reporter*. Retrieved from: http://www. hollywoodreporter.com.

Bates, B. R., Lawrence, W. Y., and Cervenka, M. (2008), "Redrawing Afrocentrism: Visual *Nommo* in George H. Ben Johnson's editorial cartoons". *Howard Journal of Communications*, 19, (4), 277–96.

Baym, G. (2009), "Stephen Colbert's parody of the postmodern", in J. Gray, J. P. Jones and E. Thompson (eds), *Satire TV: Politics and Comedy in the Post-Network Era*. New York: New York University Press, pp. 124–44.

Entman, R. M. and Rojecki, A. (2000), *The Black Image in the White Mind: Media and Race in America*. Chicago, IL: The University of Chicago Press.

Gallagher, V. and Zagacki, K. S. (2005), "Visibility and rhetoric: The power of visual images in Norman Rockwell's depictions of Civil Rights". *Quarterly Journal of Speech*, 91, (2), 175–200.

Germeroth, K. and Shultz, D. (1993), "Should we laugh or should we cry? John Callahan's humor as a tool to change societal attitudes towards disability". *Howard Journal of Communications*, 9, (3), 229–44.

Gring-Pemble, L. and Watson, M. (2003), "The rhetorical limits of satire: An analysis of James Finn Garner's *Politically Correct Bedtime Stories*". *Quarterly Journal of Speech*, 89, (2), 132–53.

Kaplan, E. A. (2004, September 30), "The Coondocks: Cartoonist Aaron McGruder's parody irks the White powers that be". *LA Weekly*. Retrieved from: http://www.laweekly.com/2004-09-30/news/the-coondocks/.

Lemons, S. (2001, December 7), "Aaron McGruder, creator of 'The Boondocks'". *Salon.com*. Retrieved from: http://www.salon.com.

McGrath, B. (2004, April 19), "The radical: why do editors keep throwing 'The Boondocks' off the funnies page?" *The New Yorker*. Retrieved from: http://www.newyorker.com.

McGruder, A. (2003), *A Right to be Hostile*: *The Boondocks Treasury*. New York: Three Rivers Press.

Meyer, J. (2000), "Humor as a double-edged sword: Four functions of humor in communication". *Communication Theory*, 10, 310–31.

Nichols, J. (2002, January 10), "Huey Freeman: American hero". *The Nation*. Retrieved from http://www.thenation.com/article/huey-freeman-american-hero.

Phillips, B. J. and McQuarrie, E. F. (2004), "Beyond visual metaphor: A new typology of visual rhetoric in advertising". *Marketing Theory*, 4, (1–2), 113–36.

Santo, A. (2009), "Of niggas and citizens: *The Boondocks* fans and differentiated black American politics", in J. Gray, J. P. Jones and E. Thompson (eds), *Satire TV: Politics and Comedy in the Post-Network Era*. New York: New York University Press.

Scott, L. M. (1994, September), "Images in advertising: The need for a theory of visual rhetoric". *The Journal of Consumer Research*, 21, (2), 252–73.

Turner, K. J. (1977), "Comic strips: A rhetorical perspective". *Central States Speech Journal*, 28, (1), 24–35.

Turner, P. A. (1994), *Ceramic Uncles & Celluloid Mammies: Black Images and Their Influence on Culture*. Charlottesville, VA: University of Virginia Press.

Ulin, D. L. (2002, January 10), "Daily Radical: How to subvert the funny papers". *LA Weekly*. Retrieved from: http://www.laweekly.com/2002-01-10/news/daily-radical/.

Young, D. G. (2004), "Late-night comedy in election 2000: Its influence on candidate trait ratings and the moderating effects of political knowledge and partisanship". *Journal of Broadcasting & Electronic Media*, 48, (1), 1–22.

—(2008), "The privileged role of the late-night joke: Exploring humor's role in disrupting argument scrutiny". *Media Psychology*, 11, (1), 119–42.

Note

1 The imaginary partition that separates the actors from the audience in a theatre production and creates the illusion that the actors are unaware of the audience's presence.

13

"Will the 'Real' Black Superheroes Please Stand Up?!": A critical analysis of the mythological and cultural significance of black superheroes

Kenneth Ghee

"A hero is only your hero if he is fighting for your cause"
(GHEE, 2010).

Historically comic books have been viewed as reading entertainment for youth with their emphasis on graphic pictures to accompany the written text. In recent decades we have witnessed a phenomenal merger and marriage of comic books with other media outlets, particularly television, videogames and movies (Jones 2002). One popular and major theme of comic book characters and their stories is what mythologist Joseph Campbell calls the hero mono-myth (Campbell 2008); that is, a singular mythos that transcends time and cultures adhering to Carl Jung's notions of the archetypal dream and collective unconscious (Jung 1936/1959; Jung 1968).

The hero myth can be categorized in four major themes: (1) the "reluctant" or "circumstantial" hero, who responds "heroically" (willingly or reluctantly) to a crisis situation, (2) the "action hero," who is a regular (but highly skilled) person who accomplishes extraordinary feats of heroism due to above average or superior intellectual, analytical, technological or physical skills (or typically a combination of them all), (3) the "superhero" who may or may not be regular human, or no longer a regular human, but has a special gift or extraordinary (super) power or technology that is used in the act of heroism, and (4) the dutiful "role hero"—the regular mom and dad, policeman, fireman, soldier, etc.—whose duty or role is to serve and protect. These are real or fictional characters who either do what is expected or go beyond the "call of duty" and they are often deemed as "heroes" in the eyes of those they serve, support and/or save, and by the culture that honors them for the familial or occupational (heroic) roles they play. Any of these four categories of hero *protagonists* may, or may not, have a physical *antagonist* (i.e. villain) but it is typical of heroes to fight something, or someone, to save, serve or support something, or someone, else. Some heroes may even perish in the act of heroism but most live to fight another day and embark on other adventures through, for example a comic book, television or movie *series*. Heroes can be non-fictional (e.g. The Black Panther Party) or fictional (e.g. The Black Panther) but it is the **fictional** heroes and stories that capture the imagination and adulation of youth and adults alike, and thus are omnipresent in comic books and other media outlets, including television, videogames and movies. Therein lays the power and potency of *fictional* heroes and the comic books and other media that tell their stories. Their imaginary acts of heroism can transcend stories, thus transcending time and space as well, and they are limited only by the seemingly infinite imagination of the writer. While action, circumstantial and role heroes can operate in either realms of fiction or non-fiction, the superhero's adventure typically operates in the realm of (science) fiction or fantasy.

Carol Pearson (1991) identifies 12 distinct archetypes involved in the mythical hero's adventure and any, or all, of these can easily be woven into a particular character, storyline or plot. Among these are the warrior, lover, creator and the sage. Such hero archetypes are common themes in comic books and action movies; their characters and stories. All hero archetypes are subsumed in the mythos of the hero's journey at one point or another in the continuity of multiple stories and adventures that could transcend time and generations. The *warrior* archetype is inherent in most comic book hero adventure stories (Pearson 1991). Pearson describes and differentiates various types and levels of warrior archetypes. She notes: "The **high level** warrior requires that we fight for something beyond our own petty self-interest … the enemy is no longer a person, group, or country, but ignorance, poverty, greed …" (p. 98). Here Pearson advocates the need for a "**high level**" warrior hero. She argues that today, most warrior heroes (comic or otherwise) are fighting not at that **high level** but at the lower levels in the secular interests of their own groups, cultures and countries. This is consistent with Joseph Campbell's (1988) notion of *cultural bound* mythology. He points out that "every mythology [hero or otherwise] has to do with the wisdom of life as related to a **specific culture** at **a specific time**. It integrates the individual into his society and the society into the field of nature ... it's a **harmonizing** force" (Campbell 1988: 55).

In American culture, and more specifically the dominant Eurocentric worldview, mythical heroes of ancient Roman, Greek, Scandinavian (Viking) and other European cultural heritages have been brought to life in the pages of books, comic books, graphic novels, videogames and on the big screen for the entertainment, inspirational, educational and *harmonizing* value of the European American masses (Cousineau and Stuart 1990; Campbell 1988). Some characters are directly (or indirectly) tied to the stories of ancient European mythology (e.g. Hercules, Thor) and other fictional superhero icons are simply created out of the vivid human imagination (e.g. Superman, X-men). In either case, such stories of heroic grandeur are highly marketed to a willing audience of young (and adult) minds on a daily, weekly, monthly and yearly bases resurfacing regularly in television series, video games and more regularly on the big screen. Like the fictional superhero icon, the "action," "circumstantial" and "role" heroes are also commonly represented in various media and are "recycled" through new weekly or yearly adventures (e.g. Rambo, Rocky, Indiana Jones).

According to psychologists and mythologists these hero characters and stories serve a major role in the developmental learning process by transmitting cultural values and allegories (Campbell 1988; 2008) and as social icons and role models (Bandura 1977). Through the process of personal (*self*) "identification" and cultural (*group*) association, fictionalized heroes and their stories, images and icons can have a profound effect on the young developing mind for both personality and identity development (Koestner et al. 1991; Pollack 1998), as well as cognitive social learning (Bandura 1977). This is especially true for young children during the critical identity stages of human development (Maslow, 1970). These media driven icons help to guide implicit assumptions and beliefs about what it means to be a male or female, Black or White, and what it means to be a good or moral citizen in a community and culture (Segar 1994; Akbar 1991; Pollack, 1998).

For children, *pretend play* is a valuable learning tool that is a natural part of the self and cultural identification process. In this regard, Jones (2002) posits:

Much of the immersion, displacement, and expression of children's play is dependent on *being* something; superheroes, monsters, army men ... But there is a special power inherent in [*popular culture*] cartoon characters and action figures; they are individualized and yet universal, human and yet superhuman, unique visual symbols that can be held clearly in the mind's eye and are instantly recognized by everyone (p. 70).

These iconic images in the "mind's eye" of a child can also have a profound effect on developing perceptions, implicit attitudes and interpretations of reality (Lind, 2004). The psychological impact of fictional and nonfictional hero icons during critical threshold stages of human development can strengthen both the individual and the collective culture (Ghee 1988; 1990).

How does cultural mythology work?

According to Joseph Campbell (1988), the value of mythology and the hero icons that stem from it, is its "relevance." "When the story is in your mind, then you see its **relevance** to something happening in your own life. It gives you perspective on what's happening to you." (Campbell 1988: 4). The key word here is "relevance." This is the same critical concept that mediates identification theory (Koestner et al. 1991), implicit learning (Segar, 1994) and cognitive social learning (Bandura 1977). The internalized experience or fantasy must be *relevant* to the fears, hopes and dreams of the reader or viewer. Without **relevance**, there is no *reference point* for grounding the message, or connecting the story, or stimulus, to personal experience for psychological identification and personal growth. As noted earlier, consistent with Pearson's observations, Campbell argues that most contemporary iconic mythologies are confined to what he calls a "bounded community." In this regard, he states: "In bounded communities, [the heroes'] aggression is projected outward ... the myths of participation and love pertain only to the **in-group** and the out-group is totally other" (Campbell 1988: 22). Thus, the hero icon and story are consciously or unconsciously, *sociologically* linked "to a particular society or culture" (Campbell 1988: 23). In other words, the archetypal theme may be timeless but the inflictions; person (*or person playing the role*), faces, language, time, place, protagonist, antagonist, environment, circumstances, etc.) are truly culture bound.

As culture bound phenomenon, the actual myths and stories themselves are rarely, if ever, universal even though the theme or archetype may be. Thus, there is always a "culture bound" context of the names, places and *especially* races and faces (i.e. heroes and villains) of the characters and story even though the deeper moral of the story may transcend cultural boundaries (e.g. the concept that good triumphs over evil). Mythology lives in the creative expression of individuals within a particular society and it is passed down from generation to generation in a culture bound context. Montuori and Purser (1995) extends this culture bound notion to all human creativity and state more emphatically: "[c]reative expression always occurs within a cultural and historical milieu. Any discussion of creativity inevitably needs to be situated within a historic, but also a sociopolitical, context" (p. 71). If indeed mythological and other fictionalized heroes are culture bound and they can play a significant role in child identification and development, then one intriguing question is: "What about Black superheroes and Black culture?"

Race, mythology, and the hero archetype

Cultural mythology has long been identified as a pervasive and functional socialization mechanism for addressing cultural concerns on multiple levels including cosmological, mystical, sociological, pedagogical and psychological (Campbell 1988; 2008). The hero myth is just one of many cultural arche-types that are transmitted through various media including comic books and movies. However, unlike in European American (White) culture, there is a dearth of serious culture bound hero archetypes available to the youth in black culture that truly "represents" the affirming African-centered values of African American (Black) culture. By contrast, White, or *mainstream* American, culture has a plethora of omnipresent positive and redeeming (real and imaginary) iconic images, symbols, characters and stories that are based in Eurocentric history, values and worldview for successfully inculcating the young developing White mind into notions of cooperative cultural values and even promoting sentiments of "white supremacy" (Welsing 1991). Further, the Euro-American's mainstream cultural promotion of altruistic human traits and characteristics (e.g. honor, duty, respect, good provider, family, love, intel-ligence, self-determination, cultural pride and even superiority) is oftentimes at the expense of, or "collateral damage" of, Blacks, whether intentional (e.g. movie: *Birth of a Nation* 1915) or unintentional (Welsing 1991). Psychological identification with these Euro-cultural icons (whether real heroes or imaginary ones) can be demonstrated psychologically and behaviorally by the iconic posters a person hangs on their bedroom or dorm room wall, the superhero costume he/she wants to wear for Halloween, the comic books they read, the videogames they play or the television shows, events and movies they watch regularly and the icons they follow, emulate, admire and idolize. Sociocultural influences on implicit attitudes, implicit cognitions and implicit memory have been demonstrated and accepted as part of the normative socialization process, particularly in childhood (Segar 1994). In White America these implicit sociocultural influences serves as an informal "rites of passage" into what it means to be an American or more specifically a "White" American

(Akbar 1984). Bandura's (1977) widely accepted theory of cognitive social learning also suggests that the more experiential reference points a child has for a character, story or image the more he/she is likely to identify with it, imitate it and model it.

In order to put the evaluative role and meaning of so-called Black super-heroes (and the comic books and movies that tell their stories) in more meaningful perspective, these critical psychosocial issues and developmental influences must be understood contextually in the sociocultural matrix of contemporary Black life—a peculiar evolutionary biculturality that exists within the historically and institutionally racist White-dominated and controlled American system (Chimezie 1988; Du Bois 1961) that is contributing to the disunity and nihilistic threat within the Black community and culture (Boykin 1986; West 1983; Gibbs 1988). The most, and perhaps only, serious and substantive discussion on Black comic books and Black superheroes in the age of the Black nihilism threat is to address the issue of the Black super-heroes explicit and redeeming cultural qualities for fostering implicit learning for positive personal growth and identification as part of the potentially "unifying force" of Black cultural mythology (Campbell 1988).

Black superheroes: Eurocentric or Afrocentric?

In the late 1970s BOCA (The Black-Owned Communications Alliance) launched a national advertising campaign addressing the dearth of fictional Black superheroes by showing a picture of a young Black boy engaged in pretend play looking in the mirror at the image of a White superhero (Browder 1992: 241). Their caption read: "What's wrong with this picture? A child dreams of being the latest superhero. What could be wrong with that? Plenty, if the child is Black and can't even *imagine* a hero the same color he or she is." In response, Tony Browder shares his own experiences as a loving father who was buying a Halloween costume for his daughter to wear to her kindergarten class party. Browder states: "While walking through the aisle of a local children's store, we saw costumes of Superman, Batman, Miss Piggy, Wonder Woman, witches and ghosts. I saw these costumes as figments of other people's imaginations, which could not reinforce within my child a healthy cultural self-image" (p. 240). Browder ultimately made his daughter a costume reflecting her African Egyptian heritage and culture and she wore it proudly. The emphatic point is that a Black child should, at the very least, be able to imagine a positive superhero or mythological archetype and icon from his/her own race or culture instead of always having to look to another culture for his/her pretend play and idolism. This notion also applies to sociocultural definitions of what it means to be "Black" when self-defeating "vile symbols" like the "N-word" takes on a iconic mythology of its own for promoting low self-worth, self-hatred and cultural devaluation (Cosby and Poussaint 2007: 144).

Today African Americans have a few more so-called Black superheroes in popular media (e.g. comic books, movies) than 30 years ago; however, many, if not most, of them, are created by European writers (e.g. Black Panther, Spawn, Blade). But how relevant are European American created African or African American superheroes for African American psychological and cultural identification and for generating trans-generational culture bound mythology? Robert Cotter (1996: 22) states:

> every Hollywood film and television narrative, though created for reasons of entertainment and profit (and sometimes art), is in fact a cultural artifact; a representation of the values, mythos, ideologies and assumptions of the culture that produced it ... these narratives shape our collective consciousness, affirming accepted ideological and cultural beliefs/mythos and, sometimes, modifying them.

This observation begs the question: do the sparse but "mainstreamed" White culture produced creations of so-called Black superheroes have any real, or redeeming, value for positive and affirming psychic identification for indigenous youth within Black culture?

Surely hero stories and icons of other races can potentially have some implicit influence on the Black child. However, social learning theory strongly suggests that a hero of the same race or "in-group" can have a significantly greater positive impact on the developing youth if the hero meets the sociological and psychological criteria outline above (i.e. culture bound relevance). We must also recognize that an out-group hero or mythos from an oppressive group (e.g. White culture) can also have an intended or unintended *negative* effects on the Black psyche (Akbar 1984). Based on humanistic and Afrocentric notions of self-knowledge, such influences (of out-group superiority) can actually be deleterious to the developing young Black psyche (Akbar 1984; Welsing 1991; Parham, et al. 2011). Thus, the Black superhero's cultural relevance and explicit identification and connection with Black culture are critical to healthy self and cultural (or racial) identity development as potential iconic role models and "path navigators" (Campbell 1988), for youth empowerment and positive growth.

For European American children such a relationship is established implicitly in nearly every story and iconic image in the culture bound nature of creativity and mythology. The preponderance of stories and mega-stories (those highly financed and powerfully marketed to the masses) are generally about White

America, in the context of a Eurocentric view of American history, and projected on the big screen and comic book pages through a Eurocentric worldview for both fiction (e.g. Harry Potter, Pirates of the Caribbean) or non fictional docudramas (e.g. *The Titanic*, *The Godfather*). White Americans play most (if not all) of the major protagonist roles and the lead heroes are predominantly (if not all) Caucasian. However the **supporting role** may be White or other. Typically a Black actor will be hired to play a supportive or subordinate role to the White protagonist, or oftentimes worst, the antagonist or villain! Further Blacks are significantly more likely to appear in comedies and sitcom than serious dramatic and hero roles (Conners 2004).

The black superhero identity complex

When a White hero is saving "America," it is an implicit assumption (in the mind's eye of those reading the story) that he (and the story) is **culture bound** and he is (rightfully, intelligently and morally so) saving his own people and culture first. By association the White hero may also save others (i.e. other out-group/minority persons) also. However, this implicit *human* assumption is not necessarily afforded the Black superhero. When, and if, a Black hero is saving America or more so, he is merely a supporting cast to a White hero (which is more typical in American media) the implicit assumptions are more complicated. Because of shameful and disturbing race relations throughout American history (i.e. from slavery to Jim Crow and institutionalized racism), saving (White) American "proper," (or more typically, helping the White protagonist to save (White) America as the thematic Black sidekick) is not necessarily viewed in the Black culture bound context as necessarily helping, or serving, or even being relevant to the concerns of, or in the best interests of, Black America. A good example of this important point can be seen in our real-life "hero" and idol recognition during Black history month each year. In February each year, African Americans publically celebrate many martyrs and real-life heroes who spent a lifetime fighting the status quo of ideological White supremacy and institutionalized American racism. From Harriet Tubman to Malcolm X, African Americans have historically lauded and cherished real-life "culture bound" heroes who have fervently worked to change (a racist White) America for the betterment of the cultural in-group (African Americans) rather than those who have fought to preserve the status quo of White supremacy. In regard to Black "real-life" heroes, the most important African-centered mediating variable and explicit criteria for collective and individual judgment, respect and veneration is that of "cultural relevance, alliance and allegiance" (i.e. culture bound). This critically important variable must be considered before we can determine if an ***individual*** Black fictional hero (created by Whites) is truly a Black hero at all. This is also the sociological function of any redeeming hero mythos; that is working to save *his own* people *first*, in the context of saving humanity, in other words "**culture bound**" (Campbell, 2008). Otherwise, a Black superhero or celebrity icon may be created and promoted in mainstream culture but nevertheless he/she can be a virtual "sell out" to the race and thus, intentionally or unintentionally psychologically destructive to the very children who identify with them by *skin color* or racial heritage (Hurt 2006). Too often we (Black people) confuse "success" with "responsibility" and oftentimes in Black culture we are as likely to reward and recognize *individual* financial or celebrity status 'success' independent of any *collective* cultural responsibility. The misconstrued message to our children is that material and celebrity acclaim (valuables) are perhaps *unintentionally* taught as more important than cultural or ethical principles (values) (Hutchinson 1994; Karenga 2002; Ghee 1988). Cultural allegiance is the most relevant evaluative critique in most successful and prospering cultures for real or mythologized "heroes" and is not unique or specific to a Black cultural critique. The success of the Black power movement of the 1960s was fundamentally based on a culture bound perspective; Black people fighting for the cause of Black people first (the future of the race) in the contextual advocacy of civil (e.g. Dr King) and human rights (e.g. Malcolm X) for all people (Asante 1988; Karenga 2002).

Real-life Black heroes are typically viewed as culturally allegiant and this culture bound and indeed they were/are necessarily antagonistic to racist forces in White American in the **interest of** Black American collective empowerment (e.g. Marcus Garvey, Martin Luther King Jr). They were not antagonistic or enemies of American people or to the White race, but rather they were antagonistic to those racist forces within America that are manifested in their actions, advocacies, practices and policies! The real-life Black heroes and their good works fit what Pearson (1991) called the "high level hero" fighting for values in the *context* of cultural allegiance, loyalty and solidarity for humanity at large.

Black superheroes: Authentically black or sellouts?

To discuss the functional utility of a Black superhero icon, one must first be aware of the cultural, developmental, cognitive learning and identification issues raised previously in this chapter. Now we can begin to analyze Black superheroes within this critical "culture bound" context. Superheroes, as mythic icons are culture bound and typically by implicit assumption are fighting for their own people (family, community, etc.) first and foremost (in-group). However, most Black superheroes do not *explicitly* fight for Black cultural integrity or relevance from a culture bound perspective and some if not most, may not fight for the (Black) community or culture (or Black people) at all! Furthermore, most were not even created indigenously within Black culture! Whether these Black hero icons, concepts and characters are merely "Whites in Black face" (dysfunctional for cultural and psychic identification) or "Black in consciousness" (functional for cultural and psychic identification) is worthy of our collective critical discourse.

So which Black superheroes are explicitly "Black" and cultural bound? To date, the most notable mainstreamed, widely popularized, marketed and circulated black superheroes are (in no particular order): The Black Panther, Storm (of the X men), Blade, and Green Lantern. Although originally created by White writers, today both Black and White writers share in the delivery of their image character and stories either in comic book form or televised media. While these and a few other superhero characters are considered "mainstreamed," there are others indigenously created and culture bound superheroes by Black writers in the underground market (e.g. Captain Africa, Brotherman) including my own character Amen Ra (Ghee 2010). Undoubtedly, there are many more so-called Black superheroes from the past and present that I did not list and more to be created in the future. The superhero comic book business is fluid. New stories are written daily changing profiles, looks and costumes, modifying the past and revising personalities (e.g. Batman), even changing racial makeup (e.g. Spiderman, Nick Fury, Green Lantern). Unfortunately, too many Black comic book heroes and their stories have little or no explicit or implicit reference points for psychological relevance to Black youth or to the Black community as cultural bound heroes; thus, they have little impact on the developing mind of the black child as a role model for advocating cultural responsibility, cultural allegiance or healthy psychological identification.

Typically such "White heroes in Black face" have little or no reference to a sustaining Black family, a viable Black community, continuity with Black history or Black culture and the character is represented as Black in **color only** while operating in an all White cultural context and worldview. Historically in comic books and movies, the Black superhero operates in a totally Eurocentric (White) context; no Black family, no Black lover, no connection to community or culture; he/she is isolated and separated from any relevant African American cultural context. *He/she is there, or solely exists; to authenticate and support the white esthetic and their culture bound (in-group) mythos and agenda, not his own.* For him (and for us and our children) there is no Black consciousness or Black cause, only a generalized "humanitarian" supportive role from a Eurocentric worldview and perspective. Thus, the Black superhero character may be contributing to the status quos of White America and may have little relevance to Black America inside, or outside, the fictionalizes story he is embedded in; thus, he is virtually irrelevant to address the institutional nihilism in Black America, or worst he may be *contributing* to it (West 1983; Hall 1995).

Typically the Black superhero is not viewed, or respected, as a culturally grounded person (with African roots) but rather as a generalized "humanitarian" (with no African roots; a characteristically disconnected *nomad*) abdicating any awareness, responsibility or interest in the Black community, its issues, plight or unique history. The Black Panther and Storm (both of African royalty) are both exceptions to this rule, particularly in the recent comic book series where they get married. The Black Panther was created in 1966 by the recognized genius of a Marvel Comics Mogul Stan Lee in the 52nd issue of the *Fantastic Four* (Lee and Kirby 1966). He was the first *mainstreamed* Black superhero. He was created and characterized as an African prince (now a king) unequivocally committed (culture bound) to his highly technological and advanced scientific, yet native and indigenous, remote and concealed African kingdom. He is also highly intelligent (a Rhodes Scholar educated in the best African, American and European institutions) and an upstanding nobleman of dignity and honor. Undoubtedly, these attributes are what endear him as the number one Black superhero in America. Although he is African, not African American, his iconic image captivated the minds and hearts of many African Americans during the 1960s and 1970s and still today. For many Black readers, the name "Black Panther" is also perhaps subliminally associated with the real-life Black Panther Party that has a definitive culture bound allegiance and history of championing the cause of African America. Further, in numerous issues of the Black Panther there are references to American racial injustice and other relevant issues and markers of Black history, heritage and culture. However, typically in the larger more dominant Western culture, most African based mythical characters are usual portrayed stereotypically as evil out-group antagonist in White culture bound story depictions of Black mythos. For example "Imhotep" a real-life historical Black Egyptian genius, is often portrayed in White media as an evil wicked villain bent on world destruction (e.g. *The Mummy* 2008). Thus unfortunately the dominant White culture continues to be an active and powerful propaganda agent for perpetuating negative stereotypes of African and African American icons and images.

In summary, it is clear that indigenous Black culture collectively needs the conscientious creation, distribution and promotion of African-centered strong, committed, honorable intelligent cultural iconic superhero characters and images as another potential sociocultural tool for educating and empowering young Black minds. It is also clear that fictional iconic images and comic book stories are used by all cultures (past and present) to nurture and foster the child and human psyche to respect and uphold notions of duty, honor in the context of culture and country.

The Black community needs a conceptual revolution for providing Black youth with fictional culture bound superhero icons and for filling the "void of positive mythos" in the culture, through comic books and ultimately on the big screen like other cultures do for themselves. African Americans have historically been severed from their African traditions and iconic fantasies and stories on national and historic level (Woodson 1933; Karenga 2002). Comic books, movies and hero stories are needed to help to rebuild the severed bridge of indigenous African and African American identification and conceptual solidarity. The strategic innovative and creative use of ancient classical African mythology for today's African American youth (e.g. Isis, Horus, Shango) is needed to inculcate redeeming messages and stories that teach each new generation about their proud history and the high moral and epistemological values of African and African American cultures (Karenga, 2002). A culture is not healthy without trans-generational mythology to pass on to each generation the ideals, values and possibilities of its kind in both fictional fantasies and non-fictional realities (Campbell 2008). Without such "larger than life" stories and images, each generation of Black youth falls prey to others' ideals and propaganda (e.g. positive White heroes; negative Black stereotypes) or they are limited to the base reality of their Eurocentric *mis-education*, oppression that serves to perpetuate the nihilistic threat (Woodson 1933; Leary 2005; Kunjufu 2010). Consistent with the precepts of Joseph Campbell, in a (Black) culture without mythology, there are fewer navigating mechanisms for advancing redeeming cultural values as a *unifying* construct (Campbell 1988).

African-centered superheroes: A demonstration

To demonstrate the creation of an African centered and *culture bound* superhero, I have created and piloted a superhero icon that fights racism and ignorance in a comic book and still framed cartoon story entitled *The Fantastic Adventures of Amen Ra*. This African centered superhero is explicitly "black in agency and consciousness," or "African Centered" (Karenga 2002) in language, purpose, mission and action and he fights a host of negative in-group and out-group antagonists such as "the evil scourge of racism," "Hatritar: the oppressor" and "Sambo Ignoramus: the back stabber." Consistent with Pearson's (1991) notion of the "high level" warrior, Amen Ra is a Black superhero fighting against powers and principalities that negatively affect *his* (Black) people and culture *in particular* (fighting both in-group and out-group antagonists) and thus benefiting all of humanity *in general*. The Amen Ra comic book was created in 1994 but was never formally published, mass marketed or distributed. However, in 1997 the comic book was made into a still life cartoon that ran for two years on cable access television in Cincinnati, OH. It was awarded the Cincinnati Blue Chip award for innovation (1998) and the regional Philo T. Farnsworth award for innovation and graphic animation (1997). The comic book was also used as part of a rites-of-passage after school program for young Black males (Ghee et al., 1997; Ghee, 1994). It was also used along with the cartoon in a subsequent comic book Reading club for Black youth in 1998. In both the after school "edu-cultural" program and comic book reading club, the Amen Ra superhero icon was favorably compared to mainstream White and Black superheroes and it successfully competed for youth identification and inspiration as part of the overall African-centered curriculum (Ghee et al. 1997). The dynamic still frame cartoon can be currently view in six parts on YouTube (Ghee 2010). Creative Black minds are needed for competing against the nihilism and dalliance that is running rampant in Black America. Through comic books and other creative media outlets, conscious African American men and women of vision can offer Black youth an alternative vision of themselves and of the culture; a vision of consciousness and solidarity and an alternative to the ineffective superficial sprawl of today's so called Black superheroes who are typically created by White writers and are basically "Black in color only," not connected to the Black experience, not culture bound, and who uses their individual superpowers to serve a Eurocentric out-group agenda. I am confident we (African Americans) can do better. Indeed, "A hero is only **your** hero, if he is fighting for **YOUR** cause!" (Ghee 2010).

References

Akbar, N. (1984), *Chains and Images of Psychological Slavery*. Jersey City, NJ: New Mind Productions.

—(1991), "The evolution of human psychology for African Americans", in R. L. Jones (ed.), *Black Psychology* (third edn). Berkeley, CA: Cobb and Henry, pp. 99–123.

Asante, M. K. (1988), *Afrocentricity*. Trenton, NJ: Africa World Press.

Bandura, A. (1977), *Social Learning Theory*. Englewood Cliffs, NJ: Prentice-Hall.

Boykin, A. W. (1986), "The Triple quandary and the schooling of Afro-American children", in U. Neisser (ed.), The School Achievement of Minority Children. Hillsdale, NJ: Lawrence Erlbaum, pp. 57–72.

Browder, T. T. (1992), *Nile Valley Contributions to Civilization, Volume 1*. Beltsville, MD: International Graphics, p. 241.

Campbell, J. (1988), *The Power of Myth*. New York: Doubleday.

—(2008), *The Hero with a Thousand Faces* (third edn). San Anselmo, CA: Joseph Campbell Foundation.

Chimezie, A. (1984), *Black Culture: Theory and Practice*. Shaker Heights, OH: The Keeble Press.

Conners, J. L. (2004), "Color TV? Diversity in Prime-Time TV", in R. A. Lind (ed.), *Race/Gender/Media*. Boston, MA: Pearson.

Cosby, W. H. and Poussaint, A. F. (2007), *Come on People: On the Path from Victims to Victors*. Nashville, TN: Thomas Nelson.

Cotter, R. (1996), "Xavier University (Cincinnati) Summer Sessions Advertising Brochure: Course and Workshop Summaries" [brochure], p. 22.

Cousineau, P. and Brown, S. (eds) (1990), *The Hero's Journey: The World of Joseph Campbell: Joseph Campbell on His Life and Work*. New York: HarperCollins Publishers.

Du Bois, W. E. B. (1961), *The Souls of Black Folk*. New York: Fawcett Publication, Inc.

Ghee, K. L. (1988), "The history, ideology, and behavior of positive Black men: Yesterday and today—A position paper. *The Griot: Journal of the Southern Conference of Afro-American Studies*, 7, (2), 3–9.

—(1990), "Enhancing educational achievement through cultural awareness in young Black males". *The Western Journal of Black Studies*, 14, (2), 77–89.

—(1994), "Edu-culture: An innovative strategy for promoting identity and scholarship in young African American males", in B. A. Jones and K. M. Borman (eds), *Investing In U.S. Schools: Directions for Educational Policy*. Norwood, NJ: Ablex Publishing Corporation, pp. 102–25.

—(2010), "The Fantastic Adventures of Amen Ra Cartoon". *YouTube*. Retrieved from: http://www.youtube.com/watch?v=iMS7Ac4Tixg (Part 1 of 5).

Ghee, K. L., Walker, J., and Younger, A. (1997), "The RAAMUS Academy: Evaluation of a two year edu-cultural after-school intervention with African American adolescents", in R. J. Watts and R. J. Jagers (eds), *Manhood Development in Urban African-American Communities*. pp. 87–102

Gibbs, J. T. (1988), "Young Black males in America: Endangered, embittered, and embattled", in J. T. Gibbs (ed.), *Young, black, and male in America: An endangered species*. Dover, MA: Auburn House Publishing Company, pp. 1–36.

Hall, S. (1995), "The white of their eyes: Racist ideologies and the media", in G. Dines and J. Humez (eds), *Gender, race and class in the media: A text reader*. Thousand Oaks, CA: Sage Publications Inc, pp. 5–17.

Hurt, B. (2006), "Hip hop: Beyond beats and rhymes". Independent Lens Film produced by God Bless The Child Productions, Inc. (60 minutes.)

Hutchinson, O. E. (1994), *The Assassination of the Black Male Image*. Los Angeles, CA: Middle Passage Press.

Jones, G. (2002), *Killing Monsters: Why Children Need Fantasy, Super Heroes, and Make-Believe Violence*. New York: Basic Books.

Jung, C. G. (1959), "The concept of the collective unconscious", in C. G. Jung (ed.), *The archetypes and the collective unconscious, collected works (Vol. 9, Part 1)*. Princeton, NJ: Princeton University Press, pp. 54–74. (Original work published 1936).

—(1968), *Man and His Symbols*. New York: Dell.

Karenga, M. (2002), *Introduction to Black Studies* (4th edn). Los Angeles, CA: University of Sankore Press.

Koestner, R. L., Weinberger, J., and McClelland, D. C. (1991), "Task-intrinsic and social extrinsic sources of arousal for motives assessed in fantasy and self-report". *Journal of Personality*, 59, 57–82.

Kunjufu, J. (2010), *Reducing the Black Male Dropout Rate.* Chicago Heights, IL: African American Images

Leary, D. J. (2005), *Post Traumatic Slave Syndrome: America's Legacy of Enduring Injury and Healing.* Milwaukie, OR: Uptone Press.

Lee, S. and Kirby, J. (1966), *The Fantastic Four #52.* Marvel Comic Group.

Lind, R. A. (ed.) (2004), *Race/Gender/Media: Considering Diversity Across Audiences, Content, and Producers.* Boston, MA: Pearson.

Maslow, A. H. (1970), *Motivation and Personality* (2nd edn). New York: Harper & Row.

Montuori, A. and Purser, R. (1995), "Deconstructing the lone genius myth: Toward a contextual view of creativity". *Journal of Humanistic Psychology*, 35, (3), 69–112.

Parham, T. A., Ajuma, A., and White, J. L. (2011), *The Psychology of Blacks: Centering Our Perspectives in the African Consciousness* (4th edn). Boston, MA: Allyn & Bacon, p. 141.

Pearson, C. (1991), *Awakening the Heroes Within: Twelve Archetypes to Help Us Find Ourselves and Transform Our World.* San Francisco, CA: HarperCollins Publishers.

Pollack, W. (1998), *Real Boys: Rescuing Our Sons from the Myths of Boyhood.* New York: Henry Holt & Company.

Segar, C. A. (1994), "Implicit learning". *Psychological Bulletin*, 115, 163–96.

Welsing, F. C. (1991), *The Isis Papers: The Keys to the Colors.* Chicago, IL: Third World Press.

West, C. (1983), "Nihilism in Black America", in M. Wallace and G. Dent (eds), *Black Popular Culture.* New York: The New Press.

Woodson, G. C. (1933), *The Miseducation of the Negro.* Washington, DC: The Associated Publishers.

14

Culturally gatekeeping the black comic strip

David DeIuliis

Although the traditional gatekeeping landscape is quickly changing, newspaper editors are, in the case of the Black comic strip, in the unique position of serving as both traditional and cultural gatekeepers. When making decisions about what news gets into the paper, newspaper editors oversee "the overall process through which social reality transmitted by the news media is constructed" (Shoemaker et al. 2001: 233). At the same time, on the comics page, they "make decisions about what images to project" (Anderson and Taylor 2006: 274). Also, just as the traditional roles of gatekeeper and the gated are ambiguously interchangeable on the web, the cultural gatekeeping that produces Black comic strips can be conceptualized in several ways, which this chapter will more fully explicate.

First, the cartoonists themselves are cultural gatekeepers in the sense that they project images within the comics that affect racial perceptions and associations. These comics are then subject to institutional forces at the newspaper that serve as a second level of gatekeeping, a more traditional form. Finally, at the third level, it is not only the images projected in the micro-level comics that influence racial perceptions, but also how much Black and White appears on the comparatively macro-level comics page itself.

Because the disadvantage or subjugation of a given social group "is created and maintained ... through cultural beliefs and stereotypes that provide narrower, more distorted, or more harmful images" about one group than another (Milke 2002: 840), clearer conceptualizations of these levels of gatekeeping that produce the Black comic strip will allow for more methodologically rigorous research on the Black comic strip.

Gatekeeping

Although the concept of gatekeeping has been applied to many fields (e.g. Bass 1969; Schultze and Boland 2000; Sturges 2001), the term "gatekeeper" was first used to describe the process through which, when passing though channels of communication, some news items make it to the public while others do not (White 1950). For both communications researchers and professional journalists, the concept of gatekeeping has been the dominant conceptualization because, in traditional media such as print, radio and television, the amount of space devoted to news is finite, making it "necessary to have established mechanisms which police these gates and select events to be reported according to specific criteria of newsworthiness" (Bruns 2003: 1). In this way, only that information considered to be suitable to a medium's audience by a small number of "gatekeepers" (Lewin 1947; 1951) would reach it.

Defined by Shoemaker (1991) as "the process by which the billions of messages that are available in the world get cut down and transformed into the hundreds of messages that reach a given person on a given day" (p. 1), gatekeeping in communication and journalism has most often considered editors, journalists and newspaper editorial staffs to be gatekeepers. Additionally, gatekeepers in print and broadcast media must not only select what content passes through to the audience, but also in what way that content is presented within the confines of a given medium and based on generally agreed-upon rules such as the inverted pyramid style of writing. With this in mind, Shoemaker et al. (2001) redefined the concept as "the overall process through which social reality transmitted by the news media is constructed, and is not just a series of 'in' and 'out' decisions" (p. 233).

Barzilai-Nahon (2008) identifies three waves of gatekeeping theories in communication research (see Barizali-Nahon, 2008, for a thorough review). The first wave focused on individual factors that influence gatekeeping, such as personality characteristics and normative and moral values of gatekeepers (e.g. Gans 1979). The second concentrated on organizational and procedural influences on gatekeeping (e.g. Bass 1969), and the third wave is interested in institutional, cultural and social influences on gatekeepers and the gatekeeping process. She then lists some key questions that have been asked about gatekeeping in the current literature and in that of the past decade, including how editors make decisions (Hardin 2005), how their roles change on the Web (Singer 2001; 2006), and whether the new media sets the news agenda differently from the traditional media (Porter and Sallot 2003).

To this point, no research on Black comic strips has considered the dual role of newspaper editors as traditional and cultural gatekeepers, or conceptualized the comics page as a societal metaphor that results from several levels of gatekeeping. Additionally, no discussion of gatekeeping would be complete without an analysis of the new forms of information control resulting from the technological affordances of online newspapers, as well as social networks and collaborative web portals.

Barzilai-Nahon (2008) points out three reasons why these new conceptualizations of gatekeeping are needed in communications research, particularly concerning the Black comic strip. The first is evident in the ambiguous nature of gatekeeping on the web compared to the straightforward, unidirectional model of the traditional media. This study embraces that ambiguity and offers a number of clarifiers. The second is that gatekeeping has become increasingly disciplinary, with definitions and conceptualizations that are inapplicable outside of a particular field of study or research agenda. This study will account for this ambiguity by positing a muli-leveled model of gatekeeping in traditional, cultural and network contexts. The third reason that Barzilai-Nahon (2008) argues for a new conceptualization of gatekeeping is because most past research has focused on gatekeepers, not the gated. Because this study will not consider the two mutually exclusive or even distinct conceptual roles, it answers Barzilai-Nahon's (2008) call for "additional theoretical refinement and clarification of network gatekeeping, and specifically understanding the spectrum of dynamics of *gated* activities and characteristics" (p. 30). How the gated respond to the Black comic strip, and the gatekeeping decisions that produce it, will allow for a clearer understanding of the social implications of Black comics.

Traditional gatekeepers and their audiences

The concept of gatekeeping has been traditionally considered a unidirectional relationship, with gatekeepers and the gated playing sender and receiver roles (Barzilai-Nahon 2005). While the gated, or receivers, are often considered newspaper readers, the gatekeepers, or senders, are most often conceived of as editors and editorial staffs. Because editors believed that their readers lacked the journalistic training to gatekeep their own content (Gladney 1996), the gatekeeper was seen as responsible for both producing and disseminating information to the gated. Additionally, even with a shift toward online news, the gated may only produce content "under the control and authorization of the gatekeeper" (Barzilai-Nahon 2005), and the ability of the gated to circumvent the traditional gatekeeping process is considered minimal, as in the case of the Black comic strip in traditional media.

Contrastingly, in print journalism, several analyses (e.g. Atwood 1970; Gladney 1996) of editors and reading audiences have shown that journalists and readers often have contradictory notions of how gatekeeping, including that of comic strips, should be defined and practiced. Some editors often underestimate the number of people reading the paper and overestimate interest in soft and fluff news (McNulty 1988; Gladney 1996), while others view readers condescendingly, perceiving reader interest as divergent from professional standards of quality journalism (Atwood 1970). Given this relationship, and despite their ontological differences and often divergent perceptions and opinions in traditional print journalism, editors and readers are psychologically similar in online news (Sundar and Nass 2001). No research has addressed the sociological implications of this psychological similarity for the Black comic strip.

Even with more politically partisan news outlets, newspaper and comic strip readers or television viewers can switch papers or channels, but are still subjected to the same traditional gatekeeping processes. However, Kelley and DeMoulin (2002) concluded that traditional news sources would be abandoned in favor of the internet as people became more comfortable with its capabilities. Research from the Pew Research Center ("Newspapers face a challenge calculus" 2009) has supported this outlook by showing that as readership of daily print publications decreases, readers are getting their national and international news from online sources. Journalists and editors who combat this phenomenon by giving the public "what it wants" (Bogart 1989), or what they think it is inclined to consume based on market research, are accused of ignoring a journalistic code based on objectivity, accuracy and balance. Also, because what readers want may not be what they need in order to be informed and participatory citizens of a democracy, reader preferences often conflict with traditional journalistic norms and values.

Much research has addressed what exactly readers expect from journalists and editors (McNulty 1988; Gladney 1996; Grotta et al. 1975). While some researchers have targeted young readers and attempted to determine readership from content characteristics, others have probed reader preferences for layout, design, and balance of hard and soft news (Gladney 1996). Still others have inferred reader perceptions and preferences from circulation and market size differences. For example, Carter and Clarke (1963) compared reader interest in what they called "disruptive" and "integrative" news in daily and weekly newspapers, and Grotta et al. (1975) found that, more so than readers in a large market, readers of small circulation newspapers value local news coverage over national or international news. Griswold and Moore (1989) scrutinized how variables such as size and closeness of community affected reader perceptions of news, and Viall (1992) suggested that the diversity or homogeneity of a newspaper's market affects reader perceptions of journalistic values. After asking journalists, editors and academics to name high and low quality newspapers, Stone, Stone, and Trotter (1981) found that a newspaper's circulation was more often a product of the size of the market than the quality of the paper. Finally, with the advent of television, online and citizen journalism, many studies (e.g. Carroll 1989) have looked at the influence of market size on perceptions of journalistic values in these new media. What has yet to be considered with the relationship between gatekeepers and readers are their attitudes toward their dual role as traditional and cultural gatekeepers, which role they believe is more important and, most consequently, their awareness of the difference.

Less is known about editor and journalist perceptions of their reading audiences. Friedland (1996) and Jankowski and van Selm (2000) observed differences between how audiences consumed information in a traditional medium and engaged journalists in an online news environment. Among others, Martin, O'Keefe and Nayman (1972) compared the findings of a public opinion poll to editors' perceptions of public opinion on the same issues; Bogart (1989) compared reader interest with what editors considered important; and McNulty (2008) found readers, not editors, to be more discreet and conservative about what should get into the paper and onto the comics page. Atkin, Burgoon, and Burgoon (1983) surveyed both editors and readers and discovered that editors assumed their readers to be indifferent to a number of journalistic standards, underrated reader interest in state, national, government, political and international news, and overrated reader appetite for sports, entertainment, cultural and fashion news. Gladney (1996), despite the aforementioned evidence to the contrary, found that both editors and readers consistently ranked standards like integrity, impartiality, and editorial independence as important, while influence and reputation were consistently considered unimportant. Nevertheless, many standards were not agreed upon, supporting past research (e.g. Atwood 1970) which suggests that overall, editors have a condescending view of their audiences.

Whereas news aggregate sites and journalistic blogs rely on the "involvement of a loyal audience with a lot of enthusiasm and expertise," the in-depth, investigative and thought-provoking reporting of print newspapers and magazines has not gained a following in the "rapid, superficial, appropriative, and individualistic" web community (Palatella 2010: 31). One reason has been the diminishing of journalistic standards online where, according to Palatella (2010), "quantity beats quality, being first beats being the best...speed is confused with timeliness, and the value of timeliness is debased by speed" (p. 26). The Black comic strip is unique in that, unlike news stories which may be fundamentally altered by the different media through which they are viewed, it changes neither when appearing in newspapers nor when forwarded through online networks.

Cultural gatekeeping

Alternatively, cultural gatekeepers must not only make decisions about what images to project to the public, but also respond to audience criticism about them (Milke 2002). Their responses to this criticism and attitudes toward those who criticize provide insight into the ways in which images of race are perpetuated by the media. Milke (2002) interviewed ten editors of national girls' magazines about the images of femininity being portrayed in their magazines and the criticism that the images fail to adequately represent reality. She found that most of those interviewed, even the highest-ranking editors, dismissed the complaints as misguided and downplayed their influence as cultural gatekeepers, attributing the images of femininity in the magazines to artistic processes, cultural forces or advertising needs (Milke 2002). Also, even when they did acknowledge the validity of the criticisms, the editors cited institutional and organizational limitations to consequential change. No research has considered cultural gatekeeping in the context of the Black comic strip.

Even when the social conditions surrounding a given group change and evolve, such as a percentage increase in a population, a scarcity of images in the media "may frame the gender or racial order as natural" (Collins 1991; Milke 2002: 840). The comics page, therefore, is a subtle means through which the resulting social ideals can be reinforced and perpetuated, with or without the knowledge or intent of gatekeepers at any of the three levels. Milke (2002) posits that, regarding femininity and the female body, simplistic and objectifying images of women and girls in the media are a systematic form of "cultural oppression" that results in a "distorted, narrow image of female beauty" (Milke 2002: 841). The consistent portrayal of women and girls in "narrow, trivializing, or distorted ways" leads to their "symbolic annihilation" in the media (Gerbner 1993; Tuchman 1978a; Milke 2002: 840) and may cause the belief, even among the group itself, that it is irrelevant or inferior (Ballaster et al. 1999; Davis 1997; Collins 1991) while more and more positively-portrayed groups are seen as normal and culturally rewarded (Kellner 1995).

From a macro perspective, the symbolic annihilation of a particular group through the media is a subtle process that often goes unnoticed by the symbolically annihilated. Comic strips are only a part of this process but, when considered at a micro level, they can become overt and explicit methods of annihilation, which can occur at three levels. This chapter will be among the first to investigate cultural gatekeeping at these three levels—the cartoonist, the comic strip and the newspaper—and to consider the color on the comics page as a metaphorical reflection of the social—and racial—world.

Levels of gatekeeping of the black comic strip

Level 1: Cartoonists as Gatekeepers: Cartoonists and comic strip artists serve as cultural gatekeepers by projecting images within comics that affect racial perceptions and associations. Just as journalists and editors must choose which individual stories and items of news from a mass of information to include in a given publication, cartoonists and comic strip artists, sometimes unknowingly, choose both what images to project and in what light to project them. However, unlike editors and especially journalists, who are often making gatekeeping decisions under harsh deadlines, cartoonists and Black comic strip artists must carefully and thoughtfully organize the visual and verbal elements of a comic to evoke their desired response in audiences of varying education and familiarity levels.

Level 2: Editors as Gatekeepers: Once completed, the comic strips are subject to organizational and institutional forces at the newspaper that serve as a second and more traditional level of gatekeeping. As mentioned, gatekeeping decisions at this level are made with less consideration for sociological implications.

Level 3: Product of Gatekeeping: Finally, at the third level, it is not only the images that appear in the individual comics that influence racial perceptions, but also the frequency with which they appear on the comics page over time. Just as the media may influence to varying degrees what audiences consider newsworthy (McCombs 1982; McCombs and Shaw 1972; Rogers and Dearing 1988), a systematic dearth of Black comic strips on the comics page "casts the group as irrelevant or inferior and provides a difficult fit between who they believe they are and who they are portrayed as being" (Milke 2002: 840). At the same time, the groups who dominate the comics page and are portrayed more and more positively throughout the media landscape are provided a "privileged fit" into cultural frames of what is normal, acceptable, and rewarded (Milke 2002: 840). A systematic and longitudinal analysis of these levels of gatekeeping is needed to determine the extent to which this is the case with the Black comic strip.

Implications

These levels of gatekeeping have implications not only in traditional and cultural contexts, but also as instances of network gatekeeping. However, they do not account for new forms of gatekeeping that result from the interchangeability of gatekeeping roles as Black comics are shared on and forwarded through social networks and collaborative web portals. Because anyone can produce, reproduce and disseminate a product on the web at a low cost and from virtually anywhere, the concept of a gate through which only some material passes becomes less relevant (Hargittai 2000). Network gatekeeping theory (Barzilai-Nahon 2005) posits that while online networks increase opportunities for the gated to produce and disseminate their own information without the approval of a traditional gatekeeper, web users "are still largely dependent on the gatekeeper's design and policy to reach users due to the fact that attention of Internet users is concentrated on a very small number of information providers" (Barzilai-Nahon 2008: 248). Barzilai-Nahon (2005) defines a network gatekeeper as an "entity (people, organizations, or governments) that has the discretion to exercise gatekeeping through a gatekeeping mechanism in networks and can choose the extent to which to exercise it" (p. 248). These network gatekeepers can prevent information from coming into or leaving a network and control the extant information within that network.

When web users with no traditional journalistic training have no political power, there is little opportunity to create and disseminate meaningful information and circumvent traditional gatekeepers. As online power and influence increase, so do the opportunities to produce content (Barzilai-Nahon 2007). Because identifying information is often nonexistent on social networks and collaborative web portals, network gatekeeping allows for far more diversity than the unidirectional and hierarchical theories of traditional media. How this increased diversity affects the levels of gatekeeping that produce Black comic strips is an intriguing avenue for future research. For the purposes of Black comic strips, the interchangeability of gatekeeper and gated roles on the web can greatly enhance the diversity of discourse in social networks and collaborative web portals. Also, because geographical and biographical markers rarely accompany network gatekeepers on the web, the homogeneity of traditional gatekeeping could also be more diversified. However, anonymity is not diversity. While a more diverse group of network gatekeepers may be more influential in sharing Black comic strips, determining if this diversity of network gatekeeping requires anonymity is an additional avenue for future inquiry.

The concept of network gatekeeping differs from the traditional relationship between gatekeepers and audiences in several other ways. The differences are categorized by Barzilai-Nahon (2005) according to gatekeeping process, focus on gatekeepers: focus on gatekeeping mechanism, relationship, information, alternatives, power, number of gatekeepers and types of gatekeepers. While the process of traditional gatekeeping is mostly selection by those in the media (Gladney 1996), network gatekeeping theory posits that in addition to selection, online gatekeeping includes channeling, shaping, integration, localization, manipulation, shaping and deletion as well. Also, although most research on traditional gatekeeping focuses on an individual journalist or the editorial staff of a newspaper as the gatekeeper, a number of other considerations, such as network service providers, governments and organizations, can also perform many of the same gatekeeping tasks traditionally left to members of the media and editors of the comics page.

Additionally, as mentioned before, while the relationship between gatekeepers and audiences can be condescending and hegemonic in traditional media (Gladney 1996), the frequent interactions between gatekeepers and the gated, and the ability for both to produce content, make this relationship inapplicable to Black comic strips. Finally, while traditional gatekeeping theories are locked into conceptualizing gatekeepers (e.g. editors, journalists, newspapers) as senders and the gated (e.g. newspaper readers) as receivers, the two roles are interchangeable in online networks where "the roles of sender and receiver are repeatedly exchanged" (Barzilai-Nahon 2005: 248).

Network gatekeeping accounts for the condescending relationship between traditional gatekeepers and audiences (e.g. Atwood, 1970) by theorizing that, because the relationship is seen, at least generally, as unidirectional, newspaper and comic strip readers have no voice or power. Contrastingly, within online networks, the ability of users to create their own information has increased their "bargaining power" and caused gatekeepers to "avoid conditions which encourage the gated to overcome gates that have been posted in networks" (Barzilai-Nahon 2005: 249).

Also, the compatibility of network gatekeeping with other communications theories such as agenda setting and framing may also have implications for the gatekeeping of Black comic strips. Prior research has found little correlation between the decisions and activities of gatekeepers of differing levels of activity, suggesting that each group uses distinct news cues and heuristics in their decision-making at each level. Future research should more fully explicate and experimentally confirm the differences among gatekeeping decisions made at the three levels posited in this chapter.

Ultimately, the web poses paradigmatic challenges not only to news production and consumption, but also traditional and cultural notions of gatekeeping. This chapter has offered a new conceptualization of the levels of gatekeeping through which the Black comic strip is produced and, through the several avenues for future research that it outlines, it has served as a framework for future research on this heretofore understudied but societally impactful topic.

References

Anderson, M. and Taylor, H. (2006), *Sociology: The Essentials*. Belmont, CA: Thomson Wadsworth.

Atkin, C., Burgoon, J., and Burgoon, M. (1983), "How journalists perceive the reading audience". *Newspaper Research Journal*, 4, 51–63.

Atwood, L. (1970), "How newsmen and readers perceive each others' story preferences". *Journalism Quarterly*, 47, 296–302.

Ballaster, R., Beetham, M., Frazer, E., and Hebron, S. (1999), *Women's Worlds: Ideology, Femininity, and the Woman's Magazine*. London: Macmillan.

Barzilai-Nahon, K. (2005), "Network gatekeeping theory", in K. Fisher, S. Erdelez, and E. McKechnie (eds), *Theories of Information Behavior: A Researcher's Guide*. Medford, NJ: Information Today, pp. 247–56.

—(2007), "Toward a theory of network gatekeeping: A framework for exploring information control". *Journal of the American Society for Information Science and Technology*, 59, 1493–1512.

—(2008), "Towards a theory of network gatekeeping: A framework for exploring information control." *Journal of the American Society for Information Science and Technology*, 59, 1493–1512.

Bass, A. (1969), "Redefining the gatekeeper concept: A U.N. radio case study". *Journalism Quarterly*, 46, 59–72.

Bogart, L. (1989), *Press and Public*. Hillsdale, NJ: Lawrence Erlbaum.

Bruns, A. (2003), "Gatewatching, not gatekeeping: Collaborative online news". Media International Australia Incorporating Culture and Policy: Quarterly Journal of Media Research and Resources, 107, 31–44.

Carroll, R. (1989), "Market size and TV news values". *Journalism Quarterly*, 66, 49–56.

Carter, R. and Clarke, P. (1963), "Suburbanites, city residents, and local news". *Journalism Quarterly*, 40, 548–58.

Collins, P. H. (1991), *Black Feminist Thought: Knowledge, Consciousness, and the Politics of Empowerment*. New York: Routledge.

Davis, L. R. (1997), *The Swimsuit Issue and Sport: Hegemonic Masculinity in "Sports Illustrated"*. Albany, NY: State University of New York Press.

Friedland, L. (1996), "Electronic democracy and the new citizenship". *Media, Culture & Society*, 18, 185–212.

Gans, H. (1979), *Deciding What Is News*. New York: Pantheon.

Gerbner, G. (1993), "Women and minorities in television. Report from Annenberg school for communication cultural indicators project, in conjunction with the American Federation of Television and Radio Artists and the Screen Actors Guild".

Gladney, G. (1996), "How editors and readers rank and rate the importance of eighteen traditional standards of newspaper excellence". *Journalism & Mass Communication Quarterly*, 73, 319–31.

Griswold, W. and Moore, R. (1989), "Factors affecting readership of news and advertising in a small daily newspaper". *Newspaper Research Journal*, 10, 55–66.

Grotta, G., Larkin, E., and DePlois, B. (1975), "How readers perceive and use a small daily newspaper". *Journalism Quarterly*, 52, 711–5.

Hardin, M. (2005), "Stopped at the gate: Women's sports, 'reader interest,' and decision-making by editors". *Journalism & Mass Communication Quarterly*, 82, (1), 62–77.

Hargittai, E. (2000), "Open portals or closed gates: Channeling content on the world wide web". *Poetics: Journal of Empirical Research on Culture, the Media and the Arts*, 27, 233–54.

Jankowski, N. and van Selm, M. (2000), "The promise and practice of public debate", in K. L. Hacker and J. van Dijk (eds), *Digital Democracy: Issues of Theory and Practice*, 149–65. London: Sage.

Kelley, C. and DeMoulin, G. (2002), "The web cannibalizes media". *Forrester Research*. Retrieved from: http://www.forrester.com/ER/Research/Brief/Excerpt/0,1317,15065,00.html.

Kellner, Douglas (1995), *Media Culture: Cultural Studies, Identity and Politics Between the Modern and the Postmodern*. London: Routledge.

Lewin, K. (1947), "Frontiers in group dynamics: II. Channels of group life; Social planning and action research". *Human Relations*, 1, 143–53.

—(1951), *Field Theory in Social Science: Selected Theoretical Papers*. New York: Harper.

Martin, R., O'Keefe, G., and Nayman, O. (1972), "Opinion agreement and accuracy between editors and their readers". *Journalism Quarterly*, 49, 460–8.

McCombs, M. E. (1982), "The Agenda-Setting Approach", in D. Nimmo and K. Sanders (eds), *Handbook of Political Communication*. Beverly Hills, CA: Sage.

McCombs, M. E. and Shaw, D. (1972), "The agenda-setting function of mass media". *Public Opinion Quarterly*, 36, 176–87.

McNulty, H. (2008), "The gap between what readers and editors think is fit to print". *Editor & Publisher*, 9, 27.

Milke, M. (2002), "Contested images of femininity: An analysis of cultural gatekeepers' struggles with the 'real girl' critique". *Gender & Society*, 16, 839–59.

"Newspapers face a challenge calculus". (2009), *Pew Research Center*. Retrieved from: http://people-press.org.

Palatella, J. (2010, June 21), "The death and life of the book review". *The Nation*, 290, 25–31.

Porter, L. and Sallot, L. (2003), "The internet and public relations: investigating practitioners' roles and World Wide Web use". *Journalism & Mass Communication Quarterly*, 80, 603–22.

Rogers, E. and Dearing, J. (1988), "Agenda-setting research: Where has it been? Where is it going?", in J. Anderson (ed.), *Communication Yearbook 11*. Newbury Park, CA: Sage, pp. 555–94.

Schultz, U. and Boland, R. (2000), "Knowledge management technology and reproduction of knowledge work practices". *Journal of Strategic Information Systems*, 9, 193–212.

Shoemaker, P. (1991), *Gatekeeping*. Newbury Park, CA: Sage Publications.

Shoemaker, P., Eichholz, M., Kim, E., and Wrigley, B. (2001), "Individual and routine forces in gatekeeping". *Journalism and Mass Communication Quarterly*, 78, (2), 233–46.

Singer, J. (2001), "The metro wide web: Changes in newspaper's gatekeeping role online". *Journalism and Mass Communication Quarterly*, 78, 65–80.

Singer, J. B. (2006), "Stepping back from the gate: Online newspaper editors and the co-production of content in Campaign 2004". *Journalism and Mass Communication Quarterly*, 83, 265–80.

Smith, D. (1990), *Texts, Facts, and Femininity: Exploring the Relations of Ruling*. London: Routledge.

Stone, G. C., Stone, D. B., and Trotter, E. P. (1981), "Newspaper quality's relation to circulation". *Newspaper Research Journal*, 2, (3), 16–24.

Sturges, P. (2001), "Gatekeepers and other intermediaries". *Aslib Proceedings*, 53, 62–7.

Sundar, S. and Nass, C. (2001), "Conceptualizing sources in online news". *Journal of Communication*, 51, 52.

Tuchman, G. (1978), "Introduction: The symbolic annihilation of women by the mass media", in G. Tuchman (ed.), *Hearth and Home: Images of Women in the Mass Media*.

Viall, E. (1992), "Measuring journalistic values: a cosmopolitan/community continuum". *Journal of Mass Media Ethics*, 7, (1), 41.

White, D. (1950), "The 'gate keeper': A case study in the selection of news". *Journalism Quarterly*, 27, 383–90.

Afterword

Jeet Heer

Race and comics

The essence of cartooning is mark-making. At least before the current digital revolution, the primordial act of cartooning almost invariably involved the impression of a black mark on a white page. Whether made by pencil, pen or brush, the black mark is the core of cartooning. Later in the production process other colors can be added on but at its root cartooning is a matter of black and white. The interplay of black and white in comics perhaps explains why the art form attracted the talents of George Herriman, one of the supreme masters of comics.

As discussed earlier in this volume, Herriman was of creole origins. He was born in 1880 in New Orleans to a very distinguished family who belonged to the city's community "free people of color." Among other relatives, Herriman's grandfather and father both fought for African American enfranchisement and legal equality in the wake of the Civil War. But by the time Herriman was born, the "free people of color" were increasingly hemmed in by the rise of Jim Crow segregation. Herriman and his family knew Homer Plessy, the light-skinned African American whose attempt to legally challenge segregation ended in the infamous Supreme Court case of Plessy v. Ferguson (1896), which entrenched segregation in the law for most of the better part of a century.

Knowing that the Jim Crow South offered them no future, the Herrimans made a radical decision in 1886 to move to Los Angeles and pass for White. Herriman grew up in a White environment but never forgot his Creole roots. He performed the role of White man impeccably, often covering his kinky hair with a derby or getting a close haircut. When he entered the newspaper business at the end of the nineteenth century, he was able to get cartooning jobs in major newspapers that would never have hired an African American. Herriman's newspapers colleagues often tried to guess his mysterious origins. Some thought he was Greek, others assumed he was Turkish, or French or Irish. Only his closest intimates knew that he was Black.

The fact that Herriman had to spend his life passing for White is worth emphasizing because it reminds us of the large inescapable reality that every African American cartoonist has had to confront: racism. There is an element of heroism in all the artists dealt with in this collection because they have made careers for themselves in a field that has been notably inhospitable for Black talent. This bravery is, of course, especially evident in such pioneers as Ollie Harrington and Jackie Ormes, who had to find a home in Black newspapers because editors and publishers assumed that their cartoons, although undeniably delightful and sharp-witted, were only of interest to a minority audience. Although conditions for Black cartoonists have improved since those days, it remains true that even in the supposedly "post-racial" twenty-first century there is a widespread assumption in the cultural indus-tries that White equals mainstream, while Black equals special interest.

As the essays in this fine collection demonstrate, Black cartoonists have made their mark on history. But these marks have often been faded, covered up, hidden away in hard to find places or unjustly ignored. So it is a great joy to read these essays and learn more about the artists who have brought to the comics page sensibilities and experiences that we all need to pay attention to.

Racism and resistance are the inescapable frameworks for understanding Black comics. In this afterword, I want to call attention to both the lasting effects of racism but also to highlight the resistance strategies used by Black artists and audiences to fight racism and to assert a positive vision of Black identity.

Appropriately enough since he was the fist major African American cartoonist, Herriman himself offers a fine example of one strategy open to Black artist living in a racist society: subversive comedy. Herriman's most famous work was the long-running strip *Krazy Kat* (which started off as an offshoot of *The Family Upstairs* in 1910 and became its own strip in 1913). A funny animal burlesque, Krazy Kat tells the story of a perpetual love triangle between a black cat, a white mouse, and a white dog. There is a constant state of emotional confusion in the strip because the animals all have amorous intentions that are at cross purposes: the cat loves the mouse and is indifferent to the dog; the mouse hates the cat and dog alike; and the dog loves the cat and hates the mouse. To top it all off, Herriman slyly empha-sizes that identity is fluid by having the characters periodically change color and even gender (Krazy is both a he and a she). A formalist fascinated by the interplay of black and white on the newspaper page, Herriman used his strip to critique the very rigid racial thinking that drove his family out of New Orleans. In Herriman's comic strip universe, black and white are not fixed categories but fluid lines constantly in play. Herriman's strong sense of the free play of identity was not shared by his White colleagues, who were largely content to reaffirm the racial and ethnic status quo.

The cartoonist Frederick Burr Opper (1857–1937) created many popular comic strip characters, notably Happy Hooligan (a good natured but hapless Irish-American tramp). Writing in The Independent in 1901, Opper reflected on the role played by ethnic characters in the comic strip universe (which he called "Caricature Country"). "Colored people and Germans form no small part of the population of Caricature Country," Opper wrote. "The negroes spent much of their time getting kicked by mules, while the Germans, all of whom have large spectacles and big pipes, fall down a good deal and may be identified by the words, 'Vas iss,' coming out of their mouths. There is also a good sprinkling of Chinamen, who are always having their pigtails tied to things; and a few Italians, mostly women, who have wonderful adventures while carrying enormous bundles on their heads. The Hebrew residents of Caricature Country, formerly numerous and amusing, have thinned out of late years, it is hard to say why. This is also true of the Irish dwellers, who at one time formed a large percentage of the population."

Opper was being either coy or disingenuous in claiming "it is hard to say why" Jewish and Irish stereotypes were on the way out. As Opper would have been well aware, Jewish-American and Irish-American groups were becoming increasingly vocal in criticizing ethnic stereotypes that targeted them. And cartoonists responded by either getting rid of those stereotypes or making them more genial: the simian Irishman of the nineteenth century became the affable lug of the twentieth century (Happy Hooligan and McManus' Jiggs). In fact, Opper would occasionally fudge the issue by saying that Hooligan was not supposed to be from any particular group, even though his facial features and name both came out of the anti-Irish tradition.

The idea of "caricature country" is a useful one, though. Nineteenth- and early twentieth-century comics dealt in caricature, not characters, and not just in ethnic and racial matters. Wives were almost always henpecking shrews (with a rolling pin in hand to bash hubby's brains with) while their feckless mates loved to flee their family so they could go drinking with their buddies. Professors by definition were absent-minded, farmers by their very nature naïve and easily fooled by city slickers. Racial and ethnic stereotypes grew out of this larger tendency to caricature. This is not to deny the racism or malevolence of the stereotype but rather to link it to the formal practices of the cartoonists. It is not just that cartoonists lived in a racist time but also that the affinity of comics for caricature meant that the early comic strips took the existing racism of society and gave it vicious and virulent visual life. Form and content came together in an especially unfortunate way.

It is not enough to say that the early cartoonists lived in a culture where blackface and minstrelsy were common. They actively participated in that culture and contributed. In 1911, there was a curious incident where it looks as if Winsor McCay (creator of the great comic strip Little Nemo) and a friend dressed in blackface attacked a man they thought was trying to blackmail the cartoonist's wife Maude McCay. (As with much in McCay's private life, the facts of the case are a bit muddy and open to different interpretations.) The use of blackface in this incident sheds some very interesting light on McCay's racial politics, showing how they grew as part of the broader minstrel culture he participated in through the dime museum and on vaudeville. In 1913, McCay performed in Montreal, doing his famous lightning fast chalk talk. Among those who shared the billings with McCay were W. C. Fields, Lew Hawkins ("The Chesterfield of minstrelsy"), the Six Musical Spillers ("Colored comedians and instrumentalists") and Asaki ("Japanese water juggler") (*Westmount News*, March 14, 1913). Blacks and Asians were spectacles: objects of wonderment and derision, not unlike the comic strips themselves. No wonder McCay would so often use racial stereotypes in his work. Because they were popular entertainers, other pioneering comic strip cartoonists partook of the broad culture of minstrelsy and corked up at some point in their lives, including George Luks and Jimmy Swinnerton. "The Olympic Club Minstrel is undoubtedly the cleverest aggregation of amateur talent on the coast," the *Oakland Tribune* claimed on December 4, 1896. One member of this minstrel troupe was Jimmy Swinnerton, who was already one of America's leading cartoonists. Interestingly, the radio show Amos and Andy had roots in comics: it was inspired by an earlier show devoted to The Gumps, Sidney Smith's comic strip. Amos and Andy was a corked up version of Smith's situation comedy about family life and get-rich-quick schemes among middle-class White goofballs.

Breaking the color line

The color line in newspaper comics seems to have started breaking up in the 1930s, the decade the Hearst syndicate (King Features) hired E. Simms Campbell to do Cuties, a daily gag panel. Campbell praised Hearst for this in a 1942 birthday poem:

> You've stood steadfast against the tide
> When people took the other side
> You've put into practice "The American Way"
> A Negro works for your papers every day …

Looking back, it is clear that the 1940s were a pivotal time in race relations, in America and in the comics. The war was the beginning of the end of Jim Crow America. With the wartime labor shortage, millions of African Americans found jobs in both industry and the army. Civil Rights groups were able to make the cogent argument that it did not make sense to fight Nazi racism in Europe while upholding segregation in America. The new African American social mobility led to a backlash among some Whites, resulting in race riots in cities like Detroit where White mobs tried to prevent Blacks from moving into hitherto segregated neighborhoods. Calls for racial equality were increasingly vocal and reached the comics page, where there was a long-standing tradition to depict Black characters in highly exaggerated forms, with rubber-tire lips and clownishly large eyes.

On November 23, 1943, and on the following day, the cartoonist Roy Crane depicted minor Black characters in his accustomed and hitherto acceptable way in his adventure strip Buz Sawyer. This led to a mild word of advice from the King Features Syndicate. Editor Ward Greene noted in an October 7, 1943 letter:

> In the background of a couple of daily releases you have a colored character. One is a Pullman porter and the other is a waiter. We feel you may be inviting trouble if you use colored characters in the comic at this time. Experience has shown us that we have to be awfully careful about any comics in which Negroes appear. The Association for the Advancement of Colored People protests every time they see anything which they consider ridicules the Negro no matter how faintly. For example, [George] Swanson did a little drawing showing a Negro baseball team breaking up to chase a chicken across the diamond. As a result, papers in cities like Pittsburgh and Chicago were threatened with a boycott by local Negro organizations. Of course, they are hypersensitive, but the sensitivity has, as you know, become more acute than ever with race troubles growing out of the war. The two Negroes you drew are no more caricatured than some of the whites in your comic, but they are caricatured just enough to give some colored brother the chance to accuse Roy Crane of lampooning his race. I know you don't want that. Please don't think we are being censorious, Roy. I am simply giving you the picture as we know it to be.

Greene's words are of course very ambiguous; he sounds slightly put upon and puzzled by the fact that Blacks are offended by racial jokes. Still, his letter is a sign that editors were increasingly attentive to Black voices of complaint.

Paradoxically, the Civil Rights agitation of the 1940s did not just lead to the disappearance of offensive stereotypes, but to a larger ethnic cleansing of the comics. With publishers and cartoonists afraid to offend Black readers, characters like Ebony White—the cringe-making sidekick to Will Eisner's The Spirit—disappeared. But they were not replaced, except in a few cases, by non-racist Black characters (who might have offended racist White readers). Instead the comics sections of the 1950s became very lily-white, with far fewer non-White characters than before. There are exceptions: Walt Kelly's character Bucky in the Our Gang stories and a Black boy briefly introduced in 1942 in Little Orphan Annie. It was not till the Civil Rights agitation of the 1960s that there was a more forceful attempt to have non-racist Black characters, as well as a more concerted opening effort to bring in Black cartoonists into the field of comics.

This then is the legacy of racism that Black cartoonists have had to contend with since the early days of comics. Yet as dire and restrictive as this racism has been, Black cartoonists like Herriman, Harrington, Ormes, and Aaron McGruder have redeemed the art form through their radical wit and stylish art. Comedy, as Herriman showed long ago, has the power to turn the world upside down and make us see the world with new eyes. The essays in this superb book are a tribute to an important tradition in American and global popular culture. May this volume produce many sequels!

Index

CPSIA information can be obtained
at www.ICGtesting.com
Printed in the USA
LVHW050630210221
679533LV00023B/1517

9 781441 135285